MERIDIAN

Crossing Aesthetics

Werner Hamacher

& David E. Wellbery

Editors

Translated by Richard Beardsworth
and George Collins

Stanford
University
Press

Stanford
California

TECHNICS AND TIME, 1

The Fault of Epimetheus

Bernard Stiegler

Technics and Time, 1: The Fault of Epimetheus
was originally published in French in 1994
under the title *La technique et le temps, 1: La faute d'Epiméthée*,

Assistance for the translation was provided
by the French Ministry of Culture

Stanford University Press
Stanford, California

Printed in the United States of America

CIP data are at the end of the book

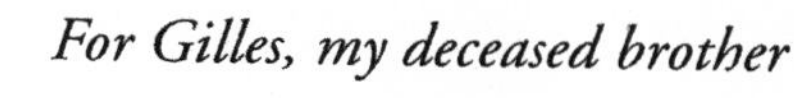

For Gilles, my deceased brother

Preface

The object of this work is technics, apprehended as the horizon of all possibility to come and of all possibility of a future.

This question still seemed secondary when, ten years ago, I was setting down its first delineations. Today, it informs all types of research, and the enormousness of the question summons us all. This calls for a work whose urgency is still hardly grasped despite the high stakes of the issue and the disquiet it arouses—a long and exacting task, as exciting as it will be difficult, stirring a necessary but deaf and dangerous impatience. Here I would like to warn the reader of this difficulty and of its necessity: at its very origin and up until now, philosophy has repressed technics as an object of thought. Technics is the unthought.

The reactions, immediate or mediate and mediatized, "epidermic" or calculated, that are provoked by the extraordinary changes characteristic of our age, in which technics constitutes the most powerful dynamic factor, must be *imperatively overcome.* The present time is caught up in a whirlwind in which decision making (*krisis*) has become increasingly numb, the mechanisms and tendencies of which remain obscure, and which must be made intelligible at the cost of a considerable effort of anamnesis as much as of meticulous attention to the complexity of what is taking place. The work presented here is nothing but a tentative approach to these questions, as subject to trial and error as it is resolute—advancing by trial and error (with the hand permitting) is the very object of this reflection.

The frenzy of time is all the more paradoxical in that, although it should open onto the evidence of a future, never before has the imminence of an impossibility to come been more acute. That a radical change in outlook and attitude is demanded induces all the more reactivity because it is unavoidable. *Ressentiment* and denegation are factors of ruin as well as irreducible tendencies, which Nietzsche and Freud placed at the heart of their reflections a century ago. They will never have been exemplified so diversely as today. The reader will know, then, that these authors, if seldom quoted in these pages, form the vanishing point of the perspectives I have attempted to open.

Unfortunately, I will not be able to acknowledge here everything I owe to so many friends and allies encountered in the course of this undertaking. I would at least like to express my profound gratitude to Gérard Granel, who, as professor at the University of Toulouse-LeMirail, awakened me, with the warm exigency that all those who have had the opportunity to study under his direction know, to the necessity of returns (to things themselves, to metaphysics) as well as to that of a major overturning.

I would also like to thank Madame Montet, Eliane Escoubas, Annick Jaulin, Madame Lévy Hébrard, and Elizabeth Rigal, whose excellent teachings find an echo here.

Jacques Derrida has made this work possible through his own, and the reader will find in these pages a reading that strives to remain faithful while taking on ("starting from," "beside," and in the deviation (*écart*) of a différance) the fascinating inheritance that the spectral authority of a master engenders—all the more fascinating when the master suspects any and all figures of mastery. Jacques Derrida's immense devotion to the *possibility of the other* not only is the object of his exemplary discourse and meditation but also governs a lifestyle, a thought of life and a life of thought where, in his relationship to students, to those who are close to him, to the private and public spheres, the author authorizes his text in the facts of existence the more he is vigilant in observing the limits of his authority.

Without the welcome extended to me by Jean-François Lyotard at the Collège International de Philosophie, and without the dialogue he so generously allowed me to enter into with him and with others (whom I also thank without mentioning their names here), steps that were decisive to my project could no doubt not have been made.

Frequent conversations with Paul Virilio, Régis Debray, and Antoine Dulaure have greatly enriched this work and have given me inestimable encouragement.

The most precious stimuli to work are often friends. I have shared with Antoine Berman, Thierry Chaput, and Michel Servière, all of whom have since died, the care and the enigma of the memory haunting this work.

Catherine Malabou has encouraged and accompanied me in the work as well as in the banal difficulties of everyday life, while setting out on her own investigations. Tenderness has been our bond in the aim of philosophical exigency, which ties together as much as it opens out the spaces of struggle—a fruitful and threatening emulation that Hesiod sings about under the name of *Ēris*, the daughter of Night. Never before has the experience of the *community of a de-fault of community*, residing magnificent and terrifying at the heart of what I attempt to explore, been more radical than with Catherine, in the concept and the circle of love, if only to conceptualize out of love for the concept—what she also names the end of love (in these times when philosophy will have wished to "lay down its name as love of wisdom in order to be effectively and actually real knowledge").

My children Barbara and Julien Stiegler had to bear, when growing up, the conception and the birth of this other progeny: a book. May this hectic period of my life have brought them some kind of joy, and may this object, now behind me, which I hope is turned toward a future already no longer my own, be for them in their own right fruitful.

I thank my students who attended my courses and often contributed to the maturing of the theses set out here. I also thank the higher administration of the University of Compiègne, which has not forgotten the urgency and necessity of an encounter between philosophy and technology. A grateful beneficiary as much as a devoted actor, I wish to recognize their unusual clairvoyance.

Lastly, I would like to express my thanks to Roger Lesgards, to Jacques Tarnero, and to the Cité des Sciences et de l'Industrie; without their help, this book could not have been published.

B.S.

Contents

Translators' Note

Most quotations appearing here in English are from published English editions, as cited in the notes. Occasionally, however, we have modified these translations to reflect the original sources or the French translations used by Stiegler. Emphasis in quotations follows the cited editions unless otherwise specified.

Stiegler's interpolations of words or phrases in quotations are enclosed in curly brackets. Our own interpolations in quotations and in Stiegler's text are enclosed in square brackets. Stiegler's omissions in quotations are indicated with spaced ellipsis dots (thus: . . .). His ellipses in his own text are marked with unspaced suspension points (thus: ...).

TECHNICS AND TIME, 1

General Introduction

> Do you admit to this certainty: that we are at a turning point?
> —If it is a certainty, then it is not a turning point. The fact of being part of the moment in which an epochal change (if there is one) comes about also takes hold of the certain knowledge that would wish to determine this change, making certainty as inappropriate as uncertainty. We are never less able to circumvent ourselves than at such a moment: the discreet force of the turning point is first and foremost that.
>
> —Maurice Blanchot

At the beginning of its history philosophy separates *tekhnē* from *ēpistēmē*, a distinction that had not yet been made in Homeric times. The separation is determined by a political context, one in which the philosopher accuses the Sophist of instrumentalizing the *logos* as rhetoric and logography, that is, as both an instrument of power and a renunciation of knowledge (Châtelet 1965, 60–61). It is in the inheritance of this conflict—in which the philosophical *ēpistēmē* is pitched against the sophistic *tekhnē*, whereby all technical knowledge is devalued—that the essence of technical entities in general is conceived:

> Every natural being . . . has within itself a beginning of movement and rest, whether the "movement" is a locomotion, growth or decline, or a qualitative change . . . [whereas] not one product of art has the source of its own production within itself.[1]

No form of "self-causality" animates technical beings. Owing to this ontology, the analysis of technics is made in terms of ends and means, which implies necessarily that no dynamic proper belongs to technical beings.

Much later, Lamarck distributes physical bodies into two principal fields: firstly, the physiochemistry of inert beings, and secondly, the science of organic beings. There are

> two classes of body: the inorganic [is] non-living, inanimate, inert; the organic [is] what breathes, feeds, and reproduces; it [is] "inevitably doomed to die" {Lamarck, *Philosophie zoologique*}. Organization becomes identified with the living. Beings [are] definitively separated from things. (Jacob 1973, 101)

To these two regions of beings correspond two dynamics: mechanics and biology. Lodged between them, technical beings are nothing but a hybrid, enjoying no more ontological status than they did in ancient philosophy. Since matter receives accidentally the mark of a vital activity, a series of objects that are manufactured over a period of time does nothing but report an evolution: a technical being belongs essentially to mechanics, doing little more than conveying the vital behavior of which it is but a thin trace.

Envisaging the possibility of a techno-logy that would constitute a *theory* of the evolution of technics, Marx outlined a new perspective. Engels evoked a dialectic between tool and hand that was to trouble the frontier between the inert and the organic. In the same period, archaeology discovered manufactured objects more ancient than those known before, and after Darwin the origins of humanity became a vexed question. Gilbert Kapp developed his theory of organic projection, which inspired the work of Alfred Espinas at the end of the nineteenth century. At the moment when historians of the Industrial Revolution began to consider the role played by new forms of technics, the discipline of ethnology amassed enough documentation on primitive industries for the question of technical development, irreducible to the disciplines of sociology, anthropology, general history, and psychology, finally to impose its importance. On the basis of this work, Bertrand Gille, André Leroi-Gourhan, and Gilbert Simondon elaborated in this century the concepts of technical system, technical tendency, and process of concretization.

Lodged between mechanics and biology, a technical being came to be considered a complex of heterogeneous forces. In a parallel development, while industrialization was overthrowing both the contemporary order of knowledge and contemporary social organization, technics acquired a new place in philosophical questioning. Philosophical reflection was now faced with such widespread technical expansion that all forms of knowledge were mobilized by, and brought closer to, the field of instrumentality, to which science, with its ends determined by the imperatives of economic struggle or war, and with its epistemic status shifting accordingly, became more and more subject. The power that emerged from this new relation was unleashed in the course of the two world wars. While Nazism took hold of Germany, Husserl analyzed the technicization of mathematical thought by algebra in terms of a technique of calculation, one that he traced back to Galileo. For Husserl, this process gave rise to an arithmeticization of geometry that

> leads almost automatically to the emptying of its meaning. The actually spatio-temporal idealities, as they are presented first hand in geometrical thinking under the common rubric of "pure intuitions," are transformed, so to speak, into pure numerical configurations, into algebraic structures. (Husserl 1970, 41)

Numeration is a loss of originary meaning and *sight*, a loss of the eidetic intentionality that underlies scientificity as such:

> In algebraic calculation, one lets the geometric signification recede into the background as a matter of course, indeed one drops it altogether; one calculates, remembering only at the end that the numbers signify magnitudes. Of course one does not calculate "mechanically," as in ordinary numerical calculation; one thinks, one invents, one makes discoveries—but they have acquired, unnoticed, a displaced, "symbolic" meaning. (44–45)

The technicization of science constitutes its eidetic *blinding*. Considered in terms of the Leibnizian project of a *mathēsis universalis*, the ensuing displacement of meaning leads to an elaboration of method that is metaphysical. Algebraic arithmetic, through which nature falls under systematic "instruction" and instrumentalization,

> is drawn into a process of transformation, which . . . becomes a mere art of achieving results, through a calculating technique according to technical rules. . . . "Original" thinking *that genuinely gives meaning to this technical process, and truth to the correct results* . . . is here excluded. (46)

Technicization is what produces loss of memory, as was already the case in Plato's *Phædrus*. In this dialogue's staging of the conflict between Sophist and philosopher, hypomnesic logography menaces the anamnesic memory of knowledge, and *hypomnēsis* risks contaminating all memory, thereby even destroying it. With the advent of calculation, which will come to determine the essence of modernity, the memory of originary eidetic intuitions, upon which all apodictic processes and meaning are founded, is lost. Technicization through calculation drives Western knowledge down a path that leads to a forgetting of its origin, which is also a forgetting of its truth. This is the "crisis of the European sciences." Without a refoundation of rational philosophy, science—having lost the object itself of any science—leads, it is argued, to the technicization of the world. This fate is announced in a historical context in which, to use the words of G. Granel,

> great humanists . . . like Cassirer and Husserl tried in the 1930's to oppose to the rise of fascist "barbarism" various forms of "regeneration" of modern rational philosophy. (Granel 1976, v)

An existential analytic (in Heidegger's sense) no longer seeks to refound rational philosophy: if the technicization of knowledge remains at the heart of the Heideggerian reflection on the history of being, *ratio* appears, in its essence, to be given over to calculation; *ratio* is a technical process that constitutes the *Gestell* (*ar-raisonnement*)[2] of all beings. And yet, at a much more profound level, destiny and "historiality"[3] are also thought by Heidegger in terms of an originary technicity, articulating the analyses of worldhood at the close of the 1920's with the "other thought" of "Time and Being" in the age of cybernetics—with the reading of *Antigone* in *An Introduction to Metaphysics*, "The Age of the World Picture," and *Identity and Difference* lying in between.[4]

The theme of forgetting dominates Heidegger's thinking of being. Being is historial, and the history of being is nothing but its inscription in technicity. If truth is itself thought in terms of this originary forgetting, it is insofar as the determination of the meaning of *alētheia* still echoes the Platonic structure of reminiscence such as it is determined in opposition to hypomnesic memory, while this memory constitutes the destiny of being as the forgetting of being.

Thinking truth as an exit from "withdrawal" and the history of being as forgetting will lead necessarily to thinking time within the horizon of an originary technicity *qua* an originary forgetting of the origin. For Heidegger, forgetting is inscribed: firstly, in the existential constitution of Dasein as instrumentality or equipmentality and, via equipment, as *calculation*; and secondly, in the (Western) history of being, thought since the pre-Socratics as *omoiōsis*, since Plato as correctness (*orthotēs*), and, with Descartes and Leibniz, according to the principle of reason that determines *mathēsis universalis* as *calculation*.

Heidegger's reflection upon technics only becomes clear, insofar as it is clear, if it is understood on these two levels at once: on the first, the existential structure of Dasein, as a relation to time determined by *intratemporality*; on the second, as the destiny of the Western history of being through the "metaphysical" history of philosophy in which being is determined as presence and is characterized by a "vulgar" understanding of time in terms of the *now* of intratemporality, determined by calculation and by the measuring instruments of time. The task of thinking is consequently to "deconstruct" the history of metaphysics by repeating it, and to return to the originary question of the meaning of being. Such a project of thought appears to consist all the more in a "critique" of modern technics given that modern technics is apprehended as the effective completion of metaphysics.

Dasein, the "entity which we are ourselves,"[5] is the guarantor of being in its temporality, a temporality that is also its truth as the history of being. It is characterized by four traits: temporality, historiality, self-understanding, and facticity.

Dasein is temporal: it has a past on the basis of which it can anticipate and thereby be. Inherited, this past is "historial": my past is not my past; it is first that of my ancestors, although it is in essential relation with the heritage of a past already there before me that my own past is established. This historial, nonlived past can be inherited inauthentically: historiality is also a facticity. The past harbors possibilities that Dasein may not inherit *as* possibilities. The facticity implied by heritage opens up a twofold possibility for self-understanding. On the one hand, Dasein can comprehend itself on the basis of an understanding of existence which is banal and "opining" (subject to everyday opinion). On the other hand, Dasein can "possibilize" this past, in that it is not its own, insofar it has inherited it: it is then on the basis of *its* possibility—such that its past is constituted therein—that it inherits possibilities of "its" factical past. Dasein is in the mode of "having-to-be" because it never yet totally is; inasmuch as it exists, it is never finished, it always already anticipates itself in the mode of "not yet." Between birth and death, existence is what extends itself [*Er-streckung*] between "already" and "not yet." This ecstasis is constituted through the horizon of death in that Dasein, in any act of self-anticipation, is always already anticipating its own death (its own end). Any activity on Dasein's part is always essentially ordered by anticipation of the end that is "the most extreme possibility" and that constitutes the originary temporality of existence.

This possibility of anticipation is, nevertheless, twofold. On the one hand, Dasein can in its activity always not "possibilize" the being-toward-the-end that forms its very essence, refusing thereby to open itself to its future insofar as it is its own, a future that is as radically indeterminate as the "when," "why," and "how" of its end. In this case, it reduces all its possibilities to those shared and recognized in the publicness of "being-in-common." It reduces them to the possibilities of others. On the other hand, Dasein can live its own possibilities *as* its incommensurable "ipseity," refusing to retreat before the essential solitude in which the anticipation of its own end ultimately always leaves it. Authentic existence is as radically indeterminable by "others" (by the publicness of being-in-common) as the death of Dasein, which can only be its own, is only its own because, radically indeterminate, death can remain nothing but unknown to it. *Its* death is what it cannot know, and to this extent, death gives to "mine-ness" its excess. Death is not an event within existence because it is the very possibility of existence, a possibility that is at the same time essentially and interminably deferred. This originary deferral is also what gives Dasein its difference to another.

The possibility of refusing the horizon of authentic possibility takes root in "concern" (*Besorgen*), a relation to the future which conceals in the future the opening of all authentic possibility. Concern is constituted by a mode of anticipation which, as foresight, essentially aims to determine possibility, that is, the undetermined. The support of all concern is "equipment" (*das Zeug*), itself the support of the system of references that constructs the significance of the world; and the horizon of anticipation, the originary structure of all worldliness, is the *technical* world—the technicity of the world is what reveals the world "firstly" and most frequently in its *facticity*. Facticity, understood as what makes possible the attempt to determine the indeterminate (to take flight from "the most extreme possibility"), forms the existential root of *calculation*. Calculation, the existential rooting of which is organized by facticity as an essential trait of technics—which also makes a heritage possible, constituting from the start the originary horizon of all authentic temporalization—is the falling of existence.

It is within these deep strata of temporality that the question of technics is located in Heidegger's work. In texts subsequent to *Being and Time*, after the "turning," the question is articulated no longer in terms of the existential dimension of the analytic of Dasein but as a motif constitutive of the very possibility of the deconstruction of the history of metaphysics. If it is true that the metaphysical side of philosophy culminates in the projection of a *mathēsis universalis* that encourages a *subject* to establish itself "as the master and possessor of nature," where the essence of reason ends up as calculation, then this turning of metaphysics forms an entrance to the technical age of philosophical thought, as a result of which technics in its modern guise brings subjectivity to its completion as objectivity. The *modern* age is essentially that of modern *technics.*

Thus the difficulty of an interpretation of the meaning of modern technics for Heidegger is on a par with the difficulty of his entire thought. Modern technics is the concern of numerous texts, which do not always appear to move in the same direction. In other words, the meaning of modern technics is ambiguous in Heidegger's work. It appears simultaneously as the ultimate obstacle to and as the ultimate possibility of thought. Among the works that deem it an obstacle, "The Question of Technics" and "The Age of the World Picture" are often quoted. However, the late essays "Time and Being" and "The End of Philosophy and the Task of Thinking" inscribe the possibility of another thinking within the task of contemplating the belonging-together of being and time in the *Gestell.* In "The Principle of Identity," *Gestell* designates

> the gathering of this challenge which places man and being face to face in such a way that they challenge each other. . . . That in which and from which man and being are of concern to each other in the technical world claims us in the manner of the *Gestell.* In the mutual confrontation of man and being we discern the claim that determines the constellation of our age. (Heidegger 1969b, 35)

To argue that modern technics is nothing but the completion of metaphysics is to consider only one side of *Gestell.* For *Gestell* also determines the co-appropriating of being and of time in terms of the "there is" (*es gibt*) of being and time. As a result the metaphysical determination of time is removed. Thenceforth the question is one of thinking being without beings—that is, without Dasein.

> The *Gestell* no longer concerns us as something that is present—therefore the *Gestell* seems at first strange. It remains strange above all because it is not an ultimate, but rather first gives us that which prevails throughout the constellation of being and man. (36)

Gestell forms a prelude to *Er-eignis* where

> man and being reach each other in their nature, achieve their active nature by losing those qualities with which metaphysics has endowed them. (37)

Identity, which is firstly identity of being and thought, constitutes the fundamental trait of being. But the principle of identity

> has become a principle bearing the characteristics of a spring that departs from being as the ground of beings, and thus springs into the abyss [*Abgrund*]. But this abyss is neither empty nothingness nor murky confusion, but rather the *Er-eignis* itself. (39)

Gestell is the global development of modern technics, and, as such, the completion of metaphysics.

"The Question of Technics" opens up a way of reflecting upon the essence of technics that moves against its metaphysical determination, specifying, moreover, the sense of modern technics in respect to technics in general. The major argument is that the traditional view of thinking technics under the category of "means" deprives one of any access to the essence of technics. This critique constitutes to a certain extent a reevaluation of the interpretation of technics given by the tradition from Aristotle onward. With reference to the *Nicomachean Ethics*[6] Heidegger contests the idea that the analysis of *Physics*, book 2, can be interpreted in terms of the categories of end and means.

> The current conception of technics, according to which it is a means and a human activity, can . . . be called the instrumental and anthropological definition of technics. (Heidegger 1977, 5)

He adds:

> But suppose now that technics were no mere means, how would it stand with the will to master it? (5)

The instrumental conception of technics is correct [*exacte*], but it reveals nothing of the essence of technics. So, the "correct" conception of technics does not go far enough.[7]

The analysis of technics in terms of end and means refers to the theory of material, formal, final, and efficient causes. The traditional interpretation of the theory of the four causes has privileged, in its understanding of technics, the efficient cause, the cause that operates—in the artisanal fabrication of an object, for example, the artist himself. The privilege accorded to the efficient cause leads to the instrumental conception of technics according to ends and means. Since the technical product is not a natural being, it does not have its final cause in itself. The final cause, appearing exterior to the product, resides in the producer, who, while being the efficient cause, equipped with the end, brings to the object the final cause—the object thereby being no more than the means.

As production (*poiēsis*), technics is a "way of revealing." Like *poiēsis*, it brings into being what is not. In the *Nicomachean Ethics* Aristotle writes:

> Every art [*tekhnē*] is concerned with bringing something into being, and looks for technical and theoretical means of producing a thing which belongs to the category of possibility and the cause of which lies in the producer and not in what is produced.[8]

If the technical product does not carry the principle of movement within itself but draws it from another—often allowing for the judgment that such and such a product is the means of which another product is the end—nevertheless, insofar as it effects a passage from a concealed state to a nonconcealed state, one of disclosure, this bringing-forth that is particular to technics constitutes a mode of truth. This means that the final cause is not the efficient operator but being as growth and unfolding: *phusis* and being are synonyms, the unconcealing of *phusis* is the truth of being as growth and bringing-forth (*poiēsis*). *Tekhnē qua poiēsis* is thus submitted to the final cause that *phusis*, working through the efficient cause, constitutes, without the efficient cause being in any way confused with the final cause. *Tekhnē*

> reveals whatever does not bring itself forth and does not yet lie here before us. (Heidegger 1977, 12)
>
> Thus what is decisive in *tekhnē* does not lie at all in making and manipulating nor in the using of means, but rather in the revealing mentioned before. It is as revealing, and not as manufacturing, that *tekhnē* is a bringing-forth. (13)

In the case of the "anthropological" conception of technics, in contrast, the efficient cause and the final cause are confused. Counter to this conception—that of subjectivity—it is, for Heidegger, only in art, the highest form of *tekhnē*, that the sense of *tekhnē* is fully grasped.

Nothing has been said yet of modern technics. It is also a form of disclosure, but one that

> does not unfold into a bringing-forth in the sense of *poiēsis*. The revealing that rules in modern technics is a challenging, which puts to nature the unreasonable demand that it supply energy which can be extracted and stored as such. (Heidegger 1977, 14)

Modern technics inflicts violence upon *phusis*; technics is no longer a modality of disclosure in accordance with the growing of being *as phusis*. Technics becomes modern when metaphysics expresses and completes itself as the project of calculative reason with a view to the mastery and possession of nature, itself no longer understood as *phusis*. And yet the being that we ourselves are is much less placed in a situation of mastery over nature by technics than it is subjected, as an entity belonging to the realm of nature, to the imperatives of technics.

So defined, modern technics constitutes the *Gestell* of nature and of humanity through calculation.

If modern technics nevertheless remains a mode of disclosure, it constitutes what is most properly to be thought. For it is through technics that the destiny of being unfolds, that is, technics is the history of being itself. As Heidegger remarks, *Gestell*,

> an in-between stage, offers a double aspect, one might say, a Janus head. (Heidegger 1972, 53)

Hence Jacques Taminiaux can write:

> It is being itself which, in its technical aspect, that is to say within the process of generalized technicization that now characterizes our world, and of which both Nietzsche and Marx, each in his own way, have correctly expressed the metaphysical essence . . . it is being itself which offers itself to us in withdrawal. But to say that, and to think what needs to be said here, this is what metaphysics cannot accomplish. (Taminiaux 1983, 275)

There is, of course, a Marxist offshoot to the above line of thinking. The thesis on technics presented by Herbert Marcuse, a student of Heidegger's, in *One Dimensional Man* (1964) determines, for example, Jürgen Habermas's position on modern technics, a position that is dependent in other respects on the thematics introduced in the Frankfurt School by Theodor Adorno and Max Horkheimer and that, in turn, furthers a dialogue already under way during the lifetime of Walter Benjamin.

In "Technics and Science as 'Ideology'" (Habermas 1987) Habermas puts in place the concept of communicative action that he opposes to technical activity and that will dominate all his later work. Marcuse's argument claims that, with modern technics, the meaning and direction of technical power is inverted: once liberating for humanity in his relation to nature, it has become a means of political domination. This thesis is supported by a critical reappropriation—influenced by Marx—of the concept of rationalization forged by Max Weber. Rationalization represents the phenomenon of an irresistible extension of the domains of society subject to the criteria of rational decision and the phenomenon of the correlative industrialization of work. It characterizes capitalism. Marcuse adds to this the idea that rationalization is in fact a hidden system of domination.

Habermas transforms and rebaptizes the concept: rationalization becomes the extension of "purposive-rational activity," linked to the institutionalization of scientific and technical progress. Habermas again takes up Marcuse's first thesis: in what Weber calls rationalization, it is not rationality that rules but rather, in the name of this rationality, a new form of political domination; one, however, which most importantly is no longer recognized *as* political domination since it finds itself legitimized by the progress of technoscientific rationality. This is an inversion of the meaning of *Aufklärung* in which the productive forces appeared as forces of demystification.

Marcuse's second thesis is that of the need to develop a new science that would be in dialogue with nature (this is the "Heideggerian inspiration," which is also an error of interpretation), free from technics as a force of domination. Referring to Arnold Gelhen, Habermas finds this project utopian. The history of technics represents that of a progressive but ineluctable objectification of purposive-rational action in technical systems. As is well known, Habermas proposes an alternative for which he coins a new concept, "symbolically mediated interaction," of which "communicative action" is an example, in opposition to work, which constitutes "purposive-rational action." Communicative action refers back to particular social norms that cannot be put on the same level as technical rules. The latter are empirically sanctioned, whereas social norms are grounded upon intersubjectivity alone. All human history can be analyzed, accordingly, as the history of the varying set of relations between communicative action on the one hand and purposive-rational action on the other. The difference between traditional societies and modern societies is characterized by the fact that, in the former, communicative action forms the basis of social authority (whether it be mythical, religious, or metaphysico-political), whereas in the latter, legitimation is dominated by technical and scientific rationality, which progressively spreads across all areas of life, including those so-called "communicative" aspects whose specificity is thereby denied. This only happens at the moment when the sciences and technics become indissociable—a marriage that makes "the sciences represent the most important productive force."[9]

Technocracy is born out of this marriage. In the context, technocracy should be considered less as the power of technicians than as technicians in the service of power, power created by technics as efficiency and as source of legitimacy, since technics has become indissociable from the sciences in which efficiency and purpose merge. The technocratic state no longer has as its aim either the encouragement of communicative action or the achievement of a critical distance toward purposive-rational action. On the contrary, it manages the dysfunctions engendered by purposive-rational action so as to reduce them and to avoid "those tendencies liable to threaten the system" (Habermas 1987, 101). Its activity consists in finding solutions to questions of a technical nature, those that escape public discussion. This situation generates a "systemic closing," in which "{social} interests define the social system so much as a whole that they coincide with the interest in maintaining the system" (105). Communicative action is progressively replaced by purposive-rational action, that is to say, by the scientific model of cybernetics as the technoscientification of language—a process that has led to the fact that "the industrially most advanced societies seem to approximate the model of behavioral control steered by external stimuli rather than guided by norms" (107). This constitutes a depoliticization of society and promotes a tendency toward the autonomization of purposive rational activities, an evolution that "does harm to language" (Jean-François Lyotard will take up this theme), that is, to socialization, to individuation, and to intersubjectivization. This tendency can go very far, being extended, for example, to "psychotechnical" manipulations (Herman Kahn).

The alternative to Marcuse's thesis proposed by Habermas rests on the idea that two concepts of rationalization must be distinguished:

> The process of development of the productive forces can be a potential for liberation if, and only if, it does not replace rationalization on another level. *Rationalization at the level of the institutional framework* can occur only in the medium of symbolic interaction itself, that is, through *removing restrictions on communication.* (Habermas 1987, 118)

The question is one of liberating communication from its technicization. It can be seen that the founding positions of philosophy still haunt these analyses.

Evidently Heidegger and Habermas are observing the same paradox concerning technical modernity. Technics, which appears to be a power in the service of humanity, becomes autonomous from the instance it empowers—technics ought to be an act on the part of humanity—as a result of which it does a disservice to active humanity, that is, insofar as humanity communicates, makes decisions, and assumes individual form. If Habermas and Heidegger are indeed interested in the same paradox, they do not analyze it in the same way, however. We must note a convergence as well as a divergence between their two approaches.

The convergence lies in the fact that both see the *technicization* of *language* as a denaturation—as if it were a question of one instance "proper to humanity" perverting another instance "proper to humanity." What is considered perverse is the possible confusion of these "properties."

The divergence resides in the fact that Habermas continues to analyze technics from the perspective of the category of "means," a category considered by Heidegger to be a metaphysical determination. Now, if technics is not a means, it can no longer be a question of having simply a "debate" on technics—through a "liberated" form of communication—nor, therefore, of ensuring for oneself a "minimum of subjectivity {or 'will and mastery'} . . . required for a democratic thought to fix limits" to technological expansion "through public decisions based themselves on public discussion and argumentation between subjects" (Ferry and Renaud 1988, 42–45). Much more radically, the preceding implies the need, today, to forge another relationship to technics, one that rethinks the bond originarily formed by, and between, humanity, technics, and language.

Thus, if Habermas and Heidegger appear to agree in considering the technicization of language as a perversion, both remaining here in the oldest philosophical tradition, we can also detect from within Heidegger's analysis the development of a completely different point of view. To give an indication: we would say that sophistic logography is also that of the *grammatist*, the ancient "tutor," without whom citizenship, as Henri Marrou and Marcel Détienne have remarked,[10] would never have been constructed in the first place. The stakes are, however, larger than the constitutive relationship between writing and citizenship.

What is more important is the relationship between technics and time. This is especially so if it is true that individuation and "intersubjectivization" are what is at stake in language. For what is given in speech is time, which is, as Heidegger says, "the true principle of individuation." The only condition on which Heidegger can oppose speech to instrumental technics in the first place is that speech bears this originary temporality of time, which calculative and technical instrumentality obscures in an intratemporality which is always that of concern. The whole question is whether such an evaluative distribution—according to which technics remains only *on one side* (of an opposition), itself not *constitutive* of individuation—in fact remains "metaphysical."

Whereas, on the one hand, the understanding of technics is now, as it has been since the Industrial Revolution and the profound social changes that accompanied it, largely determined by the categories of end and means, on the other hand, technics has itself achieved a new opacity, which will be more and more difficult to explicate with the increasing breakdown of knowledge into separate domains. During the past few years—a period placed under the sign of "modernization" and of politico-economic deregulation, in immediate relation with technoscientific development—this difficulty has become perceptible in all social spheres. The critical question of the relationship between technics and time is assuming its place on the public stage, daily, superficially, but in a more and more evident way. Each day brings its technical novelty, as well as the demise of things obsolescent and out of date. Innovation is inevitably accompanied by the obsolescence of existing technologies that have been superseded and the out-of-dateness of social situations that these technologies made possible—men, domains of activity, professions, forms of knowledge, heritage of all kinds that must either adapt or disappear. What is true of the largest political and economic structures is true of our life-world as well. The "understanding that Dasein has of its being" finds itself profoundly—and dangerously—shaken. It is as if a divorce could now be pronounced between, on the one hand, the technosciences and, on the other, the culture that claimed to have produced them, engulfed by technology. To quote Jean Ladrière:

> If, in certain respects, science, as a particular system of representation, and technology, as a particular system of action, are only subsidiary constituents of culture, in another sense, they have come to detach themselves from culture, instituting systems that are for the most part autonomous, in interaction with culture, but in opposition to it, as the universal is to the particular, the abstract to the concrete, the constructed to the given, and the sys-

> tematic to the existential. This is why it has become an urgent matter to question the modalities of interaction between science and technics on the one hand and culture on the other, and more particularly to ask how science and technology affect the future of culture in general, whether it be in the sense of a progressive disintegration or in the sense of an elaboration of new cultural forms. (Ladrière 1977, 18)

That these eventualities are today envisaged in the widest spheres of the world community is made obvious by the weight of ecological concern in recent geopolitical events. The "Heidelberg appeal," propounded at the world summit in Rio de Janeiro, just as the "counter-appeal" that was given in response, testify to the increasing importance of these questions in the highest echelons of science, technics, industry, the economy, and diplomacy.

Bertrand Gille, who anticipated these difficulties in the conclusion to his "Prolegomena to a History of Technics" (Gille 1977), shows that industrial civilization rests on an ever more intense development of the process of *permanent innovation.* It results in a divorce, if not between culture and technics, at least between the rhythms of cultural evolution and the rhythms of technical evolution. Technics evolves *more quickly* than culture. More accurately put, the temporal relation between the two is a tension in which there is both advance and delay, a tension characteristic of the extending [*étirement*] that makes up any process of temporalization. It is as if time has leapt outside itself: not only because the process of decision making and anticipation (in the domain of what Heidegger refers to as "concern") has irresistibly moved over to the side of the "machine" or technical complex, but because, in a certain sense, and as Blanchot wrote recalling a title of Ernst Jünger, our age is in the process of breaking the "time barrier." Following the analogy with the breaking of the sound barrier, to break the time barrier would be to go faster than time. A supersonic device, quicker than its own sound, provokes at the breaking of the barrier a violent sonic boom, a sound shock. What would be the breaking of a time barrier if this meant going faster than time? What *shock* would be provoked by a device going quicker than its "own time"? Such a shock would in fact mean that speed is older than time. For either time, with space, determines speed, and there could be no question of breaking the time barrier in this sense, or else time, like space, is only thinkable in terms of speed (which remains unthought).

Clearly, it is not the development of technics in general that generates in this form the foregoing reflection. This reflection can only acquire meaning when certain effects of technical development are carefully examined: namely, those that in computing one calls "real time" and in the media "live"—effects that distort profoundly, if not radically, what could be called "event-ization" [*événementialisation*] as such, that is to say, the taking place of time as much as the taking place of space.[11] And if it is true that genetic manipulations constitute the possibility of a radical acceleration of the differentiation of life forms, but also and especially the threat of indifferentiation, then we meet again the question of speed.

The Heideggerian existential analytic inscribes temporal advance and delay within the originary horizon of existence, existence being temporal and factical. In other words, Dasein only comes into the world insofar as the world has always already preceded it in its facticity, is always already the "already-there." Dasein is always behind its "already-there"; and yet, simultaneously, because its temporality is grounded in the anticipation of its end, Dasein is also always already ahead of itself, caught, thereby, in an essential advance.

The following reading rests on a confrontation between the Heideggerian existential analytic and the myths of Prometheus and of Epimetheus in their most known versions (Hesiod, Aeschylus, Plato). In classical Greek culture a mythology of the origin of technics is to be found which is also a mythology of the origin of mortality, a thanatology, the absence of analysis of which in Heidegger's work strikes us as highly revealing. For, as Jean-Pierre Vernant has admirably demonstrated (1982), *ēpimētheia* and *promētheia* form, in their very inseparability, two figures of temporalization. What is of particular interest for us in this analysis is the fact that the Promethean advance and the Epimethean withdrawal (which is also the fault of Epimetheus as the one who *forgets*) bring together *promētheia* as foresight and *ēpimētheia* as both unconcerned distraction and after-thought [*méditation après coup*]. It is their inextricability which gives mortals *elpis*, both hope and fear, which compensates for their consciousness of irremediable mortality. But this counterbalance is only possible given the de-fault of origin [*le défaut d'origine*] in which Epimetheus's fault consists—namely, the originary *technicity*, from which *ēpimētheia*, idiocy as well as wisdom, ensues.[12]

The interpretation of the meaning of the fault of Epimetheus will be the main leitmotif of this work. Along with this leitmotif, the major themes from the existential analytic will be interpreted and submitted to a critique that I sketched out above as much in respect to Habermas as to Heidegger.

With reference to Epimetheus's brother Prometheus, we will also be concerned, however, to draw out the possibilities for an analysis of technical dynamics that is reducible neither to mechanics not to biology nor to anthropology. I shall show in the first part of this work how various contributions to a theory of technical evolution permit the hypothesis that between the inorganic beings of the physical sciences and the organized beings of biology, there does indeed exist a third genre of "being": "inorganic organized beings," or technical objects. These nonorganic organizations of matter have their own dynamic when compared with that of either physical or biological beings, a dynamic, moreover, that cannot be reduced to the "aggregate" or "product" of these beings.

There is today a conjunction between the question of technics and the question of time, one made evident by the speed of technical evolution, by the ruptures in temporalization (event-ization) that this evolution provokes, and by the processes of deterritorialization accompanying it. It is a conjunction that *calls for a new consideration of technicity.* The following work aims to establish that organized inorganic beings are originarily—and as marks of the de-fault of origin out of which there is [*es gibt*] time—*constitutive* (in the strict phenomenological sense) of temporality as well as spatiality, in quest of a speed "older" than time and space, which are the derivative decompositions of speed. Life is the conquest of mobility. As a "process of exteriorization," technics is the pursuit of life by means other than life. I will show through a critical reading of Heidegger here and of Husserl in the second volume that when life becomes technical it is also to be understood as "retentional finitude." This retention, insofar as it is finite, is caught in the dynamic that a technical tendency determines. It is what neither existential analytic nor phenomenology could think, although the latter at the end of its Husserlian versions confronts the problem under the name of "writing." Existential analytic, inheriting the opposition that Husserl sets up in his analysis of the temporal object between primary, secondary, and tertiary retention (we call tertiary retention what Husserl designates by "image-consciousness"), did not give to what *Being and Time* calls the world-historial [*weltgeschichtlich*] its constitutive dimension of temporality, prior to and beyond the opposition between authentic temporality and intratemporality. We shall see how Simondon, with his analysis of psychic and collective individuation, allows one to conceive through the concept of "transduction" an originarily techno-logical constitutivity of temporality—without Simondon adopting such a conception himself. We shall thereby call in question Heidegger's claim that "the essence of technics is nothing technical" (1977, 35).

PART I

The Invention of the Human

Introduction

Our attempt will be to conjugate the question of technics with the question of time. We will take up this conjugation in the first place as the question of technics *in* time, and this first section will treat the history of techniques from the point of view of this history's concepts. To work on the concepts of the history of techniques rather than on the factuality with which the concepts can be exhumed is to attempt the theorization of technical evolution.

Today, we need to understand the process of technical evolution given that we are experiencing the deep opacity of contemporary technics; we do not immediately understand what is being played out in technics, nor what is being profoundly transformed therein, even though we unceasingly have to make *decisions* regarding technics, the consequences of which are felt to escape us more and more. And in day to day technical reality, we cannot spontaneously distinguish the long-term processes of transformation from spectacular but fleeting technical innovations.

More profoundly, the question is to know if we can predict and, if possible, orient the evolution of technics, that is, of power (*puissance*). What power (*pouvoir*) do we have over power (*puissance*)? If this question is not new, it comes to us in an entirely original way in contemporary technics: the confidence that has ruled this question since Descartes, at least, no longer holds. This is also the case because the division originarily made by philosophy between *tekhnē* and *ēpistēmē* has become problematic. If the conditions of a new relation—economic, social, and political—began with the Industrial Revolution, this novelty was actually declared a crisis only at the beginning of the twentieth century, with the First World War.

It constitutes the very grounds of contemporary philosophical debate, whose antagonistic figures are, in Europe, Heidegger and Habermas.

Confronted with this modernity, thinkers of technics as different as Simondon, Heidegger, and Gille express, each in his own idiom, a concern that they all share: that of envisaging a new relation between the human and technics.

Simondon thus calls for the development of a new knowledge: "technology" or "mechanology," founding a competence which is not spontaneously that of the engineer, the specialist of technical ensembles, or the worker, a specialist of technical elements. It is the competence of a specialist of technical individuals, who considers technics as a *process of concretization*, a competence manifestly made necessary by the new developments of technics.

Having characterized present-day culture as a defense mechanism against technics perceived as inhuman, having criticized this culture, which opposes technical reality and by that very fact opposes the human to the machine, having called for the development of a technical culture, for a new relation between culture and technics, Simondon wonders "what sort of human can achieve in itself the realization of technical reality and introduce that reality into culture" (1958, 12). This realization is not possible either for "the person attached to a sole machine by his or her work and to the fixity of daily objects (the relation of usage is not favorable to the realization)" or for the person directing "a firm using machines," who judges the machine "for its price and the results of its functioning rather than for itself." With regard to scientific knowledge, which "sees in the technical object the practical application of a theoretical law, it [knowledge] is not at the level of the technical domain either" (12).

Simondon would argue that culture has lost its "truly" general character when, with the appearance of the machine, it loses its "true" relation to the technical object. To become conscious of contemporary technical reality is to understand that the technical object cannot be a utensil (Simondon 1958, 13, 15), a fact that has become clear to us with the industrial-technical object, whose evolution, to the extent that it derives from what Simondon calls the process of concretization, excludes a simple end/means relation.[1]

We will deal here with the evolution of technics considered in general as a system, and in particular as a system that leads to the contemporary technical system. If there is a need, in Simondon's terms, for a new knowledge and a new competence, or in Gille's terms, for a new power, which, for Heidegger, is more profoundly the need for a thinking radically other than that predominant since the beginning of the West, the reason resides in the specificity of modern technics, that is, of the modern technical system, characterized precisely by the fact that it opens up a new epoch of technical systematicity. We will simply introduce here the question of this specificity (it will be dealt with in its own terms in the second volume of this study).

From this vantage, the specificity of modern technics resides, in essential part, in the speed of its evolution, which has led us to the conjugation of the question of technics with the question of time. Here the issue will be to understand the specificity of modern technics from the standpoint of a general history of technics, taken up in terms of a history of acceleration that, in the view of Ferdinand Braudel, also determines history itself.

Simondon characterizes modern technics as the appearance of technical individuals in the form of machines: hitherto, the human was a bearer of tools and was itself a technical individual. Today, machines are the tool bearers, and the human is no longer a technical individual; the human becomes either the machine's servant or its assembler [*assembliste*]: the human's relation to the technical object proves to have profoundly changed. Heidegger characterizes this "mutation" with the notion of *Gestell* (the systematization of the principle of reason). The semantics of *Gestell* is not foreign to that of system, and, in Gille's view, the concept of a technical system grounds a scientific history of techniques.

A "system" in ordinary language is "an apparatus formed by the assemblage of organs, of analogous elements."[2] "Apparatus" is a possible translation for the German term *Gestell*. As for the question of the organ, it will have a central place in our reflection; modern technics is dominated by cybernetics as the science of organization, in the largest sense, going back to the *organum* as instrumental to organization as characteristic of life. This is how Norbert Wiener's project (1950) for a cybernetic science is programmed, and it is also with the notion of cybernetic science that Heidegger characterizes modern technics (1972).

If it is true that systematicity informs the entire history of technics, in what respect, then, can modern technics be characterized as *Gestell*?

We have singled out from within Heidegger's analysis of modern technics that technics in general cannot be understood through the category of "means." Modernity, in this view, makes this manifest: modern technics is concretized in the *Gestell* apparatus of all resources. Posing exoterically the stakes of such *Gestell*, we will ask whether the human is the master of such an apparatus, the master of human destiny, given that the human is a part of "all the resources" and that the evolution of such an apparatus is the evolution of the human world. For Heidegger, systematicity, in terms of that which "challenges," is what absolutely distinguishes modern technics from any other epoch. Technics commands (*kubernaô*, the *etymon* of cybernetics) nature. Before, nature commanded technics. Nature is consigned by technics in this sense: nature has become the assistant, the auxiliary; in similar fashion, it is exploited by technics, which has become the master. For nature to be thus exploited and consigned, it has to be considered as ground, reserve, available stock for the needs of the system that modern technics forms. To exploit and "consign" nature is to realize the project of making oneself "as its master and owner."

This reflexive—making oneself—designates us, us humans. Now, is technics a means through which we master nature, or rather does not technics, becoming the master of nature, master us as a part of nature? It is first of all in this sense that Heidegger, in "The Question Concerning Technology," argues that technics cannot be defined as a means. And yet, by saying that it is a "mode of unconcealment," he carries the question beyond this anthropological level.

Technics constitutes a system to the extent that it cannot be understood as a means—as in Saussure the evolution of language, which forms a system of extreme complexity, escapes the will of those who speak it. This is why Heidegger is opposed to Hegel's definition of the machine as an independent instrument (a definition close to Simondon's, as we will see):

> When applied to the tools of the craftsman, his characterization is correct. Characterized in this way, however, the machine is not thought at all from out of the essence of technology with which it belongs. . . . {Seen in terms of the standing-reserve,} the machine is completely unautonomous, for it has its standing only from the ordering of the orderable. (Heidegger 1977, 17)

Like the machine, the human of the industrial age is dependent on the technical system, and serves it rather than making it serve itself; the human is the "assistant," the auxiliary, the helper, indeed the means of technics *qua* system.

It remains the case that the systematicity of technics, which excludes its being a means, dates from before modern technics, and is constitutive of all technicity. How then are we to pinpoint and describe, from a historical point of view, the systematic functioning of modern technics as challenge? We find in Gille a concept that attempts to give a historical answer that reverts to the question of decision and anticipation, that is, of time: the concept of programming.

Gille exposes the necessity, demanded by modern technics, of a new social competence in technics, highlighting, in a sense close to that of Heidegger in "The Age of the World Picture," the planifying and programmed character ("calculated" rather than "projected") of modern technics. The programming of the development of technics *qua* planification effects a rupture in the conditions of technical evolution. But as programmed intervention on the technical system itself, techno-economic planification has noncalculated consequences on the other constitutive systems of society (the "social" and the "cultural" systems)—and this is what has not yet been adequately taken into account and "regulated" by planification (Gille 1977, 78). Hence the programming of technical evolution harbors the threat of a general disequilibrium.

Gille's hypothesis is that we are moving into a new technical system that requires adjustments to the other social systems. The question that evidently comes to mind is knowing whether the social and the cultural systems are themselves "adjustable" in the sense of "programmable." Above all, this hypothesis presupposes the installation of a stable novelty. Now, along the lines of our hypothesis on speed, is not the new technical system chronically unstable? In this case, what might be the conditions of such "adjustments"?

Leroi-Gourhan will enable us to broach the question of the adjustment between the technical and the social from an anthropological point of view. More precisely, with the unity of the social being named the *ethnic*, a relation between the *ethnic* and the *technical* is set forth as grounding all anthropology. Leroi-Gourhan's question is that of an essential, and thereby originary, characterization of the anthropological by the technological. In his first works, Leroi-Gourhan elaborates the project of a technology's grounding of an anthropology. He approaches the subject from the viewpoint of the diffusion of technical objects. Then, posing the concept of a technical tendency informing history and geography, independent of ethnic determinations, he strives to question the process of invention at the level of ethnic groupings.

The necessity of technics *qua* the science of technical evolution or technogenesis makes up the terms in which Marx carries out his critique of the traditional point of view on technical invention:

> A critical history of technology would show how little any of the inventions of the eighteenth century are the work of a single individual. And yet such a book does not exist. Darwin has directed attention to the history of natural technology, that is, the formation of the organs of plants and animals, which serve as the instruments of production for sustaining their life. Does not the history of the productive organs of man in society, deserve equal attention? . . . Technology reveals the active relation of man to nature, the direct process of the production of his life, and thereby it also lays bare the process of the production of the social relations of his life, and of the mental conceptions that flow from these relations. (Marx 1976, 493 n. 4)

Gille and Simondon, as much as Leroi-Gourhan and Marx, essentially tie the scientificity of a technics to such a critique. We will deal here with the relation of technics and time as the question of invention. At bottom, the issue will be to understand the dynamic of the "technical system," to study the possibilities of a theory of technical evolution. We will see the question of a technical determinism arising in a permanent oscillation between the physical and biological modalities of this evolution, the technical object, an organized and nevertheless inorganic being, belonging neither to the mineral world nor simply to the animal. A central question will be that of the limits of application of the analogy between the theories of technical and biological evolution. This is equally the question of the traditional opposition between technical entities and entities deriving from *phusis*, an opposition whose line of demarcation is, as we saw with Aristotle, that of self-production, and which will need to be problematized.

We will first study what Gille calls the technical system, a notion existing in various forms in other authors' works which do not use it explicitly but which describe technics following the same idea. As for Gille, a technical system designates in the first instance a whole play of stable interdependencies at a given time or epoch. The history of techniques is essentially designed to account for the possibilities of passing from one technical system to another.

We will next see how Leroi-Gourhan deploys the concept of technical systematicity differently from Gille. The former develops the hypothesis of a systematic evolution of technics, which he deals with through the notion of technical tendency. The question he thereby introduces regarding the relations between the ethnic and the technical is central to the specificity of modern technics, if it be true that the latter "uproots" peoples, blurring, even effacing, ethnic differentiations.

With Simondon, we will address the question of the contemporary technical system in its relation to the industrial technical object within the process of concretization. We will envisage the possibility of using the concept of concretization to describe the evolution of the technical system in general by considering the system itself as individual and object.

At the end of the first chapter, having come full circle in our investigation of technical evolution, that is, of technics in time, the possibility will arise that technics, far from being merely in time, properly constitutes time. This hypothesis will be opened through our study of the relations between technology, or technogenesis, and anthropology, or anthropogenesis, and particularly through a reading of Rousseau, whence we will return to Leroi-Gourhan's work in prehistory. The full scope of the hypothesis will not be fully envisaged, however, until, in the following section, the anthropological point of view has been abandoned and its consequences then set off against the thesis of temporality that comes out of the Heideggerian existential analytic.

§ 1 Theories of Technical Evolution

General History and the History of Techniques

The general concept of a technical system is elaborated by Bertrand Gille from the perspective of a historical science. Strictly speaking, in Gille's work there is no one technical system but a succession of technical systems. In the course of a historical period, a system is constituted as a stabilization of technical evolution around previous acquisitions and structural tendencies determined by a play of interdependencies and inventions complementing one another, in relation to other dimensions characteristic of a particular historical period.

This is a proposal in historical method not only for the history of techniques but for general history: it is a question of elaborating "a history bound, so to speak, by the material world" (Gille 1978, ix), a history that can account for the everyday material world throughout history, initiate a dialogue with the specialists of other systems (economic, linguistic, sociological, epistemological, educational, political, military, and so forth) on the question of the site of technics [*la technique*] in the global coherence of the "human system," and determine the periods of technical development.

Beyond this, what is in question is an apprehension of the possibilities of passage from one technical system to another. From the vantage of a synchronic principle, Gille proposes to describe and explain the diachrony of ruptures, mutations, revolutions, of what in general is called "progress" in the specifically technical sense of the term: "What may appear, in scientific progress, not so much simple as clear and rigorously ordered, appears infinitely less so in technical progress" (1978, x). How does invention take place? Through a process unlike scientific progress: "if there is a certain logic to technical progress, this logic is not perfectly autonomous. Firstly, a certain coherence is necessary in that an isolated technique does not exist without reference to attendant techniques" (x): the logic of this progress for a particular technique is primarily determined by the technical system to which it belongs.

Lucien Febvre called attention to the necessity and the lack of an actual history of techniques within general history, to the necessity of a concept founding its method: the history of techniques is "one of these numerous disciplines that are entirely, or almost entirely, to be created" (Febvre 1935, 16). This necessity appeared notably in the thesis of Lefèbvre des Noëttes, which assigned to technical innovation—to the harnessing and saddling of the horse—a determining role in the disappearance of slavery, and highlighted the problem of the role of technics in human development and of a technical determinism in history.

The stakes are high. The incorporation of the history of techniques into general history is particularly difficult.

There is first of all the problem, intrinsic to the object "technics" [*la technique*], of not falling into a specialized, parceled history *of techniques*: *technics* is the object of a history of techniques, beyond techniques.[1] At present, history knows only techniques, because technics is essentially specialization. Technics is not a fact but a result. The history of techniques, then, needs this result to become organized into *a* history of technics.

There is on the other hand a problem in establishing the actual connections with other historical aspects; this places the preceding problem at a more general level. There are economic, political, demographic facts, and so forth. But it is the unity of the historical fact that gathers this diversity into *a* general history. Here again, the result must provide the unity of the operation from which the result results.

The concept of a technical system aims at the solution of these problems. Such a result returns after the event [*après coup*] as the possibility of a new, more stable beginning.

The Technical System

As in linguistics, here the point of view creates the object, and the concepts will have to order reality according to the static and dynamic aspects of the general system that reality forms. As in linguistics, here the system is the major concept.

Technical structures, ensembles, and channels are static combinations in which phenomena of retroaction appear: by using the steam engine, the steel industry produces better steel, allowing in turn for the production of more efficient machines. Here, then, the necessity of a concept of technical system becomes urgent. The various levels of combinations are statically and dynamically interdependent, and imply laws of operation and processes of transformation. Each level is integrated into a superior level dependent upon it, right up to the global coherence that the system forms.

A technical system constitutes a *temporal unity. It is a stabilization of technical evolution around a point of equilibrium concretized by a particular technology*: "The establishment of these connections can only take place, can only become efficient, once the common level of the ensemble of techniques is realized, even if, marginally, the level of some of the techniques, more independent than others, has remained below or above the general level" (Gille 1978, 19). A sort of technical mean is thus established around the point of equilibrium.

The evolution of technical systems moves toward the complexity and progressive solidarity of the combined elements. "The internal connections that assure the life of these technical systems are more and more numerous as we advance in time, as techniques become more and more complex." This globalization [*mondialisation*] of such dependencies—their universalization and, in this sense, the deterritorialization of technics—leads to what Heidegger calls *Gestell*: planetary industrial technics—the systematic and global exploitation of resources, which implies a worldwide economic, political, cultural, social, and military interdependence.

The Technical System in Its Relation to Economic and Social Systems

The question posed to history is that of the relation between the technical system and what we shall call the "other systems." In the first place, it is obvious that links exist between the technical and economic systems: there is no work without technics, no economic theory that is not a theory of work, of surplus profit, of means of production and investment.

There are two opposing points of view on what determines the relations between these systems: "Some have been led to think that the technical systems were, from the beginning, more astringent than the economic systems. Conversely, a technique must be incorporated into a system of prices, into an organization of production, failing which, it loses its economic interest—its proper finality" (Gille 1978, 24).

The economy may constitute a brake on the expansion of the technical system. Thus, the practice of preserving outlived techniques for economic reasons is commonplace—and only one example of the problem of adequacy between the evolutional tendencies of technics and economico-political constraints. The aim of state interventionism is the regulation of their relation—for example, through a system of customs regulations, or through public investment.

The transformations of the technical system regularly bring in their wake upheavals of the social system, which can completely destabilize it when "the new technical system leads to the substitution of a dominant activity for an out-dated activity of a totally different nature" (Gille 1978, 26). Hence the very general question of technology transfer arises. What is of interest to us here is the ever-present necessity of solving this problem in the twentieth century, which is characterized, as we shall see, by economic activity based on ever more rapid technological innovation. The relation between the technical and social systems is thus treated as a problem of consumption, in which the economic system is the third component: the development of consumerism, accompanying constant innovation, aims at a greater flexibility in consumer attitudes, which adapt and must adapt ever more quickly, at a pace obviously not without effect on the specifically cultural sphere. The twentieth century thereby appears properly and massively uprooting—and this will always provide the theme, in terms of alienation and decline, of the great discourses on technics.

The Limits of the Technical System

The limits of a system order its dynamism. Structural limits can be detected "either in the problem of increasing quantities, or in the impossibility of reducing production costs, or in yet another impossibility, that of diversifying production" (Gille 1978, 26). Economic crises are due to these structural limits.

The report *A Halt to Growth*[2] characterized our age from 1970 as one threatened by the limits of the development of technics in its relation to the terrestrial ecosystem. Gille criticized the report in its failure to apprehend technics *qua* system and its consequent inability to analyze correctly the complex nature of its limits: the limit, exhibiting a negative and a positive side, is the principle factor in the transformation of the technical system. Technical progress consists in successive displacements of its limits. The steam engine, as it becomes more powerful, becomes more cumbersome. Below 5,000 horsepower, it is not profitable, and "above a certain capacity, no gain is possible: dimensions, turnover, costs, all necessarily linked to one another, impose a limit that it would be unthinkable to surpass" (Gille 1978, 32–33). Such limits, which can "block a whole system, . . . can just as well . . . create disequilibriums inducing crises," engendering evolutions and decisions. "If . . . all techniques are interdependent, reaching a limit in a given sector may stymie the entire technical system, that is, stymie its general evolution. . . . Around 1850–1855, the replacement of the iron rails of railroads threatened to become a financial disaster if the weight and speed of the trains continued to increase" (34). One had to await the invention of the Bessemer smelting furnace, which allowed for the production of steel rails, before railroad transport would show a marked improvement. This is a case of an endogenous limit to the technical system. But there are also exogenous limits. This is, for example, the case with French techno-economic protectionism in the nineteenth century: it was because of the imposition of duties on the importation of English iron, that is, because of "customs protection, that a country like France . . . was unable to surpass certain limits"; in other words, protectionism stalled the evolution of the steel and iron industry and its global technical system. Conversely, dynamic analysis "highlights structural limits that induce invention and lead to mutations of the systems" (35). When a set of conditions is grouped into a system, a decision to evolve takes place. In other words, there is on the one hand progress *qua* the development of the consequences of a technological invention within a stable technical system, without obligatory crises, without brutal discontinuity—a development Gille calls "technological lines"—and on the other hand, progress as destabilization of the technical system, reconstitution around a new point of equilibrium, and the birth of a new technical system. New technical systems are born with the appearance of the limits of the preceding systems, owing to which progress is *essentially discontinuous.*

Rationality and Determinism in the Process of Invention

The question, in sum, is to know how an evolution of the system is decided: this is the problem of the logic of invention. The horizon of a mutation is a play of limits within a system, forming an evolutional potential; the effectuation of the mutation is the technical invention itself, *qua* the catalyst of this potential, *qua* the act of evolutional potentiality.

The explanation of this actualization is not to be found on the side of scientific discovery. Although technical and scientific progress may converge, and scientific discovery engender technical innovation, there are in each case two different processes of invention or discovery, possibly complementary but irreducible to one another. Technical discovery cannot be typified by the mere development and implementation of a scientific discovery. Such an "implementation," when it occurs, is itself autonomously inventive, following a logic that is not the logic of science.

There is, then, a singularity in the logic of technical invention. Réné Boirel speaks of a "diffuse rationality" (Boirel 1961). The term "rationality" is indeed apt, since technics, in functioning, enters into the causal chains of the principle of reason, is inscribed in the real while transforming it, thereby respecting its laws. But this rationality is nevertheless "diffuse" to the extent that the necessity it entails would be "looser" than that in scientific rationality. Technical invention, not being guided by a theoretical formalism preceding practical operation, remains empirical; however, the inventive operation cannot be said to be produced by chance, for an essential part of innovation is accomplished through transfer, whereby the functioning of a structure in a technical apparatus is analogically transposed into another domain. There is, then, a combinatory genius in technical invention. This also implies the cumulative nature of technical knowledge, although in another sense than in scientific knowledge. One should speak of technological lineages, of paths through the empirical realm [*empirie*], of tentative groundbreakings [*frayages*] in the development of the potential of a technique whereby invention deploys itself. The rationality of technical invention, "situated on a determined technological line," would then be diffuse "to the extent that choices may be made, various combinations set up. For the inventor, the whole question is knowing whether the road to follow is wide or narrow" (Gille 1978, 40).

As for this apparent possibility of *choice*, Gille speaks, with J. L. Maunoury, of "loose determinism." The difference of this from strict determinism would consist in the impossibility of anticipating technical evolution a priori, although this evolution appears necessary a posteriori—and Maunoury speaks here of chance (in Gille 1978, 41). Everything comes about as if technical innovation accomplished randomly, but certainly, the fulfillment [*remplissement*] of a technical, or techno-logical, "intention." We shall see this theme taken up in much more depth by Leroi-Gourhan and Simondon, when, once again, the hypothesis of a combinatory genius will arise, a hypothesis of such genius's random but ineluctable adjustment, an actual process of *selection of technical archetypes* recalling in singular fashion the play of chance and necessity in molecular biology.

Gille distinguishes between simple invention (for example, John Kay's flying shuttle), development (successive perfectings that improve a technique without modifying its fundamental principles), and invention as a mounting operation (for example, the internal combustion engine); it is not a matter of a unique technical lineage, but of a series of technical lines. In technical invention, other levels intervene above the technological lineage as such: scientific knowledge and interdependencies with other systems, along with external constraints in general, for example economic constraints (as was the case with the Bessemer smelting furnace), but above all, *technical systematicity itself*, that is, the play of constraints imposed by the interdependencies between technical elements and those intrinsic to the system. *The system's dynamic offers the possibility of invention, and this is what is essential to the concept of technical system: the choice of possibilities in which invention consists is made in a particular space and particular time according to the play of these constraints*, which are submitted in turn to external ones.

As a consequence, rationality "appears difficult to put into question to the extent that the number of usable combinations is not infinite, given that, basing itself on existing structures, it must follow quasi-obligatory paths." Determinism "is not less obvious. Technical determinism, scientific, economic, even social or political determinism" (Gille 1978, 47).

Throughout all this, Gille significantly restrains the role of genius in inventiveness: if there is rationality in the inventive operation and determinism of the system,

> whatever the level chosen, whatever the epoch considered, the freedom of the inventor is severely bounded, severely limited by the demands that invention

> must meet. Thus not only are choices imposed . . . but also the moments in which the invention arises, determined by scientific progress, by the parallel progress of all techniques, by economic necessities, etc. (Gille 1978, 48)

In other words, the logic of invention is not that of the inventor. One must speak of a techno-logic, of a logic literally driving technics itself. Must one speak of a technological reason? A proof of techno-logical universality would then be required, which Gille does not offer; the question as such does not arise. It is, however, the very object of reflection for Leroi-Gourhan, for whom a universal technical tendency exists, largely independent of cultural localities where it becomes concretized as technical fact, and where it can precisely enter into conflict with local cultures that accomplish it since it is universal while they are particular. We shall then see how Leroi-Gourhan transforms Gille's problem (in terms of an articulation between the technical system and others) into a veritable opposition between technics *qua* a universal tendency and what Leroi-Gourhan will name the ethnic *qua* a factor of diversifying diffraction from which the universal tendency will nevertheless profit.

Invention and Innovation

Two phases in the process of invention must be distinguished—the phase of adjustment and that of development—and a difference must be introduced (taken from François Perroux) between invention and innovation. Innovation accomplishes a transformation of the technical system while drawing the consequences for the other systems. In other words, the rules of innovation are wholly different from those of invention. The rules of innovation are those of socialization, as analyzed mainly by economists: "Innovation is mainly of an economic order" (Gille 1978, 52).

Innovation destabilizes established situations: it thereby creates resistance. The socialization in which innovation consists is work on the milieus it crosses through (social, economic, political, etc.). Beyond the fear of change, socialization also encounters the problem of technological investment and anticipation: there is always a possibility that an innovation will be made obsolete by another innovation arising to replace it. This is especially true in contemporary technics, given its speed of transformation and the decision-making problems this speed implies. This is all the more true since such anticipations suppose a vantage on the technical system as a whole, a system increasingly complex and interdependent.[3] These questions are the object of difficult calculations, which evidently suppose modelings of the technical system in relation to economic models: it is a matter of calculations of the "production function," which is a "series of technical relations in an industrial branch between the factors of the function and its products" (Gille 1978, 54).

One could say that the logic of innovation is constituted by the rules of adjustment between the technical system and the others. There is for each age a typology of the conditions of innovation that are possibilities of adequacy between the technical system and the other systems. Along these lines a French iron master, Rambourg, examined the reasons for resistance to the transfer of English iron and steel industrial technology to France,[4] finding that the variables conditioning the process of innovation stem from the geographical system (physical and human geography), the technical system itself, and the educational system. Rambourg next introduced the question of capital, that is, the question of adequacy to the economic system.

A historical approach to these conditions and to tempos of distribution of an innovation would thus lead to the creation of a typology, "being simultaneously a typology with regard to purely technical elements, which would therefore mesh well with a typology of invention; a typology according to factors of production that are not of a technical nature; and finally a typology following a chronology to be determined" (Gille 1978, 60), which would account for rhythms of transformation, cycles of acceleration and deceleration of the evolution of the technical system.

Industrial Investment: A Joint Evolution of the Technical System, the Economic System, and the Apparatus of the State

The question of investment—that is, of the adjustment between the management of capital, the management of the existing means of production, and the development of the potentialities of the technical system—deserves particular attention, to the extent that the nineteenth-century industrial technical system imposed a profound reorganization of the economic system. From the point of view of relations between the industrial technical system and the economic one, the latter separates into two subsystems, the banking system and the productive (or entrepreneurial) system as such. This essential question points to a supplementary characteristic of modern technics, inscribed in the framework of what Gille calls the canals of innovation, capable of operating at "individual, collective or national" levels (1978, 62).

Innovation cannot exist without investment, and investment implies available capital. To mobilize this capital, innovation must be sufficiently attractive; it must in the strongest sense of the term create credit for itself. This necessity, regularly born out during the expansion of the Industrial Revolution, became dominant with the thermodynamic revolution, which presupposed large-scale investment and required that the economic system readapt its financial subsystem to the newly created conditions of the technical system. This is the context in which the limited company and the stock-market system developed, with the aim of assuring the mobility of capital (what Max Weber calls the "rationalization of speculation" [1958, 10]). This recently finalized transformation of economic organization, in which the financial sector becomes autonomous with regard to production, is today undergoing developments that are disturbing for the theoretical economist as well as the manager and the speculator: the so-called "financial bubble" is becoming autonomous to such an extent that it is often cut off from productive realities, and functions according to a logic of belief (or of credit) *massively determined by the performances of telecommunication and computer-based systems* in the management of financial data. Capital exchanges have become a problem of informational management effected "in a nanosecond." These exchanges are data that are exchanged and processed, and no longer monetary masses. Decisions made "in a nanosecond" are calculations performed on series of indicators dealing primarily with the stock markets themselves and with macroeconomic decisions interfering with them, and not evaluations of the macroeconomic situations of particular enterprises.[5]

If in fact there seems to be a technological determinism in the evolution of the economic system, the birth of modern capitalism appearing required by the birth of industrial technics, then conversely it could be said that the possibility of the technical system of thermodynamics and, beyond that, of industrial technics in general is conditioned by a new organization of the economic system, which itself supposes an accumulation of capital. In effect, there is a singular techno-economic conjugation whose consequence is the appearance of "technocracy" and "technoscience": the transformation of the economic system facilitates a convergence between the "propensity toward work of available capital" and the propensity of technical activity toward innovation and improvement. Favoring this convergence becomes an actual state politics (according to a tradition that would refer back to Colbert). The point is as much acculturation and national scientific and technical information as it is that of a form of intervention and investment on the most collective scale possible.

To understand the dynamic of innovation is to understand how cascading convergences operate. The innovative dynamic, which conditions all the others (and would tend to render the technological determinations preeminent), "is of a purely technical order. It is indeed necessary that, on the plane of production itself, innovation be incorporated into a balanced technical system" (Gille 1978, 64) and consequently, that a stabilization take place at the end of a process of transformations that first appears as a disturbance of the existing system: the logic of innovation is properly that of the evolution of the technical system itself. In question here is what is today referred to as *development*,[6] understood as perpetual modernization or constant innovation. We have rapidly examined the question of the relation of these convergences "of a purely technical order" to the economic system. But the innovator must also include in his calculation—for it is indeed a matter of accomplishing the process by calculation—social, political, and institutional constraints, which can constitute in certain cases temporarily insurmountable obstacles. And if resistance to technics is not recent, it has nevertheless become a day-to-day, worldwide problem, inscribed in the program of governments and international organizations; in fact, development constantly intervenes to modify everyday life, a life in which industrial technics is omnipresent. This inevitably engenders a new consciousness of development's opacity, even of its "autonomy," and a more or less organized resistance. Gille's description of the accentuation of reactions through time, and the collective measures taken by states and "decision makers" to attenuate them, paints a clear picture of mounting discontent, as diversely interpreted as it may be, in which what will constitute modern technics as we know it today takes on form.

Constant Innovation: A New Relation Between *Tekhnē* and *Ēpistēmē*

Carrying certain hypotheses of the above viewpoint to their extreme limits, one might surmise that the French Revolution was perhaps less a realization of the exigency that the rights of the human be guaranteed, less a capture of power by the bourgeoisie, than an adaptation of the society to a new technical system through the full development of what Weber calls *free work.* All the analyses presented above, issuing in the formulation of such hypotheses, assign a considerable role to the engineer: to manage a technical system is to intervene in the social and economic transformations at a much more profound level than in what peoples, political organizations, and managers in the ordinary sense believe they decide. The intersection of technical and economic systems, today worldwide, issues in the techno-economic question of growth.

If we have been stressing, in order to analyze major characteristics of technical progress, the difference between scientific discovery and technical invention, we should now, nevertheless, underscore the tightening of the links between science and technics *qua* an essential aspect of contemporary technics—by which the conditions of scientific discovery itself are transformed. From the very beginning of modern technics, the transfer time of scientific discovery to technical invention and then to technical innovation has considerably shortened: "One hundred and two years elapsed between the discovery of the physical phenomenon applied to the photograph and photography itself (1727–1829)" whereas the transfer time was reduced to "fifty-six years for the telephone, thirty-five for radio, twelve for television, fourteen for radar, six for the uranium bomb, five for the transistor" (Gille 1978, 39). This reduction in delays is a result of what Weber, Marcuse, and Habermas call "rationalization." Its price is a totally new relation between science and technics (and politics), established by way of the economy.

Four factors of technical evolution have appeared: technical progress as invention, technical progress as innovation, economic and social progress, and scientific progress. Starting from the Industrial Revolution—with Watt and Boulton—and preeminently with contemporary industrial technics, the economic process has been based on constant innovation, that is, on an ever more rapid and more radical transformation of the technical system and, as an indirect consequence, of the "other systems," that is to say, of the world, resulting as well in a transformation of the relation between *tekhnē* and *ēpistēmē*. Gille points out two combinations, characteristic of modern technics, involving scientific progress, technical progress as invention, technical progress as innovation, and economic and social progress: scientific progress—invention—innovation; and invention—innovation—growth (1978, 70).

The first combination would posit scientific discovery as pressure encountering a convergence on the side of innovation (in industry), with invention the middle term. Initiative is then on the side of science, valorized by industry. In the second combination, where innovation is the middle term, initiative becomes much more economic, research is incorporated into the enterprise, science is commanded by development: it seems that in this case, the pressure comes

> above all from the necessities of growth, either in order to accelerate the installation of a new technical system, or to remedy distortions in technical progress as in the economic or social systems. In all domains, there is a passage to collective movements. The inventor has less importance than the entrepreneur who decides and establishes the junction between families of innovations. (Gille 1978, 72)

Here we see the beginning of what will become research and development in the modern sense, and which is the origin of what has been called technoscience. On the grounds of this new relation between science, technical system, and economic system, the state develops *qua* "technostructure" or "technocracy," aiming at the regulation of the transfer processes within each system. This is the transformation analyzed in "The Age of the World Picture" (Heidegger 1977) from the vantage of the history of being. With contemporary technics, in which "scientific and technical progress are . . . increasingly linked," in which "economic and scientific progress can no longer function separately" (Gille 1978, 73–74), *there is a reversal of meaning in the general scheme: no longer is innovation what results from invention; it is a global process aiming to incite invention, it* programs *the rise of invention.* "Before, invention, to be applied, had to wait until technical, economic, and social conditions and so forth had become favorable. Henceforth, the desire for innovation incites invention" (74). Research and development rest on this inversion, illustrated by the example of the creator of the Philips company, Doctor Holst, who inaugurates the time of actual industrial research, with his own laboratories at his disposal: this is what can be called technoscience as such.

The reduction in transfer delays mentioned above as characteristic of contemporary technics literally leads to a confusion between technical invention and scientific discovery. Research orientations are then massively controlled by industrial finalities. Anticipation, at the most global level, is essentially commanded by investment calculation—collective decision-making, temporalization—in short, destiny is submitted to the techno-economic imperatives regulating this calculation. This is as well the domination of a certain understanding of time. An increasingly crucial question is nevertheless posed by this understanding: that of the adjustment with the "other systems" (referred to globally under the name "culture" in our introduction) of a technical system in which the relations between science, invention, and innovation have been transformed in such a way that technological evolution is accelerated on a scale incommensurable with the former technical systems. Even if Gille does not situate the difficulty of such an adequacy between systems in the speed of development, he considers that we have not yet seriously envisaged the question, and that it is necessary to bring about a new understanding of the relation of the human to the technical. "If we are heading today toward a new technical system . . . , it is a question of assuring not only its internal coherence but also its coherence with the other systems" (1978, 76). In his view, this necessity finds expression in an excerpt from the French Fifth Economic Plan, which in effect poses the question of planning the technological transformation of society. At a rhythm of constant innovation, unknown factors are no longer possible; the movement must be controlled at the risk of collapsing the global coherence whereby the systems operate complementarily: at stake is the organization of the future, that is, of time:

> It is no longer a matter of undergoing uncertain technological progress in its realizations, . . . of accepting willy-nilly what occurs in the technical domain and of effecting after a fashion the necessary adaptations. In all domains, in the economic as well as the military domain, the future must be organized. (Gille 1978, 77)

The problem is one of organization *qua* the programming of technological progress, which implies that time must be included as calculation. Without calling into question such an implication, Gille deplores in his conclusion the inadequate realization of the stakes at hand and hence the inadequacy in the reigning conception of development planning of all the constitutive systems of society (what Simondon will interpret as the necessity of a new technical culture):

> When technical progress used random or apparently random channels, the adjustments of new technical systems to the other systems were carried out willy-nilly, by the play of a certain number of freely acting forces, with all the mistakes, all the retreats that this would imply before reaching a satisfactory equilibrium. If technical progress is henceforth to become something programmed, that is, ordered in fact, in space and time, the programming should spread to all the necessary compatibilities, in all domains—the economic domain, which is the one most often mentioned, but also the social, the cultural, and so forth. Without such research, it would undoubtedly be vain to seek to impose a technical progress falling short of the indispensable conditions of general equilibrium. (Gille 1978, 78)

Nevertheless, if, as we believe, the technical system has entered into an age of perpetual transformations and structural instability, one can surmise that the problem should be set out in other terms: those of the necessary reexamination of the originary relation between the human and the technical, *qua* a *phenomenon of temporality.*

Technical Universality

Should one speak of technological *reason*? The presence of a technological universality would then have to be proven, which Gille not only fails to do but does not even begin to do. André Leroi-Gourhan, on the other hand, starts from this very hypothesis. We have just seen the historian of technics taking up mainly two questions: firstly, that of a dynamism inherent in technics organized into a system, functioning according to its own at once rational and determinist logic; and secondly, that of a relation of such a dynamic system to the other systems, and hence of its incorporation into the global historical scheme. Leroi-Gourhan's viewpoint on these questions is no longer historical but ethnological. *Man and Matter* [*L'homme et la matière*, 1943] proposes the hypothesis of *universal, technical tendencies*, independent of the cultural localities that *ethnic* groupings compose, in which they become concrete [*se concrétisent*] as *technical facts.* Leroi-Gourhan thereby deals at once with the immanent technological dynamic and with the relation of the technical system to other systems. The tendency, in its universality, enters into a complex relation with particular ethnic realities that produce technical facts, from which facts it must be distinguished, although they alone give it reality. In "crossing through" ethnic milieus, the tendency "diffracts" into an indefinite diversity of facts. This will lead, in a reading of Leroi-Gourhan's *Milieu and Techniques* [*Milieu et techniques*, 1945], to a study of the relation between the *technical*, whose essence lies in the universal tendency, and the *ethnic*, whose manifestation as a particular concretization envelops its universality. The question of invention will once again be approached under this heading. This set of hypotheses on technical evolution depends on an analogy with biology and zoology. The theme of the combinatory, already present in Gille's work, is here much more clearly akin to *a theory of the selection of the best technical forms* effected along combinatory possibilities.

The ethnologist observes facts, between which he looks for links. Then he attempts to explain the principle of the linkages. In the field of technology, where this principle is also the driving force of evolution, the ethnologist's error has generally been to attribute the principle of universality deriving from the links between facts not to the technical tendency as such but to the genius of a particular culture: Indo-European culture. The concept of technical tendency is opposed to this ethnocentric illusion, formalized in the so-called theory of "concentric circles." The agreement between the historian and the ethnologist is clear: there is no genius of invention, or at least, it plays only a minor role in technical evolution. Conversely there is a systematicity that here implements tendencies, realized in a coupling, which should be brought to light, of the human with matter.

The Coupling of the Human with Matter

Man and Matter sets down the principles of a "technomorphology based on raw materials," following an approach that studies the so-called primitive peoples spread over the globe, certain of whom have entered into practically no commerce with others, on whom we have only limited, unhistorical documentation (these are peoples "without writing systems"), and for whom technics is much less complex than it is in historical epochs.

The ethno-anthropology of Leroi-Gourhan is grounded in an interpretation of the technical phenomenon, which for him is the principle characteristic of the human, through which peoples distinguish themselves more essentially than through their racial and cultural characters in the spiritualist sense of the term. This interpretation has two objectives: to furnish a theory of *anthropogenesis* corresponding point by point, as we shall see, in its paleoanthropological dimension (which will be taken up in the third chapter), to a *technogenesis*; secondly, to allow on this basis for the comprehension of cultural differentiations between ethnic groups.

Through the introduction of the concept of tendency (inspired by a reading of Bergson, to whom he sometimes refers),[7] Leroi-Gourhan interprets this technical phenomenon and legitimates his project for a technomorphology by comparing the task of the anthropologist to those of the botanist and zoologist between the seventeenth and nineteenth centuries: these two disciplines were able to elaborate their taxonomic principles—which have since proven definitive—while "the majority of species remained to be discovered" (1943, 13). Likewise, anthropology, for two thirds of a century, "has provided itself with classifications, it has divided races, techniques, and peoples, and experience has proven on the occasion of each new expedition the solidity of several old conceptions. In zoology or in ethnology, this is due to the permanent nature of the tendencies" (13). Leroi-Gourhan adds the following remark, which introduces the concept of the line—or of the *phylum*—close to the concept of technological lineage, along with the question of choice, that is, of determination, already found in Gille:

> Everything seems to happen as if an ideal prototype of fish or of knapped flint developed along preconceivable lines from the fish to the amphibian, to the reptile, to the mammal, or to the bird, from form-undifferentiated flint to the polished knapped tool, to the brass knife, to the steel sword. This should not lead us into error: these lines render only an aspect of life, that of the inevitable and limited choice that the milieu proposes to living matter. (Leroi-Gourhan 1943, 13)

This comparison between *technological and zoological facts*, between the technical object and the living being, is crucial for the hypotheses that will follow. The explanation of the technical phenomenon will analyze as a particular case of zoology the relations established between the human *qua* living matter and inert matter *qua* the "raw material" out of which technical forms appear. Leroi-Gourhan brings to bear a quasi-biological determinism that does not exist in Gille, but in which, here too, the "paths of invention are narrow": "For one must choose between water and air, between swimming, crawling or the race; the living being follows a limited number of large lines of evolution" (Leroi-Gourhan 1943, 13). The same limitation, the same principle of the molding and inscription of the living in conditions established by the inert matter of the milieu, will determine the form of tools. The texture of wood imposes forms on blades and hands and

> technical determinism is as marked as that of zoology: like Cuvier discovering the jaw of an opossum in a hump of gypsum, and deciding to invite his unbelieving colleagues to pursue with him the uncovering of the skeleton and predicting for them the discovery of marsupial bones, ethnology may, up to a certain point, draw from the form of the blade of a tool previsions on that of the handle and on the use of the complete tool. (13–14)

Technical evolution results from a coupling of the human and matter, a coupling that must be elucidated: technical systematicity is here embedded in a "zootechnological" determinism. From the very fact of the zoological character of one of the terms of the relation, that is, the human, the phenomenon must be interpreted from the perspectives of the history of life, although the technical objects resulting from the coupling come from matter that must be called inorganic since this matter is inert, albeit organized. Hence we understand the need for a reflection on the meaning of the organization of matter in general in its relation to the organism, but also on what is called the organ, whether that be taken to indicate the part of the organism or the *organon qua* technical instrument. The investigation will proceed by analogy with the methods of zoology—the whole question being *up to what point* the analogy holds.

Tendency and Facts

The experience and organization of the coupling of the human and matter through universal technical tendencies, one analyzable in zoological terms up to a certain point, constitutes the founding axiom of Leroi-Gourhan's approach. A second view aims at giving an account of the factual diversity of technical evolution, for instance in the traces found in ethnological and archaeological raw material. The question then becomes that of distinguishing the technical tendency within technical facts. The tendency is realized by the facts, and the examination of the links between facts affords us a view of the conditions for the realization of the tendency. A classification of the facts must be carried out, and the unity in the apparent diversity in which it presents itself discovered.

A problem arises here that implies a crucial choice, depending on the way the problem is solved, in the interpretation of technological development in general—a problem that Cuvier ran up against in his field because he had not firmly established the absolutely essential difference between determining tendency and material fact. "There are general tendencies that can give rise to identical techniques without being materially linked," that is, without contact between the peoples where they occur, "and [there are] the facts that, whatever degree of geographical proximity they may have, are individual and unique" (Leroi-Gourhan 1943, 14). The technical objects that the facts consist in are diverse, even though they may belong to the same tendency. One must therefore provide an account of the causes of this diversity, a fact closely linked to their belonging to a technical ecosystem, by placing oneself on another level than that of the tendency, which this causality can no longer explain. The question is to distinguish the determining universal tendency and its local appropriation, singularized by the "genius" of an ethnic group.

We see arising here the issue of the relation between the technical and the ethnic. "The custom of planting wood or bone ornaments in the lower lip is found . . . in the Eskimos of Alaska, the Indians of Brazil, and the Negroes of Africa. Here there indeed is technical identity, but hitherto no serious effort has succeeded in proving the common roots of these human groups" (Leroi-Gourhan 1943, 14). Everything seems to point to the presence of a determined tendency, a universal fact, but one inexplicable by the play of reciprocal cultural influences, given the absence of contacts between these civilizations. Inversely, "the Malaysian, Japanese, and Tibetan plows represent three related forms that were certainly in contact in the ancient history of the three peoples: each one, however, in the cultivated soil, in the details of its construction, in the details of its yoking, in the symbolic or social meaning attached to it, represents in fact something unique and categorically individualized" (14). In this case, the temptation will be, in bringing together these facts, to draw conclusions as to the conditions for the spread of the same archetype's situating itself in particular forms, oscillating between a purely determinist point of view, which gives no account of diversification, and a historico-culturalist point of view, which seeks to identify the original locus of invention and genius that influenced the other two loci through its proximity to them. From here, the more general thesis of the spread of a technical invention by concentric circles starting from several hubs of civilization will be easily taken up. Finally, "everything seems to be on the order of a 'plow' tendency realized at each point of time and space by a unique fact and indubitable historical relations on sometimes considerable scales of time and space" (14).

There are at one and the same time phenomena of diffusion, of reciprocal influences between cultures—which explain the presence and the diversification of a technical fact in a given space and time—and a causality of another nature, linked to a quasi-zoological determinism of the relation of the human to matter, the problem being their distinction. "The slightest slip has the specialist jumping from one to the other and surpassing the measure of reality" (Leroi-Gourhan 1943, 14–15). This reality is a combination [*mixte*] of two causalities that can be confused, that of cultural diffusion by borrowing—which is immediately evident—and that of the technical tendency, less directly discernible but more essential, constituting the very principle of the technical tendency from the point of view of the history of life in general.

Within this viewpoint's framework and limits, first of all the validity of the determinist viewpoint must be established, and *then* the unquestionable historical phenomena of diffusion be explained by cultural influence. The entire interpretation of the technical phenomenon is at stake. The "culturalist" point of view will give a miraculous, even magical (in any case ethnocentric) interpretation of this phenomenon. It will ascribe to one or several peoples a technical or civilizational genius in which the absolute origin of the technological lineage will be found. Leroi-Gourhan considers that such a point of view totally misunderstands the nature of the technical phenomenon, whose principle always remains the determining tendency. There is no "genius of peoples" at the origin of the phenomenon: there are facts that, inserting themselves into ethnic milieus, take on their concrete aspects as technical objects; but their emergence always results from a more profound determinism, beyond ethnic characteristics, which alone can account for the clear-cut cases of universal technical tendencies. There is a necessity proper to the technical phenomenon, whose factual diversities are but the effects of its encounter with ethnic particularities. The technical event follows much more fundamentally from a zoologically rooted systematicity than from human genius. "Technological lineages" are a relation of the human to matter analogous to zoological lineages in which evolution has since Darwin been seen to consist.

The zootechnological relation of the human to matter is a particular case of the relation of the living to its milieu, the former passing through organized inert matter—the technical object. The singularity of the relation lies in the fact that the inert, although organized, matter *qua* the technical object itself evolves in its organization: it is therefore no longer merely inert matter, but neither is it living matter. *It is organized inorganic matter that transforms itself in time as living matter transforms itself in its interaction with the milieu.* In addition, it becomes the interface through which the human *qua* living matter enters into relation with the milieu.

The enigma of this matter goes back to that of *hylē qua dynamis.* Matter *qua* potentiality would be seen in its organization as the act of this potentiality. It would then be tempting to say that the organization of matter is its form, *qua* the act of this potentiality. But here the question cannot be that of a purely hylomorphic relation: matter organized technomorphologically is not passive; *the tendency does not simply derive from an organizing force—the human—it does not belong to a forming intention that would precede the frequentation of matter, and it does not come under the sway of some willful mastery: the tendency operates, down through time, by selecting forms in a relation of the human living being to the matter it organizes and by which it organizes itself, where none of the terms of the relation hold the secret of the other.* This technical phenomenon is the relation of the human to its milieu, and it is in this sense that it must be apprehended zoo-logically, without its elucidation being possible, for all that, in terms of the common laws of zoology.

Ethnic Differences and Technical Differentiation

"The Technical Structure of Human Societies" (Leroi-Gourhan 1943, 23) shows how the paleontological approach (that is, zoological), which must be followed "up to a certain point" in analyzing technical human realities, quickly reaches its limits, by the very fact of the absolutely singular character of the technicity of the human, singling it out in the world of living beings.

The desire of paleontology is apparently fulfilled in the case of the human, as compared to the cases of other species: "If the desire of researchers is to know as much about the hominid family as is known about the past of the Equidae and the Rhinoceros, that curiosity is already more than satisfied" (Leroi-Gourhan 1943, 22). However, this is only an illusion. The human is a technical being that cannot be characterized physiologically and specifically (in the zoological sense), for a diversity of human facts ruins the possibility of such scientific satisfaction related to the knowledge of the human *qua* human, and not only *qua* living being; and from this point of view, "the paths of paleontology cannot be traveled by the paleontologist *because human society would appear as a group of vertebrates who, in the course of centuries, would exchange, one, some wings for a shell, another, a trunk for a few extra vertebrae*" (22, my emphasis).

The problem arising here is that the evolution of this essentially technical being that the human is exceeds the biological, although this dimension is an essential part of the technical phenomenon itself, something like its enigma. The evolution of the "prosthesis," not itself living, by which the human is nonetheless defined as a living being, constitutes the reality of the human's evolution, as if, with it, the history of life were to continue by means other than life: this is the paradox of a living being characterized in its forms of life by the nonliving—or by the traces that its life leaves in the nonliving. There is consequently an evolutionary determinism that is not only biological but also, for reasons we have seen earlier, quasi-zoological.

The above remark about strange human exchanges, compared to unthinkable exchanges among animals, sheds unusual light on the question of the relations between cultures and provides an altogether different perspective on combinatory evolution and, in the case of human life, on combinatory genetics, which reveals according to statistical laws the necessity of natural selection: "While the possibilities of intersection between animal species are extremely limited, while felines pursue their evolution alongside bears for millennia without ever intersecting, all human races can be crossbred, all peoples are fusible, and all civilizations are unstable" (Leroi-Gourhan 1943, 24–25). For their evolution is techno-logical, and this evolution is not submitted to the genetic isolations that guarantee the unity and the stability of the animal species. This fact offers at the same time the limits of the zoological dimension of technical evolution and the dynamic principle of the latter, that is, the diversity of facts, by which it enriches and crosses through, while realizing, the other, more profound principle of the determining tendency. At this point, the question of the relation between the technical and the ethnic proves crucial. For technical differentiation itself will now proceed from ethnic differentiation cut across by the tendency's universality and hence the effective realization of the tendency, that is, the selection of the best technical forms for its realization. The history of life can thereby continue according to new laws: in interethnic relations, insofar as human groups do not behave as species in these relations, a diversity of technical facts opens out within which the universality of technical tendencies is concretized, progressively penetrating the totality of the biosphere.

The problem is then to know how these "cross-breedings" work. This is the whole question of diffusion, which occasions numerous problems owing notably to the parceled nature of ethnographic documentation.

Technical differentiation, silently propelled by the tendency, is effected *qua* fact at the ethnic level either by invention or by borrowing:

> The tendency has an inevitable, predictable, rectilinear character. It drives the flint held in the hand to acquire the handle, the bundle hung on two poles to equip itself with wheels, the society founded on matriarchy to become patriarchal sooner or later. (Leroi-Gourhan 1943, 27)

This differentiation applies like a law cutting across the local technical ecosystems and guides the global process of their evolution and, hence, their exchanges. Whether this evolution operates by invention or by borrowing is of minor importance,[8] since the facts of unilateral or reciprocal influences brought to light by the culturalist theory in no way contradict this systematic determinism in its essence. Here, technical expansion functions like an actual "fulfillment," and this is why there is no profound difference between borrowing and invention: what is essential is that an invention, borrowed from the exterior or produced locally, become acceptable and necessary in what Leroi-Gourhan calls the logical order with respect to "the state in which the affected people find themselves" (1943, 28).

The problem is to distinguish the logical from the chronological when they coincide and when the factual origin of evolution is not attested.

Whatever this origin may be, it is only possible in the field of the tendency that is the techno-logical condition of possibility of the fact:

> The fact, contrary to the tendency, is unpredictable and whimsical. It is just as much the encounter of the tendency and the thousand coincidences of the milieu, that is, invention, as it is the pure and simple borrowing from another people. The fact is unique, inextensible, an unstable compromise established between the tendencies and the milieu. (Leroi-Gourhan 1943, 28)

As in Gille, the fact is a catalyst, the act of an evolving potentiality. It is the tendency's concretization, effected as a compromise, whereby various elements, determined not by the tendency but by the milieu *qua* both physical and cultural system, finally envelop its universality.

This envelopment of the universal tendency by the diversity that appropriates it is effected by layers setting up the degrees of the fact; the first degree—essentially technical—expresses the tendency itself without fully realizing it, while the other degrees—essentially ecologico-ethnic—constitute the layers wherein the first is embedded, in the local and diverse reality in which the fact is realized. In other words, the kernel of the fact is its technical essence; its flesh is an ethnic essence. The clarification of the relation between the technical and the ethnic, both technical and ethnic, can be observed here: it is less a question of an opposition than of a composition, as if the compromise between the universal tendency and the particular locality, being translated as fact, smothered the possibilities of a conflict while concealing and maintaining in reserve the universal essence of the tendency.

The first degree is the universal archetype expressing the tendency. The concretization of the tendency, its localization, its spatial inscription *qua* the effective process of technical evolution, stems from the following degrees, witnesses "the mechanism of progressive individualization of facts" (Leroi-Gourhan 1943, 32). The example of a hunting instrument, the "propulsor," shows that the second degree marks localization depending on the factors composing the technical ecosystem, which can account, "by means of the most diverse of elements (geo-physical milieu, game, graves, dwellings, stone carving, religion, etc.)," for factual convergences between different geographical centers, for example between the people of the Reindeer Age and the Eskimos. These localizations mesh with those of ethnic units. In turn, however, these units are decomposed into subgroups in which the technical fact is once again individualized, in a third degree which thus is "that of the major breaks inside ethnic groups" (34). Lastly, the fourth degree "ends in a detailed description of the fact and of its fixation in a specific group; it can mark the trace of delicate relations between the facts of the third degree" (35).

The ethnic groups for which the layers envelop the kernel belong to the "steps" of technical evolution:

> The fact is that there are not techniques but technical ensembles commanded by general mechanical, physical, or chemical knowledge. Having the principle of the wheel gives one that of the chariot, the potter's wheel, the spinning wheel, the lathe; knowing how to sew provides not only a piece of clothing of a particular form but also vases of sown bark, sown tents, sown dinghies; with the mastery of compressed air comes the blowpipe, the piston lighter, the piston bellows, the hypodermic needle" (Leroi-Gourhan 1943, 41)

Technical ensembles thereby determine the ages of technical evolution, the "technical states of peoples" that Leroi-Gourhan classes in five categories: the very rustic, the rustic, the semi-rustic, the semi-industrial, and the industrial.

Geography as Origin and Ethnic Genius as "Unifying Process"

The conditions of technical differentiation, invention, and diffusion, are examined in the last two chapters of *Milieu and Techniques* from the viewpoint of the ethnic group, defined, here again, in an original way, by its future rather than by its past. This inversion allows one to dismiss the question of the origin, or a traditional way of not really posing it, be it a matter of the origin of techniques or of the origin of peoples in which they develop.

These analyses are designed to shed light on an ensemble of facts through which geographical localizations of technical phenomena are established, and to support an argument opposed to the theory of technical centers of high civilizations (of ethnic geniuses) diffusing their skills in concentric circles of cultural influence: the determining factor is geographical rather than cultural. "At the beginning of historical times, the major techniques are the privilege of proportionately restrained geographical zones, arranged around an axis extending through temperate Eurasia." The question is then one of diffusion, on the subject of which it must be remarked that "in the technical domain, the only transmittable traits through borrowing are those that mark an improvement of procedures. A less flexible language, a less developed religion can be borrowed, but the cart cannot be traded for the hoe" (Leroi-Gourhan 1945, 303–4). Just as there is no regression of the living, but an increase in negentropy through the ineluctable complexification of genetic combinations, so also there is only technical progress. There is a teleologism in technics linked to the principle of tendency. We have already met with this idea in Gille, where the technical system develops in ever-growing complication and integration; it will be found again in Simondon, in the domain of industrial technical objects, as the phenomenon of concretization, that is, of their tendential path [*acheminement*] toward perfection.

The major techniques are linked to geographical zones that favor their appearance. It is no less the case that the conditions of progress, that is, of invention and of borrowing, are ethnic as well as geographical (ethnic characteristics being themselves largely determined by the life conditions imposed on peoples by geography), and it is then a question of specifying the definition of the concept of ethnic group, given that invention and borrowing remain, *qua* procedures for the realization of the tendency, phenomena "intimately linked to the ethnic personality" (Leroi-Gourhan 1945, 306).

The point is to know what links are established between a general human phenomenon and the ethnic group—in what way the ethnic group is characterized through originally marking the phenomenon in question: how, for example, the phenomenon of language in general, specific to humanity in general, yields a particular language belonging to one particular ethnic group. "In linguistic matters, agreement has long since been reached: language corresponds only accidentally to anthropological realities" (Leroi-Gourhan 1945, 307), that is, to zoological characteristics of particular human groups, for example the Australians or the Chinese. On the other hand, one notices that languages, techniques, religions, and social institutions very often correspond to geographical centers—as for example in current-day China, a convergence that does not result from a zoological unity of the Chinese race, for "one grants that the 'Chinese race' is composed of disparate elements, and, on analysis of them, one finds such a diversity of dialects, of skulls, of homes, and of social laws that Chinese reality may be called into question" (307). What does the unity of an ethnic group consist in? by what processes? why these rather than others? why does such and such a technical phenomenon develop there in such and such a manner?

The unity of the ethnic group is governed by the relation to time, more precisely, the relation to a collective future sketching in its effects the reality of a common becoming:

> The ethnic group . . . is less a past than a becoming. The initial traits of the distant group that created political unity become indistinct if not completely effaced. Having become a people, the mass of disparate men tends to unite successively at the linguistic, social, technical, and anthropological levels. (Leroi-Gourhan 1945, 308)

Although expressed in a completely different register, this proposition is compatible with the Heideggerian conception of time that accords primacy to the future: we shall see up to what point.

Ethnic unity is essentially momentary and in perpetual becoming; it is never acquired, since it does not itself proceed from an origin that would be shared by the people composing the ethnic group: ethnic unity is conventional, without any other origin than a mythical one. Contrary to the theory of concentric circles, there is no ethnic genius of technics that would itself be the product of an originary race "more gifted" than others, disposing of more advanced zoological attributes and finding itself thereby favored by nature for cultural domination.

This is why the determinism that makes the logic of the development of technical tendencies understandable, stemming from the relation of the human to matter, is first of all geographical. As Gille shows for Egypt and Mesopotamia, the system of physical geography originally holds a privileged relation to the technical system, and, contrary to what the theory of concentric circles would suggest, "if one examines impartially the chart of the last three millennia, it is not the central-Asiatic hub that diffuses civilization; civilization materializes around an axis running from Great Britain to Japan, cutting across all those regions benefiting from a temperate or moderately cold or hot climate" (Leroi-Gourhan 1945, 311). When this system of physical geography is considered from the standpoint of ethnic reality, it can be seen as a system of human geography, which will be referred to further on by the name "milieu," a combination of geographical and historico-cultural determinations, itself divided into interior and exterior milieus. Under these geographical conditions, peoples appear as developers of technical tendencies, inventors or profiteers of the inventions of other peoples, and as the principle vectors of technical evolution. They form strong ethnic units—that is, they are always empowered with a unifying ethnic becoming that is their "genius" (314).

Interior and Exterior Milieus in the Technological Dynamic

The fertile fields of the Eurasian axis are at the origin of the technical centers whose farmers and metalworkers emerged at the end of the Paleolithic era. Before the Neolithic revolution, there were two groups: the men of the reindeer, and the Paleolithics of the camel and ox. For the latter, this is the most favorable climate, enabling them to pass into the technical stage of farmer-cultivators and finally leading them into historical times. This is the moment when the thesis of a radical determination of the field of general history by technics appears, recalling the problem posed by Lefèbvre des Noëttes: if one can, in linguistics, in the history of art and religions, in sociology, disregard the difference between "savage" and "civilized," "in comparative technology, we are obliged to recognize it, and since in the final analysis equipment solves political questions, we gain in the same stroke insight into the point of view of historians: general history is the history of peoples possessing good tools for laboring the land and forging swords" (Leroi-Gourhan 1945, 320).

Technological superiority is the profound reality of the "superiority" of historical peoples. By this very fact, "civilization" is a technical state, a relation of technical forces, rather than cultural in the limited sense of moral, religious, artistic, scientific, or even political. The following question remains: what are the causes of the appearance of this type of "technical state" *qua* factor of "civilization"?

Another categorization can be used, that of static and dynamic human groups. The Australians, hampered by a specific geography and undergoing its limitations, belong to the static group, as do the Chinese, whose technical system is found to be stymied by the cultural milieu.

In order to understand the conditions of technical immobilism or dynamism, the behavior of humans living in groups as technical animals should be analyzed under the double condition of their "interior milieu" and their "exterior milieu." These concepts, once again, are taken from the field of biology; through them the ethnic group is apprehended as a living structure—and the metaphor becomes here an actual analogy:

> The human group behaves in nature as a living organism . . . the human group assimilates its milieu through a curtain of objects (tools or instruments). It burns its wood with the adze, consumes its meat with the arrow, the knife, the cauldron, and the spoon. Within this interposed membrane, it nourishes and protects itself, rests, and moves. . . . The study of this artificial envelope is technology, the laws of its development belong in technical economy. (Leroi-Gourhan 1945, 322)

The point is to understand the human at the level of the group in its functioning as an organism. Because the technical object is inscribed in the technical system, technical evolution implies the comprehension of human groups rather than of individuals—individual genius explains nothing about invention. Thus technical economy will study the laws of technological development *qua* the "artificial envelope" of this quasi-living organism that is the human group, thereby explaining its very evolution according to quasi-zoological laws.

With this concept of *exterior milieu* "is first apprehended everything materially surrounding the human: the geographical, climactic, animal, and vegetable milieu. The definition must be . . . extended to the material signs and ideas which may come from other human groups" (Leroi-Gourhan 1945, 333). With the concept of *interior milieu* "is apprehended not what is proper to naked humans at birth, but, at each moment in time, in a (most often incomplete) circumscribed human mass, that which constitutes its intellectual capital, that is, an extremely complex pool of mental traditions" (334). The interior milieu is social memory, the shared past, that which is called "culture." It is a nongenetic memory, which is exterior to the living organism *qua* individual, supported by the nonzoological collective organization of objects, but which functions and evolves as a *quasi*-biological milieu whose analysis reveals "used products, reserves, internal secretions, hormones issuing from other cells of the same organism, vitamins of external origin" (334). The exterior milieu is the natural, inert milieu, but also the one carrying "the objects and the ideas of different human groups." As inert milieu, it "supplies merely consumable matter, and the technical envelope of a perfectly closed group will be the one allowing for the optimization of the 'interior' milieu's aptitudes." As for what comes from foreign groups, these influences "act as veritable vitamins, causing a precise assimilative reaction of the interior milieu" (334).

The problem to be elucidated is that of the conditions of transformation of the interior milieu by the exterior one, as a combination of geographical and cultural elements. How do crossovers and mutations take place? It must be asked what the conditions are for the group's receptivity to foreign cultural influence, analogous to the "plasticity of the interior milieu of the biological cell" (Leroi-Gourhan 1945, 334). There may be mutations without foreign influence, through the sole relation to the geographical exterior milieu. But knowing whether a technical innovation is borrowed or properly invented appears here as almost secondary, since the innovation's adoption can only take place in "an already favorable state of the interior milieu. The adoption can be considered an almost accessory trait, the important aspect being that the group is ready, in the absence of innovation, to invent or borrow" (335). The Gillean notion of technical system had the same consequences; the potentialities accumulating in the system, even in the form of limits, practically implied innovation. Here, the technical returns to the fore to the extent that, when favorable conditions are encountered, it organizes the potential receptivity of the group either to borrowing or to innovation proper. The point here is to understand how the play of the interior and exterior milieus, articulating themselves onto one another, determines the technical fact and "frees" the tendency's potential. Both are quite variable according to groups, and this is why the tendency presents itself never as such but only as a diversity of facts. The phenomenon of the tendency offers, more profoundly than ethnic singularity, an explanation of all possibility of evolution and reveals the essence of the relation between the two milieus. The techno-logical combinatory is finite, and the problems to which it responds, as well as the solutions resulting from possible combinations, forming the horizon of the tendency—but also of all facts—are limited in number.

The Two Aspects of the Tendency

In order to "distinguish this altogether special property of evolution making the consequences of 'exterior milieu / interior milieu action' predictable," Leroi-Gourhan adopts "the philosophical term 'tendency,'" which he sees as "*a movement, within the interior milieu, that gains progressive foothold in the exterior milieu.*" (1945, 336). This movement, this gaining foothold, which is close to what determines the morphogenesis of organisms in their milieus, excludes any possibility of a priori classification of tendencies: it appears only through facts, and the tendencies "only become explicit in their materialization, then cease to be tendencies in the strict sense. This is why we have conflated the particular tendency and the fact in the first degree" (337). This also means that, as we shall see with Simondon, form does not precede matter, and the process of individuation (in which technical evolution *qua* differentiation consists) must be inscribed in another categorization. But with Simondon, the industrial technical object concretizes this dynamic in itself, without the intervention of an interior milieu, and thus tends toward techno-logical perfection by incorporating or overdetermining functions. This implies a new concept of milieu: the associated milieu. The interior milieu is absent because it is diluted into the interior milieu when the technical object becomes industrial. By the same movement, the milieu in general no longer constitutes an exteriority.

With Leroi-Gourhan, the tendency proceeds, on the contrary, from the encounter of two sources, respectively intentional and physical, coming from the interior and exterior milieus (this reasoning's limit being the apparent forgetting of the specificity of the Industrial Age). The encounter between the two milieus is the coupling of the human *qua* social being to matter *qua* geographical system, comparable to the structural coupling of the living and its ecosystem.[9] The relation of the interior milieu to the exterior milieu, the expression of the coupling of the human to matter carried to the level of the group, is to be interpreted as the *selection* of the best possible solutions, a selection in which the tendency, its criterion as well as its driving force, is based "in one whole aspect," that of criteria, on the same laws of the universe. This aspect of the tendency yields the concept of technical convergence:

> Each tool, each weapon, each object in general, from the basket to the house, responds to an architectural plan of equilibrium whose outlines give a purchase to the laws of geometry or rational mechanics. There is then a whole side to the technical tendency involving the construction of the universe itself, and it is as normal for the roofs to have a V-shaped slope, hatchets to have handles, and arrows to be balanced at a point the third of their length as it is normal for gastropods of all times to have a twisting shell. . . . Next to the biological convergence, there is a technical convergence, playing from the beginnings of ethnology a role in the refutation of the theories of contact. (Leroi-Gourhan 1945, 338)

The concept of associated milieu that we shall find in Simondon constitutes the complication of this hypothesis: there is a transformation of the universe by the technical tendency. The ecological problems characteristic of our technical age can only acquire meaning from this point of view: a new milieu emerges, a technophysical and technocultural milieu, whose laws of equilibrium are no longer known. The convergence is creative of new reality and values—but it can also be imagined as engendering in the same movement unknown forms of divergence.

Here, the tendency is a double movement whereby the interior and exterior milieus *adhere*, under diverse conditions, subject for example to what Leroi-Gourhan calls the restrained tendency, or again, the tendency's obstacle: local phenomena whereby the tendency translates into diverse facts in which the singularity of localities can resist the universality of the tendency.

The other aspect of the tendency, its driving force, comes from the interior milieu: stones do not spontaneously rise up into a wall, and the clear determinism of the tendency is in no way a mechanism. Coming from an enigmatic *intention* of the interior milieu, the tendency diffracts into a diversity of facts, like a ray of light passing through an aqueous milieu when it is reflected by the exterior milieu, and in this sense its determinism remains "loose" and its rationality no less enigmatically "diffuse." There is a "technological intentionality" that "diffracts" through an opacity proper to a locality that is not only physical but human as well:

> The tendency is proper to the interior milieu; there can be no tendency of the exterior milieu: the wind does not propose a determined roof to the house, the human gives to its roof the most favorable profile. . . . The exterior milieu behaves like an absolutely inert body into which the tendency collides: the material sign is found at its point of impact. . . . Empowered, thanks to its universal nature, with all the possibilities expressible in general laws, the tendency cuts across the interior milieu, which is suffused by the mental traditions of each human group. It acquires therein special properties, as a ray of light acquires diverse properties in crossing through different bodies, and encounters the exterior milieu, which offers to the acquired properties an irregular penetration; and at the point of impact between the interior and exterior milieus this membrane of objects constituting the furniture of humans materializes. (Leroi-Gourhan 1945, 339)

A subgroup of the interior milieu is constituted as the agent of intention and the corrector of diffraction: this is the technical milieu.

The Technical Milieu as Factor of Dilution of the Interior Milieu

The unity of groups must be conceived in the way in which they "face up to the future," relying on an ensemble of social coherencies, which themselves are synthesized into a global coherence, undergoing constant change, as in the case of the cell. In the ethnic group apprehended as an interior milieu, the technical milieu itself can be isolated, organized into "technical bodies" combining with other subgroups, equivalent to the Gillean "other systems," all of which are "given quite different rhythms," the ethnic group being the complex of a certain human mass considered over that period of time during which its constitutive elements do not lose all parallelism. The solidarity of the technical milieu, which itself comes in its concrete aspects from the universal technical tendency, with the other subgroups implies that the tendency is only realized as the diversity of technical facts, and that "each group possesses technical objects absolutely distinct from [those of] other groups" (Leroi-Gourhan 1945, 342). In order to discern the tendency in the technical milieu, the tendency must be abstracted from objects impregnated "by the traces left by the whole interior milieu" (342). The question is to know under what conditions the technical milieu is capable of dynamism, to know its "permeability": "Everything happens as though the technical milieu were constantly undergoing the effect of all technical possibilities, that is, as if the entire determining tendency directed onto itself the totality of its excitations at every moment" (342). And if "the permeability of the technical milieu is variable" (342), the irresistible negentropy in which technical dynamism consists implies its constant increase.

Anticipating a reading of Simondon, one could ask whether the permeability of the tendency would not also lead to an ever-greater dilution of the interior milieu into the exterior one and conversely, and would do so all the more with the increase of points of contact between the diverse interior milieus that tend to accentuate the general permeability of the technical tendency of all groups.

Just as the Gillean technical system consists in relations of interdependence of technical elements, so too the technical milieu is *continuous.* And once again as in Gille, technical continuity excludes "pure invention, *ex nihilo*" (Leroi-Gourhan 1945, 344); the inventive genius is combinatory, close to a "logic of the living": evolution, indeed technical evolution, must be thought in terms of reproduction. This is also the meaning of continuity, which here is diachronic as well as synchronic, even though the effects of rupture manifest themselves on our scale as the most apparent phenomena of technical evolution. For the idea of continuity does not exclude that of mutation. A mutation is a catastrophic phenomenon on the inside of an essential continuity that, as a combinatory, makes it possible.

Just as a technical milieu detaches itself from within the interior milieu, so a technical subgroup is detached from within the ethnic group. And in the same way, "the ethnic group is the materialization of tendencies cutting across the technical milieu" (Leroi-Gourhan 1945, 347). Here again we can ask whether today the technical groups still belong to the ethnic group, or if they may not extend well beyond it, to the point of calling its unity into question: the phenomena of deterritorialization and acculturation are the telling marks. It is as if the technical groups tended to become autonomous with respect to the ethnic groups, owing to the very fact that techno-industrial units have become worldwide. Thus, "it is obvious that if the technical milieu is continuous, the technical group belongs to the exterior milieu," which is not only geographical but a vector for foreign influences, displaying "a large part of discontinuity" (347). This discontinuity affects in the first instance the technical milieu itself, but by reaction, it also affects the interior milieu as a whole. One may conclude that the technical group then gains an *advance* with respect to the ethnic group to the extent that, as is the case today—with technical evolution accelerating and becoming too fast for the possibilities of appropriation by the "other systems"—one must wonder if we might not be in the presence of a separation and progressive opposition between, on the one hand, cultures, or an ensemble of interior milieus, and on the other hand technologies, which are no longer only a subgroup of the technical milieu but the external milieu become worldwide technology: the dilution of the interior milieu into the exterior milieu has become essentially technical, firstly as an environment totally mediated by telecommunications, by modes of transportation as well as by television and radio, computer networks, and so on, whereby distances and delays are annulled, but secondly as a system of planet-scale industrial production. This is undoubtedly not Leroi-Gourhan's hypothesis here, but he makes it thinkable when he shows how the exterior milieu can perturb and reorganize the interior milieu through the intermediary of the technical group, which is capable, at a given moment, of entering into conflict with it so as to facilitate the permeability of the tendency, that is, the realization of the consequences coming from the exterior milieu.

An analysis of the impact of the technical group on the interior milieu first requires the exclusive study of those cases in which the exterior milieu does not carry foreign influences, and in which there are therefore no borrowings: the result will be a decisive confirmation of the tendency's determinism. Having succeeded, for all intents and purposes, in definitively establishing the tendency thesis, the next step will be to understand the logic of borrowing and the outcomes to which it can lead.

The Permanence of Evolution

Within "groups of the same exterior milieu," "real borrowings" and "simple convergence" should be distinguished (Leroi-Gourhan 1945, 355). But to understand borrowing, the exterior milieu should nevertheless not be treated specifically: the influence of a foreign cultural factor carried by the exterior milieu is basically the same problem as the influence of the exterior milieu on the interior milieu in general. Thus, there is no fundamental difference between the fact of invention and the fact of borrowing. In both cases, the question is that of the plasticity of the technical milieu, and through it, of the availability of the interior milieu to evolution.

Given the correct understanding of this nondifference, there are, regarding the rhythm and the consequences of a given transformation, cases where it would seem that

> the borrowed element is incorporated into the technical milieu without significantly changing it: it makes the milieu richer without giving the impression of a transformation. . . . The progressive accumulation of these discreet borrowed elements ends up in fact changing the interior milieu. . . . For convenience the other extreme can be apprehended; a borrowed element such as agriculture translates in a rather short period of time into a total mutation of a major part of the technical milieu. If fact . . . it is a question of scale rather than one of essence. (Leroi-Gourhan 1945, 364)

We meet here once again the continuity thesis, which distinctly recalls the Leibnizian motif of little perceptions, and *what is said here about borrowing could be said as well of invention.* There are indeed "catastrophic" effects in the evolution of technical systems, which precisely concern the passage of one system into another (or, following Simondon, the passage from one stage of concretization to another). But this in no way contradicts the continuity hypothesis, which holds that the dynamic of evolution is systematic and *therefore permanent*, as thinking is for Leibniz, and that no transformation (by borrowing or invention) can take place without ulterior consequences that extend the effects, even if the moments during which these effects are concretized take place suddenly and provoke a brutal reorganization of the technical milieu and, by counterreaction, of the interior milieu. *Brutal* has never meant discontinuous, but here means only fast, and the question is once again that of speed.

The question of speed belongs to that of a logic of transformation, whereby the interior milieu and, within it, the technical milieu and the technical group allow for transformation. At bottom, the possibility of borrowing always comes in the first instance from the interior milieu itself, and it must be dealt with exactly as a phenomenon of counterreaction of the exterior milieu in general, as for example the presence of lithic material in a given geographical milieu; that is, borrowing must be dealt with not specifically as a cultural influence but as an event coming from the exterior milieu in which at a given time the interior milieu invests its technical tendencies, according to the permeability afforded it by the technical milieu. Just as stones will never rise up spontaneously into walls without their being invested by the interior milieu's tendency, so too cultural influence will never operate on a particular interior milieu without the latter having accomplished the work by which, "in hesitant steps" or at the height of a crisis, this influence may end up enriching a technical milieu or group. To consider borrowing as a phenomenon of invention and inversely, invention as borrowing, is tantamount to considering foreign influence and invention as ordinary phenomena of influence of the exterior milieu, composed of natural and technical elements issuing from the other group.

What becomes of the exterior milieu with the advent of modern technics, when the equipment of ethnic groups, the "membrane" within which they form their unity, acquires performances such that each group finds itself in constant communication with the quasi-totality of the others without delay or limits in distance? What happens when there is no longer any exterior milieu as such, so-called "physical" geography being saturated with human penetrations, that is, technical ones, and the principle relations of interior to exterior milieus being mediated by a technical system having no "natural" remainder in its wake? One wonders if the technical system, being now worldwide, does not form a realm in which the distinction between interior and exterior milieu, having totally altered their relations, has become highly problematic, and if the technical group does not find itself totally emancipated from the ethnic group, an archaic remnant.

Leroi-Gourhan answered this question in the negative in 1945 but changed his mind in 1965, when he spoke of a mega-ethnic group.

Influence does not necessarily have effects, and groups can resist the realization of technical tendencies and maintain differences between themselves. This is a promise and proof of diversity. However, if it is true that the phenomenon of foreign influence should be considered as a phenomenon of the exterior milieu in general, if it is true that they have the same possibilities of constraint on the interior milieu (as when a very cold winter in Alaska forces the Indians to develop snow techniques), if, finally, it is true that the technical system, becoming worldwide, incorporated, and overdetermined, puts more and more constraint on the interior milieus that are maintaining themselves therein, one must at least envisage the hypothesis that the conditions of possibility of differentiations between groups have radically changed—and notably, that the ethnic dimension of groups is waning. This Leroi-Gourhan refuses, because such a position seems to be necessarily inscribed in the ethnocentric teleologism of the theory of cultural technical centers progressively influencing their vicinities in concentric circles. However, the thesis of the tendency, reconsidered from the vantage of the process of concretization *qua* the dynamic of industrial technical objects, leads to the hypothesis that the ethnic structuring of groups is outdated, presupposing not a culturalist and ethnocentric logic of technical evolution, which would necessarily imply a phenomenon of uniformization and destruction of diversity, but new conditions of multiplication, reproduction, and diversification.

Industrial Technical Evolution Imposes the Renunciation of the Anthropological Hypothesis

In the explanation of technical evolution by the coupling of the human to matter, cut across by the technical tendency, an essential part of this tendency, coming from the ethnic interior milieu as intention, remains *anthropologically determined.* Simondon has this interior milieu becoming diluted. The tendency no longer has an anthropological source. Technical evolution stems completely from its own technical object. The human is no longer the *intentional actor* in this dynamic. It is its *operator.*

This analysis concerns the industrial technical object, whose appearance, somewhere in the eighteenth century, transforms the conditions of technical evolution. *On the Mode of Existence of Technical Objects* [*Du mode d'existence des objets techniques*] aims to "create a new consciousness of the sense of technical objects" (Simondon 1958, 9), a consciousness that is necessary because, especially since the advent of the machine, "culture has made itself into a system of defense against technics, in which the defense is presented as a defense of humanity, supposing that technical objects do not contain human reality."[10] "If there is such a thing as the alienation of humanity (or of culture) by technics, it is caused not by the machine but by the misunderstanding of its nature and essence." To know the essence of the machine, and *thereby* understanding the sense of technics in general, is also to know *the place of the human* in "technical ensembles." There is general agreement on the change in technics since the advent of the Industrial Revolution, insofar as it causes the appearance of machine apparatus of production that call into question the traditional relation of the human to the technical. A new form of knowledge, founding the competence of the "technologist," becomes necessary to confront this change, and first of all to determine its true nature.

To understand the machine, the point of view of its "idolaters" must be destroyed. They believe that "the degree of perfection of a machine is proportional to its degree of automatism. . . . Now, in fact, automatism is a rather low degree of technical perfection. To render a machine automatic, many possible uses must be sacrificed" (Simondon 1958, 11). The characterization of the machine by automatism misunderstands its virtue, its perfection as an industrial technical object, which is also its actual autonomy, that is, its indetermination. This renders the machine sensitive to the functioning of other machines, allowing in turn their incorporation into technical ensembles. The place of the human is among these technical ensembles, in the organization of the coordinated functioning of objects, and if the industrial technical object that the machine is achieves its perfection in the setting up of a margin of functional indetermination, its task, in industrial technics, is to determine this functioning within technical ensembles, in order to harmonize the undetermined technical objects.

The human here has less place in technogenesis than in Leroi-Gourhan's ethnotechnology. In the industrial age, the human is not the intentional origin of separate technical individuals *qua* machines. It rather executes a quasi-intentionality of which the technical object is itself the carrier.

Mechanology, the Science of the Process of Concretization of the Industrial Object

If there is a discrepancy between contemporary technics and culture, it is because the latter has not been able to incorporate a new dynamic of technical objects, a failure that engenders a disharmony between the "technical system" and the "other systems" in which it consists: "Present-day culture is ancient culture, incorporating as dynamic schemes the state of craft and agricultural techniques of past centuries" (Simondon 1958, 14).

Adjusting culture to technology means taking into account the "dynamic schemes" of present-day technics and casting aside those issuing from a reality that today has disappeared. It means, too, admitting that the technical dynamic *precedes* the social dynamic and imposes itself thereupon. The tasks of a knowledge allowing for the articulation of a relation between the human and the technical ensemble are those of an analysis of the new dynamic schemes and an understanding of the *necessity* of an *advance* of the industrial technical dynamic upon other social aspects. The issue is neither that of the traditional skill of the worker nor that of the engineer-contractor, whose relationships to machines are too intimate and too interested: at stake is *doing technology as one does sociology or psychology.* There is in technical objects a dynamic that stems neither from the soul nor from human societies, but that, like these, plays a determinant role in the movement of human becoming and must be studied for its own sake. The *dynamic of objects, qua industrial technology,* is a *science of machines,* and as such, it will be named *mechanology.*

"That which resides in machines" is certainly only "human reality, the human gesture set and crystallized into functioning structures" (Simondon 1958, 12). But the industrial technical object, although being realized by humans, nevertheless results from an inventiveness that *comes from the technical object itself.* It is *in this sense,* resulting in the indetermination of the machine's functioning, and not under the category of autonomization, that one may refer to the *autonomy* of the machine—the autonomy of its *genesis.* This analysis goes further, in the affirmation of a technological dynamic, than does the thesis that the technical tendency overrides the will of individuals and groups, who are subject to rules of technical evolution proceeding both from laws of physics and from laws of a universal human intentionality that no longer has a purchase here. Accounting for the technical dynamic non-anthropologically, by means of the concept of "process," means refusing to consider the technical object as a utensil, a means, but rather defining it "in itself." A utensil is characterized by its inertia. But the inventiveness proper to the technical object is a *process of concretization* by functional overdetermination. This concretization is the history of the technical object; it gives the object "its consistency at the end of an evolution, proving that it cannot be considered as a mere utensil" (Simondon 1958, 15). The industrial technical object is not inert. It harbors a *genetic* logic that belongs to itself alone, and that is its "mode of existence." It is not the result of human activity, nor is it a human disposition, only registering its lessons and executing them. The lessons of the machine are "inventions" in the ancient sense of the term: exhumations.

There are technical elements, individuals, and ensembles. The elements are the tools, the separated organs; the individuals implement the elements; the ensembles coordinate the individuals. Industrial technics is characterized by a transformation of technical individuals, which allows for the comprehension of the genesis and breaking down of the present-day relation of the human to the machine. The dramaturgy of modern technics begins in the eighteenth century with a phase of optimism. A crisis ensues with the advent of industrial technics exploiting the resources of the thermodynamic machine. The machine does not replace the human: the latter supplements, up to the Industrial Revolution, the absence of machines. The appearance of the tool-equipped machine, *qua* a new technical individual, however, strips the human of its role as technical individual as well as of its employment.[11] However, a new optimism is ushered in during the twentieth century with the cybernetic machine capable of producing negentropy. More profoundly than the relinquishment of the human's place as technical individual beside the machine, the threat of entropy makes possible the anguish in which the human experiences technical evolution. Against this, optimism is justified through reference to a thought of life, because technical evolution appears as a process of differentiation, creation of order, struggle against death.

With the machine, a discrepancy between technics and culture begins because the human is no longer a "tool bearer." For culture and technics to be reconciled, the meaning of "the machine bearer of tools" must be thought, what it means for itself, and what that means for the place of the human. Our age, which calls for the thought of this new relation, harbors the evidence of a positivity of technics insofar as technics becomes regulative, which is also the essence of culture. "Technical reality, having become regulative, will be able to be incorporated into culture, which is essentially regulative" (Simondon 1958, 16).

The Genetic of the Industrial Object as Functioning Matter

The machine *qua individual* has its own dynamic: technology as mechanology studies the machinic dynamic of industrial technical objects, that is, of objects that *function*. Objects that function accomplish functions by *synthesizing* them, in the double sense of *incorporating* them—which is the process of concretization by functional overdetermination—and in the sense of *reproducing* them to realize them in place of ... But reproduction, here as in life, produces a new, unique individual, maintaining a family resemblance with the ascending individual but remaining no less absolutely singular.

The concretization of the object, or the integration of its functions through overdetermination, is its history, having absolutely left its matter and, in the same move, become absolutely singular. Understanding the technical individual that the machine is means understanding its genesis. And understanding this genesis as the development of a coherence and an individuality is to observe the passage from an abstract phase to a concrete phase of the object. If, wanting to know what a concrete object is, one seeks to construct series of objects to establish a classification, "one only encounters the problem of defining technical objects under the heading of a species . . . for no set structure corresponds to a defined use" (Simondon 1958, 19). Indetermination, which is the virtue gained by the modern machine but which tendentially constitutes the essence of all technical objects, bars a classification of technical objects on the basis of these exogenous criteria for the uses to which they are put. It is rather the procedures, implemented in the most diverse domains of use, and not the uses themselves, that constitute the families of technical objects. "The same result can obtain from quite different functionings and structures," and that is why "there is more real analogy between a spring engine and a bow than between the latter and a steam engine" (19). The series of objects that can be observed accomplishing the process of concretization, the very genesis of the concrete object, will find their rationales in procedures. Use is misleading in that the object is subject to an anthropological logic that remains absolutely foreign to it, "grouping heterogeneous structures and functionings under genus and species which derive their signification from the relation of this functioning to another, that of the human being in action" (19). At issue, then, is understanding the genesis of technical objects and their functions *independently* of human functionings that establish the use behaviors of technical objects.

Despite appearances, this indetermination does not contradict the determinism of the technical tendency. The technical tendency is moreover revealed as precisely the tendency to indetermination and adaptability by Leroi-Gourhan himself, when, in "Memory and Rhythms," he describes how the tendency to exteriorize memory became, in the twentieth century, concretized as machinic exteriorization of the nervous system—of which the programmable Jacquard machine was the harbinger. Moreover, what determines the tendency from the vantage of the interior milieu is not a use but a function, in the quasi-zoological sense of the term. The Simondonian dynamic of the industrial technical object is nevertheless found to be much more autonomous as regards the human dynamic itself than the analysis of the technical tendency in the human/matter relation would make it appear. One must here be able to dispense with the first term of this relation, in order to observe what derives exclusively from a dynamic of *matter that, to accomplish a function, functions.* The dynamic of organized inorganic matter, bearing tools, calls into play a force that is no longer of zoological (animal or human) origin, nor ecological (water and wind), but *industrial, that is, available independently of all territorial considerations.*

Technical functionings can be observed only at the level of technical *individuals.* These in turn can be understood only with reference to their *genesis*: the individuality of technical objects is modified in the course of its genesis, it develops within that genesis—it is the history as well as the driving force of these modifications:

> The individuality and the specificity of the technical object can be defined in terms of genetic criteria: the individual technical object is not this or that thing given *hic et nunc*, but that for which there is a genesis. The unity of the technical object, its individuality, [and] its specificity are the characters of consistency and convergence of its genesis. The genesis of the technical object is a part of its being. (Simondon 1958, 19–20)

There is a *historicity* to the technical object that makes its descriptions as a mere hump of inert matter impossible. This inorganic matter organizes *itself*. In organizing itself, it becomes indivisible and conquers a quasi-ipseity from which its dynamic proceeds absolutely: the history of this becoming-organic is not that of the humans who "made" the object. Just as the living being has a collective history in the sense of a genetic history informed and inscribed in a *phylum*—a phylogenesis—and an individual history—an epigenesis—regulated by its indetermination in confrontation with a singular milieu and regulating in turn its morphogenesis, the technical object calls into play laws of evolution that are immanent to it, even if, as in the case of the living being, they are effected only under the conditions of an environment, to wit, here, that of the human and the other technical objects. "As in a phylogenetic series, a defined stage of evolution contains within it structures and schemes that represent the principle of an evolution of forms. *The technical being evolves by convergence and adaptation to itself; it becomes unified interiorly according to a principle of internal resonance*" (Simondon 1958, 20). This is the process of concretization. Characteristic of the technical object *qua* individual, which can be apprehended in its essence only from the standpoint of its genesis, this process is here again a quasi-biological dynamic. It is, however, not a biological dynamic: whereas the living being *maintains* its unity, the technical object *tends* toward unity—just as does the ethnic group caught up in a unifying becoming operating from within a history crystallized into a "body of traditions."

The dynamic of concretization is a morphogenesis by adaptation to self, a convergence by functional overdetermination of organs that is always difficult to consider separately. These organs, in the becoming-organic that is the genesis of the object, function more and more as parts of a whole. This dynamic can be highlighted by a comparison between the abstract phase and the concrete phase of a technical object such as the internal combustion engine: "In a current-day engine, each important component is so linked to the others by reciprocal exchanges of energy that it cannot be other than it is" (Simondon 1958, 21). There is a necessity to the form of components of the object that is immanent to it. The process of concretization is the realization of this necessity, its deployment, its coming into existence, its invention. The concretization of the technical object is its individuation, its becoming-individual, that is, its organization as a becoming-indivisible. This determinism calls upon, as in Leroi-Gourhan, the idea of a convergence that means here too that the number of technical solutions is limited. As the factor of a tendency, it carries a teleology that is not foreign to the "technical tendency." But, completely on the side of matter, of a matter that invents its form, in a process of transduction that will be analyzed in the second volume of this work, this tendency must do away with all anthropological provenance. Such a teleology is not a human process.

The Predominance of Technology in the Becoming of Industrial Societies

The concretization of technical objects, their unification, limits the number of their types: the concrete and convergent technical object is standardized. This tendency to standardization, to the production of more and more integrated types, makes industrialization possible, and not the converse: it is because there is one or another tendency in the process of technical evolution in general that industry can appear, and not because industry appears that there is standardization.[12] It is not an industrial invention that imparts form to them. "The handicraft technical object made to measure is contingent," a contingency interior to the technical object itself, but corresponding to an exterior contingency that determines the "measures" of the object. Since the technical object is not concrete, it is not determined in its uses, it must adapt itself to precise contexts that constrain it, in the absence of which it cannot function. In an apparent paradox, the more concrete the object, the less determined it is, the less "to measure." Intrinsically universal and necessary, it is adapted to itself, and not determined by what surrounds it, while the "technical object made to measure is in fact an object without intrinsic measure," without *self-determining* measure. Industrialization is the affirmation of technological necessity. It is the sign of the immense power of the technical object over industrial society, of technical evolution in general over becoming in general, of the "technical system" over the "other systems." "At the industrial level, . . . the system of wants is less coherent than the system of the object; wants are formed around the industrial technical object, *which thereby takes on the power of modeling a civilization*" (Simondon 1958, 24, my emphasis).

The actual measure of the technical object is its concrete becoming, its genesis *qua* process of concretization, in which the limits play a dynamic role, as in the Gillean technical system. "The evolution of the technical object is accomplished by the passage from a separate analytical order to a unified synthetic order," and the causes of this evolution "reside in the imperfection of the abstract technical object."

> Thus, in an internal combustion engine, the cooling could be arranged by an entirely autonomous subgroup; if this subgroup stops functioning, the engine may deteriorate; if, on the contrary, cooling is assured by an effect in solidarity with the functioning of the whole, the functioning implies cooling. (Simondon 1958, 25)

The relation of functional overdetermination is a relation of objective implication—coming from the object itself—through the solidarity of the constitutive elements of the object. This is not a logical implication: it is not imposed in the immanence of the experience. The evolution of technical objects thus does not stem from the nontechnical environment of "other systems." There is obviously a common dynamic to all systems: "there is a convergence of economic constraints (matter, labor, energy) and properly technical demands." But the technical system, and above all the technical object in its proper dynamic within the technical system, "prevails in evolution" (Simondon 1958, 26). The analyses by Gille and Leroi-Gourhan of technical evolution must be radicalized. The technical system, the universal tendency that it carries, are no longer the partners of the "other systems"; the technical object lays down the law that is its own, it affirms an auto-nomy with regard to which, in the industrial age, the other layers of society must regulate themselves, with an actual possibility of negotiation. The indetermination of uses may well leave open possibilities for adjustments to the "system of objects," but at bottom the object bestows the horizon of all possibilities, essentially preceding the fixation of uses.

The Unpredictability of the Object's Becoming

The dynamic play of the limit implies a discontinuity at the heart of all evolution in the sense of concretization. Ruptures mark the successive epochs in which the technical object gains its autonomy. These epochs are the fruit of the self-conditioning of the object that, to pass from the abstract to the concrete phase, is "its own cause" (Simondon 1958, 27)—a self-conditioning that upsets the Aristotelian divide between physical and technical entities. The "successive systems of coherence" establish relations of reciprocal causality, which are equally characteristic of the living being wherein the part does not exist without the whole, implying through their sole effectuation in the functioning of the object the discovery of the object's limits, that is, of the system of coherence that it forms:

> *The incompatibilities born of the progressive saturation of the system of subgroups harbor a play of limits whose crossing constitutes a progress*; but owing to its very nature, *this crossing can only take place in a leap.* (27, my emphasis)

This discontinuity is still lodged on a backdrop of continuity, of an individuation, of a history, outside of which it would lose all meaning: the relations of reciprocal causality are a co-implication of functions, a complication. Their incorporation is thus not a simplification, but a differentiation of the technical object that "allows the secondary effects which were once obstacles to be suppressed (through their incorporation into the functioning)"; such a differentiation is strictly speaking the reversal of a limit, the production of a new order through noise. This phenomenon is analyzed in the case of the electronic tube, in which one can see how the tetrode is invented by the internal necessities of the triode, then the pentode by the necessities of the tetrode.

As in the morphogenesis of the living, "specialization does not occur function by function, but synergy by synergy; the synergetic group of functions, and not the function alone, sets up the actual subgroup in the technical object" (Simondon 1958, 27) Functional overdetermination means that the part becomes what it is only through its insertion into the whole. The concrete being of the object, the essence of the "technical being," the acting tendency in morphogenesis, is the technical object "that no longer struggles with itself, in which no secondary effect hampers the functioning of the ensemble or is left outside of it" (27). What is proper to the industrial technical object is a tendency toward the unification of parts in a whole, which tendency is not due to the person making the object and thinking by functions, but to the synergetic necessity that most often is unplanned, and that is affirmed within the object in the course of its functioning, whereby the technical object invents itself independently of a "fabricating intention":

> Each component in the concrete object is no longer one whose essence is to correspond to the accomplishment of a function intended by the constructor, but a part of a system in which a multitude of forces operates and produces effects independently of the fabricating intention. (Simondon 1958, 35)

Whereas the anthropological basis of the technical tendency conceived of by Leroi-Gourhan, even if the tendency only becomes concretized in passing through the laws of matter, affords impetus to the "fabricating intention," what engenders the industrial technical object in the tendency to concretization is the organized matter that the technical object itself is, the system of constraints that it forms and that, as a play of limits, of a combination of forces, frees ever-new possibilities—in this sense invents them. There is here an actual techno-logical *maieutic*. Certainly, what is invented, exhumed, brought to light, brought into the world by the object exists in the laws of physics. But in physics they exist only as possibilities. When they are freed, they are no longer possibilities but realities, irreversibly—pure possibilities that have become effects which must from that point on be taken into account. They become reality only through the technical object's potential of inventiveness, in the process of concretization characterized by the fact that the human has no longer the inventive role but that of an operator. If he or she keeps the inventor's role, it is *qua* an actor listening to cues from the object itself, reading from the text of matter. To draw further on the metaphor, the actor is not the author—and that is why existing technical objects are never thoroughly concrete; they are never consciously conceived and realized by the human from out of this "logic," which is strictly speaking empirical, experimental, and in a sense quasi-existential (it is the object's *mode of existence*), the sense, namely, that this logic is revealed only in its realization, in the experience of the object itself, or, as it were, on stage, and not at the time of conception. In this move the logic of invention becomes in essence unpredictable, as in Maunoury; and this is why "the technical object is never totally known." For this very reason, it is never totally rational nor "ever totally concrete, except in the quite rare case of a fortuitous encounter" (Simondon 1958, 35). Thus does concretization call on technics to transform itself into technoscience and on technoscience to replace science. But this means that concretization calls for technoscientific *experimentation* to replace scientific *deduction*.

This dynamic, in which experience has the essential role, can be compared to what distinguishes organic matter from inert matter, to what makes biology a science irreducible to physicochemistry. If a mechanology is necessary, this is because the laws of physics, no more than those of sociology or psychology, or of all of these as a whole, cannot suffice to explain the phenomenon of the technical object *qua* the genesis of an individual and the production of an order. But on the other hand, biology cannot be the science of machines, since the organic beings it observes are always already individualized. The problem in distinguishing between inert matter, organized objects, and organic beings is on the scale of the problem of situating biology with regard to physicochemistry. But this is a problem *specific to a third order of phenomena* (neither organic nor inorganic).

The maieutic proper to the empiricism of what we are calling the *experience* of the technical object, which is its *functioning*, corresponds here as well to a *selection of combinations*. Operating on a backdrop of chance, the selection follows phyletic lines whose necessity is their horizon, dotted with mutations whose accidental effects become the new functional principles.[13]

Mutations, Lineages, and the Becoming-Natural of the Industrial Object

There are two types of perfectionings: major ones, which "modify the distribution of functions, significantly increase the synergy of the functioning," and minor ones, which "without modifying this distribution, diminish the harmful consequences of residual antagonisms" (Simondon 1958, 38). Now a diminishing of this sort is itself harmful insofar as it prevents the play of the technical object's limits from imposing a rupture. Things occur here as they do when an economic system artificially attenuates the weaknesses of a technical system by protectionist measures. The minor perfectionings, by concealing the discontinuity of technical evolution, cover over the profound meaning of the technical object's dynamic, just as, on a certain temporal scale, the apparent continuity of the genetic drift of living beings can conceal the fact that the mutation is the reality of this evolution (Jacob 1974, 244). The fact remains that these "mutations" operate from within lineages, on a backdrop of continuities. Concretization is effected in series of objects, of which the last term, never reached, is the perfectly concrete technical object. The question then is knowing "to which first term" one "can go back to reach the birth of a specific technical reality" (Simondon 1958, 40).

It is not only "the result of its functioning in exterior apparatus" that makes the technical object exist, but also the "fecundity" of "nonsaturated" phenomena that the object carries and that give it a "posterity." From then on, the first term of a series, the "primitive technical object," is defined as a "nonsaturated system," and the process of concretization is a progressive "saturation" of the complex of phenomena defining the object. In evolving, the technical object constitutes a series of objects, a lineage or a line, a "family" of which "the primitive technical object is the ancestor," and this generation is a "natural technical evolution." At the origin of the lineage is a "synthetic act of invention constitutive of a technical essence." The technical essence is the *identity* of the lineage, its family resemblance, the specificity of its patrimony, which is the secret of its singular becoming: "The technical essence is recognized in the fact that it remains stable through the evolutional lineage, and not only stable, but productive as well of structures and functions by internal development and progressive saturation" (Simondon 1958, 43). If one can speak of a *natural* technical evolution, this is because the technical object, in becoming concretized, is in the process of *naturalization*: the concretization of the abstract technical object is its progress toward a naturalness that allows it as well to escape being known, its filiation improbably engendering its becoming beyond the "intellectual system" that gives birth to it. The difference between *phusis* and *tekhnē* thus fades, as if the industrial technical object had engendered a *third milieu* in which it "becomes more and more like a natural object. At its beginning this object was in need of a regulative exterior milieu, the laboratory or the workshop, sometimes the factory. Little by little, . . . it becomes capable of dispensing with the artificial milieu" (47). Just as the living being is more than its physicochemical constituents, the technical object is *more* than the sum of the scientific principles that it implements; it witnesses "a certain mode of functioning and a compatibility that actually exists and that was fashioned *before being planned*: this compatibility was not contained in each of the separate scientific principles that served for the object's construction, it was discovered empirically" (48). From this point, like "natural objects spontaneously produced," technical beings must be submitted to an inductive study from within a "science of correlations and transformations that would be a general technology or mechanology" more akin to biology than to physics (47–48). Nevertheless, an "abusive assimilation of the technical object to the natural and especially the living object" must be avoided. "Mechanology" must not be cybernetics, for one must not "found a separate science that would study the mechanisms of regulation and command in automates built to be automates"; and contrary to Wiener, "it can only be said that technical objects tend toward concretization, whereas natural objects such as living beings are concrete from the start" (49). The organizing principle of the technical object is in this object *qua* tendency, aim, and end. As for the tendency's *driving* principle, it remains in the living, for "without finality, *driven and realized* by the living, physical causality could never alone produce a positive and efficient concretization" (49, my emphasis). Once again, then, the question of the relation between living matter and organized inorganic matter arises. The industrial technical object has brought us to the suppression of the intentional anthropological part of the techno-logical dynamic. But a part still remains, namely that the living, who no longer *commands*, *operates*. It is in returning to the theme of a third milieu undercutting the opposition of *phusis* and *tekhnē*, engendered by the object itself in the course of its "naturalization," that the nature of this operation will be brought to light.

Anticipation as the Condition of the Appearance of the Associated Milieu

By becoming naturalized and engendering its own milieu, the object avoids the phenomenon of hypertelia, which limits the object's indetermination by leaving it dependent upon an artificial milieu. Hypertelia is an "exaggerated specialization of the technical object which renders it unadaptable to change, however slight, taking place in the conditions of its use or fabrication" (Simondon 1958, 50).

The technical object is the point of encounter of two milieus, the technical and the geographical, and must be incorporated into them. It is a compromise between these two worlds. For example, the electrical power unit is doubly articulated: onto the electrical network, which transmits electric energy from the technical milieu that it transforms into mechanical energy; and onto the form of the landscape, a varied geographical milieu onto which the electrical network and the railroad bring mechanical energy to bear. Through the traction engine, the two worlds act upon one another. If we compare this traction engine to the electric engine of the factory, we find that the latter "functions almost entirely in the interior of the technical world," that it is not in need of adaptation to a non-technical milieu. Its conditions of functioning being highly determined, it may be specialized, but it may just as well not be concrete. On the contrary, "the necessity of exclusive adaptation not to a defined milieu but to the function placed in relation to two milieus both in evolution, limits the adaptation and specifies it in the sense of autonomy and of concretization" (Simondon 1958, 53). The technical object would tend to emancipate itself from all specialization just as the human being is susceptible of adapting itself to the most varied of milieus owing to the *removability* of its organs.

The case of the Guimbal turbine highlights the stakes of the problem, allowing for the delineation of the concept of associated milieu and indicating to what sort of ecology the process of concretization in general leads. "This turbine is immersed in a pressure pipeline and coupled directly to a quite small generator contained in a crankcase filled with pressurized oil" (Simondon 1958, 54). Its originality is that the water in which it is immersed, which "affords the energy" that starts it, is a natural milieu that becomes "plurifunctional" for the technical functioning itself, since it "evacuates the heat produced by the generator." But the oil, an element of the technical milieu, in its relation to the water, an element of the natural milieu, also becomes plurifunctional:

> The oil lubricates the generator, isolates the coil, and brings the heat from the coil to the crankcase, where it is evacuated by the water; lastly, it prevents water from entering the crankcase. . . . This suppression is itself plurifunctional: it accomplished a greasing under the permanent pressure of the stages

> at the same time as it prevents water from entering should the stages not be waterproof. Now . . . owing to this plurifunctionality, this concretization and this relational adaptation have been made possible. (54)

In other words, here the "natural" milieu itself is found to be incorporated and functionally overdetermined: the concretization is effected outside the object itself, which does not effect here a mere addition of a technical milieu to a geographical one—and the associated milieu is more that the sum of the two.

> *Adaptation-concretization is a process conditioning the birth of a milieu* rather than *being conditioned by an already given milieu.* It is conditioned by a milieu that has only virtual existence before the invention. There is invention because a leap is accomplished and justified by the relation that the leap sets up on the inside of the milieu it creates: *the condition of possibility* of the turbo-generator couple is its realization. (Simondon 1958, 55, my emphasis)

The object self-conditions its functioning, bringing with it its conditions of functioning, thereby reducing the phenomenon of hypertelia. The technical object creator of a milieu "frames" nature. The natural aquatic element encounters the technical object: the natural element not only subjects itself to the technical object's functioning but favors it (the Guimbal turbine provides the profound sense of that dam on the Rhine to which Heidegger refers). The technical object submits its "natural milieu" to reason and naturalizes itself at one and the same time. It becomes concretized by closely conforming to this milieu, but in the same move radically transforms the milieu. This ecological phenomenon may be observed in the informational dimension of present-day technics, where it allows for the development of a generalized performativity (for example in the apparatuses of live transmission and of data processing in real time, with the fictive inversions engendered therein)—but it is then essentially the human milieu, that is, human geography, and not physical geography, that is found to be incorporated into a process of concretization that should no longer be thought on the scale of the object, but also not on the scale of the system.

To create one's own milieu is to build. This construction—which is ineluctable given that technics has become largely a matter of data processing and counts on the largest possible indetermination in the functioning of machines, presupposing a maximum decrease in hypertelia and in the same stroke a generalization of associated milieus—is not a "humanization of nature," first of all because it is not a human construction. The ever more concretized object tends toward naturalness, and "this process might well appear as the naturalization of the human." However, Simondon adds a remark that opens the question at the heart of our treatise:

> Between humanity and nature a technogeographical milieu is created which only becomes possible with the help of human intelligence: the self-conditioning of a scheme by the result of its functioning demands the use of an inventive function of anticipation found neither in nature nor in already constituted technical objects. (Simondon 1958, 57)

If there is, then, a dynamic proper to the technical object tending toward its concretization, it nevertheless supposes a possibility of anticipation on the part of the operator, of the driving force, the human *qua* efficient cause of the technical object.

We shall seek to show here that this capacity of anticipation *itself supposes the technical object*, and no more precedes it than does form matter.

§ 2 Technology and Anthropology

> But mankind, made for peace as much as for war, writes laws with his hands, raises altars and statues to Gods, builds a ship, constructs a flute, a lyre, forges a knife, pinchers, produces the instruments of all the arts; in his writings, he bequests memoirs on the theoretical aspects of these arts, in such a way that, thanks to the written works and to the use of his hands, you may converse with Plato, Aristotle, Hippocrates, and the other ancients.
>
> —Galen

Paradoxes of the Question of Technics *qua* the Question of Time

Gille shows why and how, with the technical system conditioning technical invention, technical evolution must be thought from the start in terms of the notion of system.

Leroi-Gourhan attempts to think the system as a quasi-organism commanded in its evolution by the technical tendency, which has two sides: the intentionality of the human, and matter in its laws.

Simondon analyzes the industrial stage in which conditioning and evolution are brought into play by a dynamism proper to the technical object and independent of all human intention—the technical object being of organized inorganic matter, tending toward naturalization. Its organizational dynamism, although no longer submitted to human intention, nevertheless requires the operating dynamics of anticipation. The object, which is not produced by the human, still is in need of the human insofar as it anticipates: the heart of the question is time.

But what is an object? The electrical power unit with its freight cars, rails, quaternaries, signal systems, furbished stations, and so on, does it not in turn constitute *an* object? Does not this object with its electrical network constitute a new object? Does not this object with its electrical network constitute *an* object? In other words, could not the contemporary technical system itself be apprehended as an object, tending toward concretization? If this were the case, and if the process of concretization essentially tends toward the generation of associated milieus, what is the third milieu engendered by contemporary technics?

We can see at this point that Heidegger is right and Hegel and Simondon wrong, providing one adds that it is from within a certain independence of the individual, which the machine actually is, that the technical system becomes thinkable, itself organized and mobilized *qua Gestell* by the dynamics of concretization. Furthermore we then meet once again the aporia of a biological formalism of the relation of (living) parts to the whole of an individual.

We suggested in the previous chapter that this concretization, relating principally to the informational plane, was realized by incorporation and functional overdetermination of the milieus of human geography and directly affected the capacities for anticipation, overdetermining them in turn. If, as Simondon suggests, anticipation remains the properly human side of the process of concretization, such an evolution constitutes an actual rupture—and we saw in the introduction to this work that contemporary technical evolution engenders reactive resistance, which crystallizes around the feeling that such a rupture literally affects the very possibilities of human decision—the destiny of humanity is suddenly alienated in a technological "destiny"; "*Gestell*" frames human reason itself. The question remains, however: is not anticipation *from the beginning—originally—constituted in the very technicity* of the object? Contemporary epochality should in this case be revised.

The first chapter, whose whole concern lay in an analysis of the question of technics in time, thereby leads us to the exposition of the primary elements of our thesis: technics *as* time, but firstly, hardly less ambitiously, as a *question of time*. We shall approach technics here as a question of time from what is still an anthropological viewpoint. If, as Simondon led us to conclude, the technological dynamism of the industrial object remains linked to human dynamism insofar as the latter anticipates, we shall set off paleoanthropology *qua* a science of the origin and evolution of the anticipating living being with paleotechnology *qua* a science of the origin and evolution of technical objects. This is why this chapter is entitled "Technology and Anthropology." We shall read in detail certain passages from Leroi-Gourhan's work *Gesture and Speech*, in which he synthesizes and enriches his original hypotheses elaborated in the field of ethnology.

The paleontology of humanity uncovers and inaugurates at the deepest levels the question of origin that Leroi-Gourhan, far from trying to elude—he never hesitates to start down the most speculative paths—attempts to handle from outside the snare of metaphysics. Does he succeed? Though attentive from the start to what materials prove, these being the initial supports of each of his approaches and the catalysts of his most audacious hypotheses, he never slips into the illusion of a pure positivity of facts, which would be nothing but a naive submission to the blandest of positivist metaphysics. One can consequently expect to see in his work not only a permanent conflict between the sciences of the origin (prehistory and archaeology) and transcendental questions but also the perpetual contamination of the one by the another. Our still-anthropological approach to the question of technics *qua* a question of time will soon lead us to a properly philosophic approach.

Gesture and Speech is given to us as the last word on paleoanthropological thinking—and undoubtedly this heritage still remains to be assumed today, either by paleoanthropology or by philosophy. This sort of escheat (absence of succession) is due not only to the size and importance of the corpus: at stake is a body of thought occasioning immense difficulties and replete with questions as yet untouched by any real research.

Leroi-Gourhan undertakes this comprehensive work by addressing the "cerebralism" of Rousseau, which neglects the systemic zoological principle that must be embraced to understand, throughout the history of life, the event constituted by the emergence of humanity—that is, in the final analysis, the emergence of technics. (This critique of Rousseau's anthropology was, moreover, formulated in different terms by Nietzsche [1986, 215–16], and was leveled as well against Kant.) It was, however, by claiming a transcendental type of approach that Rousseau was able to get behind the facts, by claiming to have the right, over against their facticity, to relate a fiction on the origin of man, from originary evidence that can still be heard through the voice of pure nature. As we will say further on, this fiction maintains that the apprehension of the question of the origin based on empirical data will always arrive too late. Rousseau's argument rests on a perfectly clear divide between the empirical and the transcendental (which also supposes the opposition of being to becoming). Given his exemplary approach, Leroi-Gourhan calls into question such a divide. He will, nevertheless, be confronted with a difficulty that will lead him to restore and repeat Rousseau's gesture even as he displaces it.

In this chapter, we shall examine a paradox of contemporary technics in which it reveals itself at one and the same time as human power [*puissance*] and as the power for the self-destruction of humanity. From within this paradox as well as the question of origin (and of time) that it opens up, a temporary attempt at definition of what should be called technology and anthropology will lead to the question and to the paradoxes of the transcendental anthropology of Rousseau. We will thereby be able to examine Leroi-Gourhan's arguments against transcendental anthropology, an examination that will issue in the next chapter in an account of his major hypothesis on the process of humanization effected between the Australopithecus and the Neanderthal.

The Question of Technics, the Question Coming to Us from Technics

In the technological context of *Gestell*, a "technicization" of all domains of life is experienced on a massive scale. In the wake of research planning recommended by the French Fifth Economic Plan quoted in the first chapter, the theme of societal modernization has risen to dominance—ever since the oil crisis of 1973, and more particularly from the beginning of the 1980's, in France and elsewhere, in the east and south as well as to the west and north of the globe. Whatever the diversity of viewpoints, the dominance of this theme resounds in all the official discourses of public and private decision makers.

In the industrialized countries with a "democratic" tradition, "technopoles" have sprung up. An attempt to reevaluate technical education has been made. The University of Technology at Compiègne, where part of the work presented here was elaborated, is itself a new variety of institution corresponding to new imperatives.

Novel technical apparatuses of all sorts are to be seen: machines for circulation, communication, for sight, speech, entertainment, calculation, work, "thought"; soon machines for feeling and for doubling oneself ("tele-presence" or tele-aesthesis, virtual reality), and for destruction. These include living machines—"chimera" and other *biological artifacts* currently translate not so much an organization of the inorganic as a reorganization of the organic.

Paradoxically, the extraordinary vitality of this generalized machinism (each day engenders its system corresponding to the law of constant innovation that dominates industrial economies) is contemporary with a veritable collapse of technocratic euphoria. Countless problems are being engendered by the expansion of technical equipment: gluts, ever-increasing risks consequent upon the increase in traffic and improvement in performance speeds; the installation of a generalized "state of emergency" caused not only by machines that circulate bodies but by data-transport networks; the growing paucity of "messages," illiteracy, isolation, the distancing of people from one another, the extenuation of identity, the destruction of territorial boundaries; unemployment—robots seeming designed no longer to free humanity from work but to consign it either to poverty or stress; threats surrounding choices and anticipations, owing to the delegation of decision-making procedures to machines that are on the one hand necessary since humanity is not fast enough to control the processes of informational change (as is the case for the electronic stock-market network), but on the other hand also frightening since this decision making is combined with machines for destruction (for example in the case of polemological networks for the guidance of "conventional" or non-"conventional" missiles, amounting to an imminent possibility of massive destruction); and, just as preoccupying, the delegation of knowledge, which not only modifies radically the modes of transmission of this knowledge but seems to threaten these forms with nothing less than sheer disappearance. In this regard, for example, everyone is concerned about the effects of the mini calculator on the arithmetical skills of future generations, or automatic spelling correctors, but the problem now extends to more complicated and "skillful" technical apparatus: data banks, expert systems, knowledge-based systems, computer-assisted decision making, and so forth. Even more massively felt is the extraordinary influence on collective behavior by the media, which control the production of news that is transmitted without delay to enormous population masses of quite diverse cultural origins, by professionals whose activity is "rationalized" following exclusively market-oriented criteria within an ever more concentrated industrial apparatus. This system is furthermore frequently and cleverly parasitized by forms of terrorism or vulgar propaganda, forms that no longer characterize simply small isolated groups but constitute actual state politics (and this does not only apply to poor or reputedly "totalitarian" states). Meanwhile, political programs, when they are *local*, appear dependent on an actual *diktat* issued by an unruly world public opinion. In this context one scarcely dares evoke the systematic exploitation of natural resources and the destruction of what is called "nature," knowing how fast ecological questions have become mundanely predominant: earth and energy exhaustion, water pollution, destruction of the ozone layer, urban disequilibrium, various contaminations, and so forth.

And yet genetic manipulations undoubtedly constitute the most striking technological development, giving rise to the most disarming discourses: worse than the possibility of sheer destruction of humanity, they make imaginable and possible the fabrication of a "new humanity," or of a pseudo-humanity, and without even having to dive into science-fiction nightmares, one can see that even their simple current applications destroy the oldest ideas that humanity has of itself—and this, at the very moment when psychoanalysis and anthropology are exhuming the constitutive dimension of these ideas, as much for the psyche as for the social body [*le faire-corps social*], beginning with ideas concerning kinship relations. Maternities, paternities, generations (by sperm banks, test-tube fecondations, and embryo implants *qua* available commodities on a new market) no longer belong to the set of unattainable realities. This is the age in which Marvin Minsky has proposed that a program of miniaturized technological equipment be developed with "nanotechnologies"—on the inside of the human brain, which would thereby be linked to new artificial organs allowing the brain to improve and diversify its sensory-motor and calculating performances through the incorporation of tele-presence-system commands and "intelligent" automatic modules at the level of the cortex itself. This is the age when vast, horrific traffic in human organs is conducted with impunity on homeless children of third-world megalopolises, kidnapped and emptied of their livers, kidneys, hearts, their very entrails. This is all taking place at a moment when a new Orphism is moved to indignation by medical experimentation on animals (however problematic), at a moment when a vast DNA research program aims at technoscientific "productions" capable of making profits upon receiving copyright, at a moment when genetic manipulations are directly affecting the organization of the human individual body, its specific memory and therefore its genetic prospects, its most "natural" "substratum," in a word, its nature.

Which "nature"?

This presentation, cursory, dramatic, but nevertheless exact, of the current state of contemporary technics and its effects, wishes to stress what today is universally felt if not clearly acknowledged: the urgency of an elucidation of the relations holding, at an ontological level (if one can here still refer to ontology), between anthropology and technology. This, at a time when technology has disquietingly cast doubt upon, while perhaps for the first time directly confronting, the very form of this question: what is the nature of the human?

The question of technics is first of all the question that technics addresses to us. The evolution of Heidegger's thinking from *Being and Time* to "Time and Being" does nothing perhaps but register the foregoing upheaval, if it is true that modern technics is the accomplishment of metaphysics, that metaphysics is the history of being, that the history of being is being itself, and that being is the question that "the being that we ourselves are" is capable of addressing to being, whereas starting from "the turn" [Heidegger's *Kehre*], it becomes a question of "thinking being without beings" (Heidegger 1972, 24), that is to say, without Dasein, without this "being that we ourselves are."

The Becoming-Astral of Man and the Power of Man as Self-Destruction

In this age of contemporary technics, it might be thought that technological power risks sweeping the human away. This is one of the possible conclusions of this dramatized presentation. Work, family, and traditional forms of communities would be swept away by the deterritorialization (that is, by destruction) of ethnic groups, and also of knowledge, nature, and politics (not only by the delegation of decision making but by the "marketization" of democracy), the economy (by the electronization of the financial activity that now completely dominates it), the alteration of space and time (not only inter-individual spaces and times, by the globalization of interactions through the deployment of telecommunication networks, the instantaneity of the processes, the "real time" and the "live," but also the space and time of the "body proper" itself, by tele-aesthesia or "tele-presence," a neologism that bears as it stands the whole weight of the contradictions that we shall attempt to think through here).

For the moment, let us refrain from asking whether the nature of the human is threatened by alteration or even disappearance, for one would first have to know whether humanity ever had a nature. Let us consider what is happening today to the human world, and ask ourselves first of all what this human world once was. These questions, according to Maurice Blanchot, have acquired today a specific and irreducible importance in the way they radically affect our very temporality, which was once conceived as that of a sublunary world whose bearings were constituted from the standpoint of the stars, until the day the human itself became a star:

> If, reading Herodotus, we have the sentiment of a turning point, do we not have, reading our times, the certainty of an even more considerable change, such that the events offering themselves to us would no longer be linked in a way according to what we are used to calling history, but in a way still unknown?
>
> . . . Today we meet an event bearing an elementary trait, that of impersonal powers, represented by the intervention of mass phenomena, by the supremacy of mechanical play, and thirdly by the seizure of the constitutive forces of matter. These three factors are named in a single word: modern technics, since technics comprises at once collective organization on a planetary scale for the calculated establishment of plans, mechanization and automation, and finally atomic energy, a key word. What hitherto only stars could accomplish, mankind does. Mankind has become astral. This astral era that has begun no longer belongs to the measures of history. (Blanchot 1969, 396)

To the measures of history belonged the divide separating the human world from the stars, and thereby constituting that world. Humanity (the human world) was history (the world of Herodotus was the human world). Humanity (the human world) has become a star (has become the world of the human having become a star). This is an astral figure of power, which speaks to a change in epoch, to modern technics. But the power of *whom* or of *what*? Of humanity, or of the "impersonal forces" of modern technics itself?

The human was history, which is here its *second origin* (the human arrives before history), the origin of the globalized Western world, the second origin of humanity as a whole in the very fact that it ends up in this worldwide extension, in this global culmination [*achèvement*] of the West. The origin of Western man, that is, of the human who writes, thinks rationally, and, in the development of this rationality, also finds the development of its world, its total territorial extension, that is, its deterritorialization—a thoroughly technological extension, whereas writing *qua* technics is not, at the origin,[1] foreign to the West's access to this extensive and domineering rationality.

This second origin that history is was the beginning of a world, the Western world. In the astral age, this world is now common to all humanity, it is "accomplished," culminated in its movement of planetary extension, *insofar as this movement would have characterized it*—"culminated" also means finished, terminated, disappeared or disappearing ("change of epoch"). The radical transformations effected by contemporary technics come to pass in this culmination. This world whose bearings are now planetary is that of Western science and technics in a new configuration that, traversing the virginity of the American continent, has become the world of technoscience.

Today, the becoming-astral of man and his technoscientific imagination project themselves not only into the mastery on the earth of "what up to now only the stars could accomplish." The astrophysicist Hubert Reeves,[2] speculating on the solution of the problem posed for the human race by the death of the sun, conceives of a human technical intervention into the star's activity, that is, a "competing scenario" to that of a definitive exile from the earth, itself another totally serious technoscientific hypothesis of which the pseudo-scientific and industrialo-cultural project named "Biosphere 2"[3] has exploited the media spin-offs.

In this global Western culmination—which has allowed for the total mobilization of all geological and geographical as well as historico-spiritual energies, and soon will allow for the literal mobilization of stellar energies themselves, resulting in an unheard-of, incalculable, unpredictable increase in the power of technics in the immediate future, that is, in the first place, in the power of humanity—a strange problem is posed: the greater humanity's power, the more "dehumanized" the world becomes. The increasing intervention of humanity in the course of nature, and by the same token in its own nature, makes it incontestable that humanity's power can reaffirm itself eminently as the power of destruction (of the world) of humanity and the denaturalization of humanity itself, if it is true that worldness is essential to the human and that the essential characteristics[4] of worldness itself have apparently been destroyed by the technoscientific "world," the germinative body of the human itself having become accessible to technical intervention—an *imminent* possibility. The "change of epoch" consists in this imminence. It is from within this imminence alone that today it may still be asked, *What is the human?*, and asked again, *What is the human world insofar as worldness is also always already technicity, technical power*, activity," and perhaps it will finally be asked, for once, *What is technology*, *qua* the power of the human, *that is to say, the human empowered?*

Technics *qua* the Question of Intervention: *Hubris* and *Metron*, Stars and Disasters, Haps and Mishaps

Reeves's text and an article by Michel Deguy indirectly echoing it[5] pose, each in its distinct way, the question of intervention—an originary, specifically Western question, if it is true that the West is engendered in philosophy in such a way that it is constituted against (and with) the Sophists, in that the latter would have instrumentalized the *logos*, denaturalizing its vocation of unveiling, putting it in the service of a power of intervention on the *doxa*. This denunciation—inseparable from the tragic prescription of *metron* [measure] before the incessant imminence of sublunary hubris, finding expression in *theoria*, in an essential relation to stars (beings "always being" in the sphere of the permanent stars [*les fixes*]), generating the question of the relation of being to becoming, the opposition of sensible and intelligible—still commands the contemporary discourse of philosophy that takes on the task of analyzing the technoanthropological process against the horizon of technoscientific rationality: a certain understanding of technics dominates all the fields of discourse (philosophical, anthropological, scientific, technocratic, mediatory-political, artistic) that are articulated by categories—ends and means, subjects and objects, nature and culture—which only function and make sense in these oppositional pairs.

The anthropology of Leroi-Gourhan, *insofar as it cannot be constituted otherwise than as a technology*, radically undermines these categorial oppositions and perhaps makes them obsolete. Such an obsolescence of the categories through which historical reason has apprehended technical reality is perhaps indissociable from the becoming astral of man (*qua* the question of intervention—and if the first volume of *Gesture and Speech* is mainly devoted to the technological origin of humanity, the second ends with an equally technological anticipation of humanity's end). This becoming-obsolete of historical categories (which we shall take up again in more detail in the second volume of this work) would be the price to pay for becoming-astral, would constitute the profound sense of the "change of epoch." A becoming whose factor is technics understood today as system, tendency, concretization, *Gestell.* Disaster. "Disaster" does not mean catastrophe but disorientation—stars guide. A loss of guides that would have affirmed itself only in its difference, god, regulating idea, eschatology of emancipation. Consequently, a disaster of the führer. Such differences are lost in the potential illimitation of technics, in which the nature of humanity is thereby threatened by its own power *qua* technics; and along with humanity's nature, nature as such is threatened by humanity, by the threat it represents for its own nature. A threat on the "nature" of "Nature": on being.

Must humanity, in the name of an anthropocentrism that is always denounced by philosophical reason (and first of all against sophistry), resist technics, that is, its own power? In the name of anthropocentrism, that is, in the name of humanity's so-called "nature" and of the danger that would constitute its own disappearance or the disappearance of what would supposedly be proper to it *qua* its "nature"? Such a postulate could never be uncritically accepted philosophically. Is humanity the term, and the aim as well, the end, the finality of becoming in life and beyond life, when, since Darwin, humanity is no longer the origin? The veritable anthropocentrism, which must be denounced when one presumes to refuse the discourse of the human-measure-of-all-things, is this teleology setting the human up *qua* the end of nature—*qua* finality and *qua* culmination.

But there is also another question: must humanity, in disappearing, accept making nature disappear? Is not anthropocentrism justified in its obstruction of becoming, for the sake of being? Must the question of being be thought in terms of humanity's becoming (or its "maintenance")—or again, and in a certain way conversely, must not becoming be thought as the question of nature and of its maintenance, implying notably the maintenance of humanity's nature?

Does a "technocentrism" that would be the counterpart of anthropocentrism constitute a danger for nature? Notably for the nature of humanity, but here this question loses its priority, for it is no longer a question of resisting in the name of anthropocentrism. Technocentrism means the development of technics "for itself," when it is an end unto itself, the autonomization of technics by which it is its own law, indeed the law;

this possible development has always been perceived as the epitome of hubris *qua* alienating violence that brings human "freedom" *qua* freedom of being to an end, brings an end to time, evacuates the future, if not becoming. But technocentrism is also, is still, a figure of anthropocentrism, is still understood as such—as mastery and possession of nature.

The nature in question here is, firstly, that of the human. If our reading of Simondon led us to see the human as the operator of technical organization, we can envisage this organization, rising to the level of its effective and systematic concretization, as the very possibility of the disappearance (or the replacement) of the operator. Questioning the nature of the human means first of all questioning its origin. In the final analysis, this is what anthropology does. But we should question the very form of the question. We cannot, and neither can anthropology in general, postulate a nature (that is, an origin) of the human, as Claude Lévi-Strauss does, assigning to science the task of solving the "problem of invariance," a problem that "appears as the modern form of a question that mankind has always asked itself" (Lévi-Strauss 1978, 35). Leroi-Gourhan interests us precisely because he apprehends anthropology *as* technology; in this respect he is an exception.

Technology

Technology is first of all defined as a discourse on technics. But what does technics mean? In general, technics designates in human life today the restricted and specified domain of tools, of instruments, if not only machines (Louis Mumford thus thinks all instrumentality from the vantage of the machine).

Technics (*tekhnē*) designates, however, first and foremost all the domains of skill. What is not skill? Politeness, elegance, and cooking are skills. However, only in the latter do we have production, a transformation of material, of "raw material," into "secondary matter" or products; and this is why cooking, as is the case in *Gorgias*, is more willingly acknowledged as technics, as productive skill in-forming matter. This is the model of the craftsman, the operator (efficient cause) of *poiēsis*, from which has developed the theory of the four causes, on the basis of which tradition understands technics.

Dance produces a spectacle. Is not elegance also a spectacle? Dance is *tekhnē*. Just as in the case of elegance, it is not necessarily produced for others (as social commerce or commercial spectacle); it might simply afford pleasure to its "efficient cause," as can any technique for that matter. Rhetoric and poetry are also techniques. And there is something of poetry and rhetoric in all language. Is not language itself, *qua* skill, a technique, and a potentially marketable commodity? The speech that presupposes a type of skill is productive even if speech is not the specialty of the person speaking: it produces enunciations. These can be marketed or not, as is the case for all products of a *tekhnē*. Hence the difficulty of delimiting the field of technics.

All human action has something to do with *tekhnē*, is after a fashion *tekhnē*. It is no less the case that in the totality of human action "techniques" are singled out. These most often signal specialized skills, not shared by all. Thus the technique of the craftsman, or the medical doctor, the architect, or the engineer, as well as that of the philosopher, the artist, or the rhetorician. A technique is a particular type of skill that is not indispensable to the humanity of a particular human. This is what is implicitly understood by the term "technique." We shall attempt to show in this section that this bespeaks an inadequate understanding, one that is already restrictive and derived, of what a technique is. This difference (specialization), however, is what allows for the constitution of technical milieus in ethnic milieus and their gradual separation from their respective territories.

Technology is therefore the discourse describing and explaining the evolution of specialized procedures and techniques, arts and trades—either the discourse of certain types of procedures and techniques, or that of the totality of techniques inasmuch as they form a system: technology is in this case the discourse of the evolution of that system.

However, technology is most often used today as having incorporated a large part of science, in opposition to traditional prescientific techniques. The corps of engineers was born with the advent of technics as "applied science." The concept of technoscience derives from this established meaning, in which technics and sciences become inseparable, in which rationality is confined to usefulness—for Habermas, the usefulness of capital as "purposive-rational action" (1987, 106). This is an inversion, even a perversion, of the initial epistemological model of philosophy by which theory, the essence of science, is defined by its independence from useful finalities, that is, anthropocentric ones. Does technoscience nevertheless serve humanity, or serve *tekhnē* itself? Is it actually usefulness that governs concretization? If technology, which for a long time has been synonymous with progress, is no longer necessarily perceived as such, or rather, if it is no longer obvious that progress is tantamount to benefit for the human race,[6] a feeling found deep in the multifarious reactions of resistance to development, can it still be affirmed that techno-science submits theory to useful finalities—usefulness still being understood as usefulness-for-humanity?

Technics would then be an end unto itself. Numerous authors suggest as much, and see in this self-finalization of technics a monstrous possibility, scandalous from the ontological vantage, from that of what is, or of "what must be." However, this type of analysis, again opposing means to ends, remains hampered by categories that can no longer speak to what technics is. If technics can be given its own finality, this means that its thinking in terms of ends and means is no longer sufficiently radical.

Anthropology

The prevailing understandings of contemporary technics, caught up in the workings of oppositions inherited from metaphysics, are by the same token hampered by the false alternative of anthropocentrism and technocentrism—and are reduced to opposing the human and the technical.

If we now wish to address the problem of the nature of the human, and if the nature, the essence, or the principle of a being lies in its origin, then we will have to question the origin of the human, with the risk, once again, of having to call into question the very possibility of an origin.

But the question of the possibility of the human, of its origin, of the possibility of an origin of the human, cannot itself forget the question of the possibility of origin as such. To discourse on the origin of the human is always also, explicitly or not, to discourse on origin in general—on what is, on the principle and the origin of being. The question of origin is that of principles, of the most ancient, of that which, ever since and forever, establishes what is in its being. The question of origin is the question of being. If the stakes are the being of the human, the origin of the human defining what it is, its "nature," its *phusis*, one will have to know how to distinguish, in the human, between what it essentially is, what establishes it from the beginning and for all time as the human, and what it is accidentally; that is, one will have to sort out the essential predicates from the accidental. We will also have to know what the stakes of humanity's becoming are. We can already sense that these distinctions, which are necessary on the subject of any being and for the discourse authorizing them (ontology), risk breaking down on "the being that we ourselves are," should we succeed in establishing that technicity is essential to humanity.

The question of origin, including the origin of the human, cannot be sustained by a simple, historical style of investigation: it is not a question of uncovering traces of what was at the beginning. A bit or piece of the principle of what is will not be found at the beginning. If the first thinkers, the thinkers of the beginning, seem to have, in a certain fashion, reasoned in this way (at the beginning, there is a piece of being: water, air, and so on), they were not thinking in terms of a historical investigation—they were reasoning from the standpoint of reason insofar as reason is a principle unto itself: the principles of being are those of reasoning, and only reasoning allows any trace, whatever its age, to be deciphered. This whole discourse is enigmatic and old, as old as metaphysics. As for the enigma of the origin, it has traditionally been untied by a thought of origin *qua* fall. This is the case from Plato to Rousseau and beyond. If "the discourse of the fall" means the discourse of the fall into the sublunary world, this always means also and at the same time, essentially, a fall into technics. This is certainly not explicitly the way Plato speaks, but it is more clearly the case with Rousseau. Contingency is what that which falls falls into, that which, stemming from what is below the stars, belongs to becoming, to unveiling, to the covering over and to the forgetting of what is: to fall is to forget. What falls is the soul. The soul is what possesses in itself the principle of its movement, the soul is its own principle, and technics, as we have seen in Aristotle's *Physics*, is fundamentally what does not have the principle of its movement in itself. The soul is also that which can know: there is a fall of the soul at the origin, at the origin of our world, of the world of becoming, into this world, from the sphere of eternal beings, from the stars. A fall into the body, into passion and particular, diverse interests, into the sensible, the only place where a conflict between the true and the false can take place. Platonic philosophy is constituted on the basis of an opposition between the intelligible and the sensible which is just as much an opposition between the astral and the sublunary, that is, an opposition between the human insofar as his essence, or the essence of his soul, is knowledge, and technics insofar as its essence is lack of knowledge, that is, the absolute privation of self-movement. For this thought it is evident that technical self-movement can only be an illusion. But we can no longer dispose of such evidence, neither immediately (doxically) nor mediately (through the philosophical detour).

This discourse comes down to us in its first version and first movement (the provenance of the soul) in the myth of Persephone recalled by Socrates to Meno, and comes to fruition (the fall of the soul), as regards its specifically Platonic version, in *Phaedrus*. *Meno* is the oldest, properly philosophical enunciation of the question of origin, and the first affirmation of the absolute necessity of a transcendental knowledge. What is virtue? Socrates shows Meno that such a question cannot be answered with examples. The definition of virtue cannot be founded in experience. Experience gives us only a collection of cases, but in no case do we have the rule for the unity of these cases. Only by speaking the essence of virtue, hence by truly answering the question What is virtue? can we come up with the unity of these various examples, the reason that gives the examples, *de jure* and not only *de facto*, as examples of virtue; this is the only way for us to gain access to the universality within the manifold. Now this universality, and this essence, are not in the manifold of experience as such, they are not in experience inasmuch as experience is always a manifold. This does not rule out the help examples can afford us in attaining to the essence. But the heuristic principle cannot be found therein. In fact, Socrates only dwells on this question on his way to another: What is being, the knowledge of being, that is, a true discourse? Responding to this question will lead Plato to the enunciation of what will inaugurate metaphysics: the myth of anamnesis.

The myth ripostes to an aporia addressed by Meno to Socrates in his discourse on the essence: If you do not rely on experience, if this recourse is in principle impossible in your search for the essence,

> how will you look for something when you don't in the least know what it is? How on earth are you going to set up something you don't know as the object of your search? To put it another way, even if you come right up against it, how will you know that what have found is the thing you didn't know? (Plato 1961, *Meno*, 80d)

According to you, Meno, says Socrates, repeating the aporia to bring out the stakes,

> a man cannot try to discover either what he knows or what he does not know. He would not seek what he knows, for since he knows it there is no need of the inquiry, nor what he does not know, for in that case he does not even know what he is to look for. (80e)

This aporia, crucial in the history of philosophy, sets out the very difficulty of a reflection on essence, on origin, on that whereby a thing begins to be. The stakes are incredibly high. "Aporia" means that if truth is truly something that is achieved, and achieved in dialogue, one cannot learn; there is therefore nothing new; one cannot say what is. A discourse of truth, which would not be a simple collection of facts but would unite *de jure* these facts in an essential unity that would speak their origin, such a discourse is a deception. Meno's aporia, left unanswered, is the thoroughgoing victory of skepticism.

The attempt at a response to this aporia will be, in the history of philosophy, the very spring of all thought, and notably of modern thought, be it that of Descartes, Kant, Hegel, Husserl, Nietzsche, or Heidegger; there is never any other question at stake. It is with modern philosophy, with Kant, that the question will take on the name "transcendental."

Such a question, ripostes Socrates, since it is absolute, since it precedes *de jure* all questions, since it determines the very possibility of questioning, is a limit question—originary—which can only be endured through a "passage to the limit." This passage is effected by Socrates in a special discourse, the story of the myth of Persephone, taken from the priests and poets

> who say that the soul of man is immortal. At one time it comes to an end—that which is called death—and at another is born again, but is never finally exterminated. On these grounds a man must live all his days as righteously as possible. . . .
>
> Thus the soul, since it is immortal and has been born many times, and has seen all things both here and in the other world, has learned everything that is. So we need not be surprised if it can recall the knowledge of virtue or anything else which, as we see, it once possessed. All nature is akin, and the soul has learned everything, so that when a man has recalled a single piece of knowledge—learned it, in ordinary language—there is no reason why he should not find out all the rest, if he keeps a stout heart and does not grow weary of the search, for seeking and learning are in fact nothing but recollection.
>
> We ought not then to be led astray by the contentious argument you

> quoted. It would make us lazy, and is music in the ears of weaklings. The other doctrine produces energetic seekers after knowledge, and being convinced of its truth, I am ready, with your help, to inquire into the nature of virtue. (Plato 1961, *Meno*, 81b–e)

There is, then, an originary knowledge, without which no knowledge of any kind would be possible, as Kant would repeat 23 centuries later and differently. We next learn, in *Phaedrus*, that this knowledge is acquired by the soul before its fall: the soul, in falling into its body, which is also its grave (true life is elsewhere), forgets this knowledge in a single stroke. However, no knowledge is possible without this originary forgotten knowledge, without this originary exposure [*découvrement*] to that which is and which must be rediscovered. This is called *mathēsis* (the science of learning) by the Greeks and *mathematics* by Kant. Mathematics, synthetic a priori judgment, is the originary knowledge conditioning access to any kind of knowledge. True knowledge is, according to Plato, the recollection of this originary knowledge. With Kant, this becomes the question of transcendental knowledge that precedes and in this sense takes leave of experience, that is not founded in the empirical realm, since the transcendental is precisely the condition of possibility and hence the very foundation of all experience: facts are facts; they are, if not fabricated, at least constructed; they are only given across possibilities of interpretation that are not themselves of the order of facts. This knowledge, dating from before all experience, just as the immortality of the soul in Plato is knowledge before the fall, is a priori. It is with a mathematical example, coming from the knowledge of idealities recollected in the observation of stars, that Socrates will illustrate the truth of the myth.

Thus understood, *mathēsis* manifests the originary character as well as the originality of thought, and this is why thought must have the principle of its movement (*arkhē*) in itself: insofar as it is its own origin, as it has its *arkhē*, the most ancient, in itself, the thinking soul does not receive its forms of knowledge from outside but finds them again in itself. Hence, the thinking soul is self-movement, which a technical being could never be.

Does not Simondon say the same thing? Certainly not: if anticipation is indeed the necessary possibility of movement, it is not sufficient thereto: the reality of movement is organization. That means there is no self-movement, only hetero-movement.

But here, this recollection—still aporetico-mythical in Meno, dogmatic after *Phaedrus*—can have as its sole "explanation" the immortality of the soul. "Immortal" means that which belongs to the world of being *qua* being, to the intelligible world, that of the stars, which is not a world of becoming. Mortality is nothing but the domain of the contingent, of forgetfulness, of becoming: passion, suffering [*pâtir*], that which is not a principle unto itself. There can be no other access to being than as an access to what, belonging to the sphere of the fixed stars or that of divine beings, is not swept away in becoming, does not fall into the sublunary world of the artifice, of facticity (*mimēsis*), that is, into error and ultimately corruption, denaturalization, nonbeing.

From *Meno* to *Phaedrus* to Rousseau: "Metaphysics"

All narratives of the origin take on a mythical turn, in that they speak what is: to speak what is *qua* what absolutely is, is always to endure Meno's aporia, to which a positive answer cannot be given. For there to be, in becoming (there can be an origin only when becoming is; the question of origin could never arise in a world of being), something after all, for being to be itself always the same, for it to have an identity in essence, a threshold should not be crossed but experienced. This is the difficulty Rousseau will encounter in thinking originary man[7] as what he is in his nature, before any determination by his becoming. This will also be the very difficulty of our question: the human / the technical. When do(es) the human / the technical begin and end?

Later, in Plato, the aporetic myth of recollection, which remains essentially a mystery and an image in *Meno*—the image of a mystery to be endured as a mystery and within which a *distinction* must be obtained—will become a dogma, no longer the experience of a limit to be endured but the schema of an explanation of the origin that will be opposed to the fall. This dogma is, in *Phaedrus*, the myth of the winged soul, which is then transformed into a "metaphysics" whereby the opposition between the intelligible and the sensible becomes real; being is in reality opposed to becoming, the opposition of the soul and the body becomes the law of all philosophical discourse—and with it, the opposition between what will later be nature and culture, the human and the technical, as well as the question of technics *qua* writing. "Metaphysics" means retreat before the limit, negation of the aporia, a facility that philosophical thought accords itself, in the form of a dogma, in the face of the infinite number of questions opened up by it. Rousseau's *Discourse on the Origin of Inequality* belongs to this tradition, in which there is never anything, at the origin, but the fall outside it. This aporetic moment is one in which the aporia always ends up hardening into a mythology opposing two moments: those of purity and corruption, of before and after—the point separating them always already diluted. This is an excellent archetype of the discourse of philosophy on technics, relating through a fiction, if not by a myth, how the man of pure nature is replaced by the man of the fall, of technics and of society. This myth is the foundation, according to Claude Levi-Strauss, of modern scientific anthropology. It is the conjunction of two *ēpistēmē*, two structures of knowledge in which anthropology plays a discriminating role.

There is the origin, then the fall, forgetting, and loss. But it is quite difficult to distinguish the origin from the fall—which is to say also difficult to distinguish what is at the origin of the fall—this is particularly true in Rousseau. At any rate, the distinction must be made; it is the price to be paid for overcoming skepticism. The distinction assures all the others. The point is nevertheless that of knowing if it must be made in the mode of simple distinction, or in that of opposition, and if it is possible to distinguish without opposing. Can a difference be thought that would not be an opposition? We shall see how the thinking of différance[8] attempts to avoid opposing differences by thinking itself *qua* the unity of their movement, by installing itself at the heart of becoming: becoming other.

We have posed the question of the nature of the human. This is also the question of the nature of its origin. This is Rousseau's question. But the question of nature, evidently preliminary, which in Plato is meshed with that of being, is not at all the question of the nature of the human. This question does not interest Plato: as long as one has not asked what being (becoming) means, asking what the human is leads to a dead end. This is why the anthropocentrism of Protagoras should be condemned. Hence, anthropology is not Greek. Nor, is it, at the origin, philosophical. Greek thought is logical (dialectical), that is, ontological (the dialogue that speaks the true speaks what is). "Philosophical" means (by enduring the question) transcendental (even empiricism, when it is philosophical as in Hume, endures the transcendental question).[9] Now anthropology is not transcendental. The anthropological (sophistic) question, and behind it anthropology *qua* science, dismiss the very question of the transcendental. This does not mean that they can eliminate it.

Hume, Rousseau, Kant: there is undoubtedly a philosophical anthropology, but it is not a question of an anthropological science, of a "human science," for such a science proceeds from metaphysics; it receives its movement from metaphysics, and this is the development of the question of a priori (of the transcendental), or, to remain in line with the formulations of a philosophical empiricism, of the reflexive. Recent anthropology *qua* human science on the contrary suspends the question of the a priori. It is first of all a descriptive science, from which there can be an "explanatory," empirico-deductive approach to the nature of the human. This is the explanation of what the human is, of what is invariant between all sorts of humans.

The heuristic anthropocentrism constitutive of the so-called "human" sciences will not be long, however, in meeting its other, in finding itself decentered:

> From the moment when man first constituted himself as a positive figure in the field of knowledge, the old privilege of reflexive knowledge, of thought making itself, could not but disappear; but that it became possible, by this very fact, for an objective form of thought to investigate man in his entirety—at the risk of discovering what could never be reached by his reflection or even by his consciousness: dim mechanisms, faceless determinations, a whole landscape of shadow that has been termed, directly or indirectly, the unconscious. (Foucault 1973, 326)

There is an invention of man by modern thought, which lulls that thought into an "anthropological slumber" that a new criticism would interrupt:

> Anthropology constitutes perhaps the fundamental arrangement that has governed and controlled the path of philosophical thought from Kant to our own day. This arrangement is essential, since it forms part of our history; but it is disintegrating before our eyes, since we are beginning to recognize and denounce in it, in a critical mode, both a forgetfulness of the opening that made it possible {critical philosophy and the discovery of finitude} and a stubborn obstacle standing obstinately in the way of an imminent new form of thought. To all those who still wish to talk about man, about his reign or his liberation, to all those who still ask themselves questions about what man is in his essence, to all those who wish to take him as their starting point in

> their attempts to reach the truth, to all those who, on the other hand, refer all knowledge back to the truths of man himself, to all those who refuse to formalize without anthropologizing, who refuse to mythologize without demystifying, who refuse to think without immediately thinking that it is man who is thinking, to all these warped and twisted forms of reflection we can answer only with a philosophical laugh—which means, to a certain extent, a silent one. (Foucault 1973, 342–43)

This Nietzschean tone denounces the reactivity of anthropologism against becoming. If apriorism is a discourse of being against sophistic skepticism which is deployed in the name of an omnipotence of becoming (for such are in fact the stakes of sophistry: negating the discourse on being by negating being itself in the name of becoming, negating in the same stroke the theoretical, the difference between *de facto* and *de jure*, truth and opinion, and so on), if here one sees Foucault, in a gesture for becoming, appeal again to the transcendental, this is because it is less a question of opposing critical philosophy as one of opposing the transcendental thought as an opposition of being and becoming, an opposition resting fundamentally on an anthropocentrism common to metaphysics and to sophistry—and engendering the bland positivism of the human sciences. For Nietzsche, one must ask not only, who is man?, but *who overcomes man*? "The most cautious peoples ask today: 'How may man still be preserved?' Zarathoustra asks: . . . 'How shall man be overcome?' Man is something that must be overcome" (1961, 279).

> We should not think of Nietzsche's overman . . . as simply a raising of the stakes . . . the overman is defined by a new way of feeling: he is a different subject from man, something other than the human type. *A new way of thinking.* (Deleuze 1983, 163)

Human, All Too Human, in the same vein, takes direct aim at Rousseau's philosophy:

> All philosophers have the common failing of starting out from man as he is now and thinking they can reach their goal through an analysis of him. They involuntarily think of "man" as an *aeterna veritas*, as something that remains constant in the midst of all flux, as a sure measure of things. Everything the philosopher has declared about man is, however, at bottom no more than a testimony as to the man of a *very limited* period of time. Lack of historical sense is the family failing of all philosophers; many, without being aware of it,

even take the most recent manifestation of man, such as has arisen under the impress of certain religions, even certain political events, as the fixed form from which one has to start out. They will not learn that man has become, that the faculty of cognition has become; while some of them would have it that the whole world is spun out of this faculty of cognition. Now, everything *essential* in the development of mankind took place in primeval times, long before the four thousand years we more or less know about; during these years mankind may well not have altered very much. But the philosopher here sees "instincts" in man as he now is and assumes that these belong to the unalterable facts of mankind and to that extent could provide a key to the understanding of the world in general {Rousseau}: the whole of teleology is constructed by speaking of the man of the last four millennia as of an *eternal* man toward whom all things in the world have had a natural relationship from the time he began. But everything has become: there are no *eternal facts*, just as there are no absolute truths. Consequently what is needed from now on is *historical philosophizing*, and with it the virtue of modesty. (Nietzsche 1986, 215–16)

Rousseau and Anthropology

Rousseau is Nietzsche's target as the father of anthropology, and above all the father of the question, what is man?, promoted to the rank of a philosophical, that is, transcendental question. But Rousseau is also, according to Lévi-Strauss, the father of anthropological science. Rousseau is the pivot between the anthropological question promoted to philosophical rank and the beginning of scientific anthropological theory:

> Rousseau was not only the penetrating observer of rural life, a keen reader of travel journals, a knowledgeable analyst of exotic customs and beliefs; without the slightest fear of being proven wrong, it can be said that this ethnology that did not yet exist was, a full century before its appearance, conceived, intended, and announced by Rousseau, giving him straightaway his rank among the already constituted natural and human sciences. (Lévi-Strauss 1978, 44)

Lévi-Strauss next quotes note 10 of the *Discourse*, in which Rousseau praises travelers who, after having traversed the diversity of ethnic groups that Enlightenment Europe had been discovering in the reports of navigators, and, especially, having come to know the most savage ethnic groups, would then construct

> the natural, moral, and political history of what they had seen, {and thereby} we would ourselves see a new world emerge from their pens, and thus would learn to know our own. (quoted ibid.)

The principle of ethnology is set down here by Rousseau as the search for the human invariant, through the diversity of men, through the cultural variations of human nature. This is indeed an admirable principle: to know oneself in the other, by the knowledge of the other; to respond to the "know thyself" quoted at the beginning of the *Discourse* with the movement toward the other. Lévi-Strauss continues:

> Rousseau did not limit himself to predicting ethnology: he founded it. First in a practical manner, by writing this *Discourse on the Origin and the Foundations of Inequality Among Men*, which poses the problem of the relations between nature and culture, and it can be considered the first treatise of general ethnology; then, by distinguishing, with admirable clarity and concision, the object proper to the ethnologist and that of the moralist and historian: "When one wants to study men, one must consider those around one. But to study man, one must extend the range of one's vision. One must first observe the differences in order to discover the properties." (*Essay on the Origin of Language*, chap. 8) (Lévi-Strauss 1978, 47)

If it is true that Rousseau "founds the human sciences," his anthropology is nevertheless not in itself a science of man: it is a transcendental anthropology. Its question is apparently that of Lévi-Strauss and the anthropologists: what is man?, or, what is the nature of man? But for Rousseau, despite appearances, this is not a question that can be answered with facts, for to question facts, necessarily human facts, would be to question nature before culture-and-history in terms of culture, in terms of history. Therefore, here too an a priori approach is called for. Rousseau "suspends" (or attempts to do so) the historical thesis (an aborted attempt according to Nietzsche). Defining man in his nature starting not from facts but from a sort of transcendental "evidence" resulting from a "reduction"—whose remainder is not an "I think," but a feeling, an "I feel," a suffering—such is Rousseau's undertaking.

Equality, Force, Difference

"Of all human sciences the most useful and most imperfect appears to me to be that of mankind" (Rousseau 1973, 43). This is the first sentence of the *Discourse.* "For how shall we know the source of inequality between men," what makes them differ, makes them vary, and become, "if we do not begin by knowing mankind," by knowing what men have in common? Already being and the origin are on one side, time and the fall outside the origin on another: "And how shall man hope to see himself as nature made him, across all the changes which the succession of place and time must have produced"—accidentally—"in his original constitution," his essential constitution, "and distinguish what is fundamental in his nature from the changes and additions which his circumstances and the advances he has made have introduced to modify his primitive condition" as culture, facticity, technicity (43)? "The human soul . . . has changed in appearance so as to be hardly recognizable" (43). This is what must be affirmed in the first place: that there is a full, pure origin, followed then by alteration, corruption, impurity, the fall. The nature of man is not in the way he changes. There is, there has to be, a nature of man before change. The human soul "has changed in appearance so as to be hardly recognizable," and what provokes this change, under the names of society and culture, is technics: progress operates an incessant distancing from the origin ("every advance made by the human species removes it still further from its primitive state," 43). This creates a problem of validation of our knowledge concerning man, a problem of an a priori knowledge:

> The more discoveries we make, the more we deprive ourselves of the means of making the most important of all; . . . thus it is, in one sense, by our very study of man, that the knowledge of him is put out of our power. (43)

This is much more a critique of reason than a critique of progress.

It is in time, in becoming, "in these successive changes in the constitution of man that we must look for the origin of those differences which now distinguish men" (Rousseau 1973, 44). If progress is profoundly a regression, it is because difference means not force (virtue, *virtus*), the marvelous and generous power of diversity, but inequality in the law of the strongest (or least strong). The law of the strongest is not originary, nor is the difference in which it necessarily consists. Nature is equality: the originary indifferentiation that is the universal. What is at stake in the *Discourse* is that nature not be the law of the strongest. Let us not forget the following: what is at stake—and this stake is above all philosophical—is a denial of an originary difference that allows one to affirm that, after the fall, there is a difference between principle and fact, here rebaptized as nature and culture. This discourse against difference passes therefore in turn through a differentiation; this is a discourse for difference as well. There is no difference at the origin, but originary equality: we must, but afterward, make an originary difference between what the origin is and what it no longer is, while recalling, reinvigorating, resurrecting in ourselves the origin *qua* indifferentiation: the problem will be to "distinguish properly [*démêler*] between what is original and what is artificial in the actual nature of man" (44) (and we will find the possibility of making this difference in the very voice of the undifferentiated origin—which can still speak to us).

This is by no means a "light undertaking." What does "distinguish properly" here mean? Is the original opposed to the artificial, or is it a matter of an a priori distinction rather than an opposition? The answer is complex, and the question full of knots. There must be in any case an original instance, and one must say what it is: the inhuman is there, everything is not permitted, history is interlaced with horrors that must be able to be denounced. But in this relation to the nonoriginary, does this "proper" strictly speaking derive from the originary? Should the original simply be opposed to the artificial? Or should one proceed as if that were the case?

The Improbability of the Origin, the Voice of Nature (What "to Distinguish Properly" Means) and the Anamnesis of the Carib

Rousseau gives a nuance to the foregoing remark, which leads us to think that it is a question both *of a distinction and of a distinction that can only be expressed as an opposition.* A distinction supposes terms that are different without being exclusive of each another, hence, an original state maintaining itself through its own transformations; an opposition is an exclusion of one term by the other: either the original state or the transformation in which this original state disappears. On this point, Rousseau is extremely prudent and cunning: the point is to distinguish properly, in the actual nature of man, the original from the artificial, and "to form a true idea of a state which no longer exists, *perhaps never did exist, and probably never will exist; and of which it is, nevertheless, necessary to have true ideas, in order to form a proper judgment of our present state*" (1973, 44, my emphasis). Even if the origin is improbable, even if what is proper to man is a fiction ("perhaps never did exist"), it is a necessary fiction. At its limit, speech calls for a "special" discourse: to distinguish, in man's nature, the original from the artificial, even if they have never been distinguished in fact, even if this state of distinction of the original and the artificial never was, never existed; a fiction will be related, a story told, if not a myth—we are not in Greece, but the approach of the *Discourse* is comparable to that of Socrates to Meno. A distinction will be related to save the principle from the fact—from the fact of force and from the force of fact. But what is a fiction, if not an artifice? An artifice will be needed to distinguish the artificial from the natural. Does this artifice not risk in turn creating confusions, concealing other things? And to do wrong in turn to law, to truth, and so on? The fiction is necessary because "it is by our very study of man, that the knowledge of him is put out of our power" and something is irremediably lost: the fall is here again a forgetting of the origin. The essence (the origin), impossible to find in the facts (the fall), calls for, through listening to the voice of pure nature, a transcendental recollection. To distinguish properly is to recall through listening.

Stressing again the difficulty of the distinction, Rousseau pleads for an experimental practice of the distinction: "What experiments would have to be made, to discover the natural man? And how are those experiments to be made in a state of society?" But experimentation would only refine a posteriori and mediately an answer received through another, a priori channel, from the instance of original im-mediacy: original equality is natural right; now, natural law, to be natural, must speak "directly from the voice of nature" (Rousseau 1973, 40). The natural is immediately there in an original evidence. The question is the origin, the principle, the most ancient, "the appallingly ancient," Blanchot would say today. The guide, the light for having access to this original immediacy, the exclusive possibility of returning to the source through a questioning back, is *evidence* as such, *self-presence*, that which remains inside, does not pass through the outside, through the artifice of cultural, worldly prejudgments, to be found in the very forms of judgment. The absence of such light would be a catastrophe. Paradoxically, one does not spontaneously remember the voice of the origin's principle, "the voice of nature," which, notwithstanding, speaks to us immediately; the immediate is not there immediately, at hand; access to it is *après coup*.

If it is indeed necessary that this law be heard immediately in order to be natural, and that it be founded in something else than these artificial reasonings and quibbles on which philosophy generally establishes law, through its sophisticated if not sophistic "metaphysics," it is no less the case that the possibility of hearing it is every bit as immediate: we are in the fall, in forgetfulness, we must remember. Hearing becomes a question, but for natural law to be natural, it is indeed necessary that everyone hear and understand it immediately, originarily, without having to use strange and studious reasonings. Natural law must be before reason itself, indeed before reasonings (those of philosophers and metaphysicians as well as those of everyman). It is reasonable to think that everyman, learned or not, can hear it. But the more learned he is, the more difficult it will be for him to hear, for his culture will obfuscate the naturalness of the law (reason, "by its successive developments," will suppress nature). He will then have to remember (putting aside "all those scientific books which teach us only to see men such as they have made themselves," Rousseau 1973, 46–47). The most originary is the most familiar, the closest, and therefore, the most removed, the most hidden. The usual structure: the simplest is the most imperceptible. Aristotle says as much of fish in his treatise *On the Soul* (423a): "animals that live in water would not notice that the things which touch one another in water have wet surfaces" (Aristotle 1984); everything that can be touched and everything that is, is for them wet. They see only what is wet, but that means that the wet is the only thing they do not see. Just as Plato says in *Timaeus*, if the world were made of gold, gold would be the only thing that we could not know, since there would be nothing for us to oppose it to; nothing to which to compare it, no notion of it, and yet gold would be the only thing that we would truly know, for only gold would be in truth, the truth of all beings, being itself.

The immediate—the incomparable, and in this sense the improbable, for one can pose and identify only by differentiation and comparison—is what is most difficult to hear, perhaps in all rigor inaudible, being immediately covered over by the mediate—the comparable, the probable. But nevertheless everyone must hear it, just as all fish must live in water; this is why only fish do not know what water is, not even that there is such a thing, although they are the only beings who know how to live in water.

The more natural it is, the deeper it is hidden in the "appallingly ancient": in order to remember, to recover the evidence prior to the fall, reason must be forgotten. Earlier than I think, I am because I feel, I suffer.

These are principles prior to reason—self-preservation and pity—"*without which it is necessary to introduce that of sociability,*" which communicate and combine with each another in the immediateness of the voice of nature, and from which derive "all the rules of natural right, . . . rules which our reason is *afterwards obliged to establish on other foundations,* when by its successive developments it has been led to suppress nature itself," to forget, to put at a distance, to mediate nature (Rousseau 1973, 47). The nature of man is neither reason nor sociability. Originary man is neither a reasonable or speaking animal, nor a political or social one. Even if this originary man is in one way fictive, even if he must be read as a mystery and an image forever lost and forgotten, which can only be depicted, but without description, this fictive figure, the closest to us in being what is most proper, essential, and true, is a figure of what *obliges* us. The originary purity of this essence, impossible to express otherwise than through fiction, absolutely contradicts tradition—yet another reason for denouncing the mediations of philosophy and its "studious detours" for understanding what natural law is: this philosophical tradition of "political and rational," "sociable and speaking" man is that of false evidence: the savages discovered by the age of Enlightenment are neither rational nor sociable. The Caribs of Venezuela are this mythico-real figure—an obviously problematic reference since Rousseau does not intend to found his discourse on factual reality. But the Carib is not a simple fact, and Rousseau does not appeal to him as proof: he finds in him a source of inspiration, with his anamnestic and maieutic virtue; an already corrupted figure of the origin, he suggests the origin nevertheless, without ever revealing it. One understands the fascination of this type of approach for Lévi-Strauss: for the first time from within the Western world, its "ethnocentrism" is stated and denounced.

Thinking Before Creation

The narrative of the origin is placed in the first section of Rousseau's *Discourse,* and is preceded by a general introduction whose second part explicates the necessity of this fiction.

The introduction first criticizes the importation, in the description of the state of nature by philosophers, of "ideas taken from society"—an argument that Nietzsche will turn against Rousseau, claiming that he did nothing else himself, believing he was doing exactly the opposite, blind as he was to the direction and meaning of time, history, and becoming. This same Rousseau, however, on the other hand, questions once again, and in a move whose radicalism is "hardly ordinary," the very idea of a state of nature:

> It has not even entered into the heads of most of our writers to doubt whether the state of nature ever existed; but it is clear from the Holy Scriptures that the first man, having received his understanding and commandments immediately from God, was not himself in such a state, and that, if we give such credit to the writings of Moses as every Christian philosopher ought to give, we must deny that, even before the deluge, men were ever in the pure state of nature; unless, indeed, they fell back into it from some very extraordinary circumstance; a paradox which it would be very embarrassing to defend, and quite impossible to prove. (Rousseau 1973, 50)

Hence the pure nature of man is paradoxical and improbable, doomed to fiction and to artifice. Rousseau's aim, the absolutely equal origin of man, is prior to the first real man. "Let us begin then by laying all facts aside, as they do not affect the question" and could never teach us anything (Rousseau 1973, 50). We are not in the historical. But we are not for all that in simple fiction either, for there is evidence dictating the account of such a fiction. Evidence dating from before all facts—transcendental evidence. Evidence beyond even that which "religion commands us to believe," and which is called up by this order itself: original sin says that there is something prior to the fall, which, however, is original, since one is *in* creation;[10] God is its organizer, with this enigma that has one speaking at once of an "immediately" and of an "after" ("God Himself having taken men out of a state of nature immediately after the creation")—but religion does not forbid us for all that from imagining what might have and even should have been a state of pure nature if God had not put an end to it "immediately after the creation." We were admiring the extreme prudence of Rousseau: now must we admire his extreme audacity. Pure nature, man in his essence come before creation. The fall outside of pure nature is creation. This is certainly an audacity that remains faithful to the spirit of religion, of original sin and of babelization: it is through an accident provoked by divine will, by Providence, that the process of the fall and the precipitation into disastrous inequality can be explained in detail, as, in the *Essay on the Origin of Language*, God's finger, tipping the axis of the planet, introduces seasonal variations and along with them idiomatic differences. But there remains the task of thinking what *precedes* creation.

Feet and Hands

The nature of man is a point through which nature will have had to go but at which it will never have stopped, being already the fall; and God, who wanted inequality among men, did not abandon the human species to itself. This is a positively unthinkable limit. And it is the reason why Rousseau can give short shrift to the comparative anatomy of his age, as we are thus forewarned at the beginning of the story:

> Comparative anatomy has as yet made too little progress . . . to afford an adequate basis for any solid reasoning. . . . I shall suppose his conformation to have been at all times what it appears to us at this day; that he always walked on two legs, made use of his hands as we do. (Rousseau 1973, 52)

Nietzsche wrote, "the whole of teleology is constructed by speaking of the man of the last four millennia as of an eternal man toward whom all things in the world have had a natural relationship from the time he began" (1986, 216). But Rousseau explicitly assumes this attitude, as though in anticipation of this critique. The whole argument postulates mankind's durability (the voice of nature), in which being is not becoming. This is what Nietzsche contests. This is the question that will have to be posed when we take up the analysis of the paleontological discourse that speaks of the human as it was four million years ago.[11] Rousseau will then presuppose a (fictive) originary man, who has "always walked on two legs, made use of his hands as we do," but will he honor his promise—or more exactly, is he aware of all the consequences? We shall soon see that walking on two feet brings along a series of transformations from which technics is not absent. Rousseau may well decide to ignore the facts; he may not, however, totally contradict them. To posit that man walks on two feet is also to posit everything implied by feet. That is where man begins: with his feet, and not with his brain, as Leroi-Gourhan will say; but also, the upright position has a meaning and consequences that are precisely incompatible with Rousseau's account of the origin of man, who already, immemorially, from the origin, "walks on two feet" and "makes use of his hands." For to make use of his hands, no longer to have paws, is to manipulate—and what hands manipulate are tools and instruments. The hand is the hand only insofar as it allows access to art, to artifice, and to *tekhnē*. The foot is these two feet of the human, this walking and this approach only insofar as, carrying the body's weight, it frees the hand for its destiny as hand, for the manipulative possibility, as well as for a new relation between hand and face, a relation which will be that of speech and gesture in what Leroi-Gourhan names the anterior field. Considering originary man as walking on two feet and making use of his hands therefore contradicts what follows in the text: Rousseau, at last beginning the account of the fiction, would rid this being of "all the artificial faculties he can have acquired only by a long process"; originary man is originary only because he is not contaminated by the artificial, the mediate, the technical and the prosthetic:

> If we strip this being, thus constituted, of all the supernatural gifts he may have received, and all the artificial faculties he can have acquired only by a long process; if we consider him, in a word, just as he must have come from the hands of nature {nature, as productive, has hands!}, we behold in him an animal weaker than some, and less agile than others; but, taking him all around, the most advantageously organized of any. I see him satisfying his hunger at the first oak, and slaking his thirst at the first brook: finding his bed at the foot of the tree which afforded him a repast; and, with that, all his wants supplied. (Rousseau 1973, 52)

Having Everything Close at Hand

Originary man is practically immobile: finding nourishment under an oak and "finding his bed at the foot of the tree which afforded him a repast," he does not change places, nor move across space, let alone desire to possess the whole of it or even a constantly greater part of it. He is not moved *excessively* because he is not truly moved, he has no passions: he has natural, vital needs, which he can satisfy in reaping the fruits of nature close at (his) hand—this hand that only grasps without manipulating anything, an organ of grasping rather than of fabrication.

> While the earth was left to its natural fertility and covered with immense forests, whose trees *were never mutilated by the ax*, it would present on every side both sustenance and shelter for every species of animal. Men, dispersed

> up and down among the rest, would observe and imitate their industry, and thus attain even to the instinct of the beasts, with the advantage that, whereas every species of brutes was confined to one particular instinct, man, who perhaps has not any one peculiar to himself, would appropriate them all. (Rousseau 1973, 53)

For this man with everything close at hand, the original fruits are just as originally there as the voice of nature, the instinct of self-conservation, and the compassion that he hears, to the exclusion of everything else. Denaturalization will be self-exteriorization, the becoming self-dependent, self-alienation, the alienation of the originary, the authentic, in the factical, the technical, the artificial death constitutive of the mediacy of a social and differentiated world of objects, and hence of subjects, for, from this point on, it is only through its objects (the objects it has) that the self can define itself and thus is no longer itself. We shall have an opportunity to speak again of this alienation of authenticity in facticity and the range of the hand, a hand having become that of Dasein. Originary man with everything immediately at hand has nothing: he is everything, he is himself in totality, he is his own fullness, and by that very fact, this hand with "everything close at hand" is no longer a hand, it no longer either manipulates or works. It has no desire; it does not have to submit its desire for pleasure to the detour and the mediacy of the principle of reality that Rousseau knew about.[12] The man of pure nature has no passions; he is not altered by the hubris always present in dependency, by the split and by differentiation. Unaltered, he *adds nothing* to nature: he only *imitates* animals. He is isolated under that tree sheltering him: the human species of pure nature is dispersed; the *grouping* is not originary.

Being Altogether at One's Disposal

The "imitation of animals" is an "advantage" man has over them; he appropriates all their instincts, without having "any one peculiar to himself." In the myth of Prometheus in Plato's *Protagoras,* man arrives because of something forgotten by Epimetheus, who had distributed "all the qualities," leaving man naked, in a default of being, having yet to begin being: his condition will be to supplement this default of origin by procuring for himself prostheses, instruments. Rousseau, precisely, wants to show that there is no originary default, no prostheses, that the claws missing in man are not stones, or, should they be stones, they are precisely not cut or fabricated, being immediately at hand and not inscribed in any process of mediation. The man of nature, without prostheses, is robust, as robust as man can be—and it is civilization that will weaken him:

> Accustomed from their infancy to the inclemencies of the weather and the rigor of the seasons, inured to fatigue, and forced, naked and unarmed, to defend themselves and their prey from other ferocious animals, or to escape them by flight, men would acquire a robust and almost unalterable constitution. The children, bringing with them into the world the excellent constitution of their parents, and fortifying it by the very exercises which first produced it, would thus acquire all the vigor of which the human frame is capable. (Rousseau 1973, 53)

There is no change in education, there is above all no education, and there is no need of it: everything repeats itself identically, and this identity guarantees the reinforcement of the same, that is, of the maximum of which humanity is capable. The maximum is at the origin, and the fall will be its *ptōsis*, its decomposition by decay, by consumption. "Nature in this case treats them exactly as Sparta treated the children of her citizens: those who come well formed into the world she renders strong and robust, and all the rest she destroys," and this is not the law of the strongest. Nature thereby guarantees, not a differentiation, but the equality of all; man is not yet in society, and it is only in society that this will become the perverse law of the strongest, a social, unnatural law "in which the State, by making children a burden to their parents, kills them indiscriminately before they are born" (Rousseau 1973, 53). The man of the original maximum thus has no need of prostheses. His body "being the only instrument he understands, he uses it for various purposes, of which ours, for want of practice, are incapable: *for our industry deprives us of that force and agility which necessity obliges him to acquire*" (my emphasis). In other words, technics is what leads us down the road to decay in depriving us of our originary power. Here, power owes nothing to technics, nor to either ingenuity or reason, and reason is technics itself, or rather, technics is reason itself, a "technoscience" already—in 1754—dooming humanity to powerlessness. If man at the origin "had had an ax, would he have been able with his naked arm to break so large a branch from a tree?" (53). Ax, slingshot, ladder, horse, these procedures and artifices are machines, already automates: they already carry the fate of all technics, which is to be substituted for the natural, originary force of the solitary man. They constitute an illusory power, always beyond the reach of the hand, unavailable and mediate, which must be prepared, transported, arranged, and in which one must enclose oneself. Whereas civilized man depends on machines that can always be lacking, the savage state has "the advantage of having all our forces constantly at our disposal, of being always prepared for every event, and of carrying one's self, as it were, perpetually whole and entire about one" (54).

The prosthesis is the origin of inequality. The man of pure nature has everything about himself, carries himself whole and entire about himself; his body is "the only instrument he understands"; he is never in himself in default; no fissure is at work in him that would be provoked by a process of differentiation on the outside of himself, nor a differentiation of an "outside" that would be essential (interiorized) to him: he depends on no outside. This must be demonstrated, for Rousseau well knows that from the moment he no longer has everything within him, whatever he has (however little), not being a part of his being, becomes differentiated, diverges, disrupts, belongs already to the fall. Everything is inside: the origin is the inside. The fall is exteriorization. This thematic of exteriorization is central to Leroi-Gourhan's definition of the process of humanization. We will see the paradox this definition struggles with as long as its own consequence is not drawn: the human is the technical, that is, time.

The man that "carries himself, as it were, perpetually whole and entire about him" does not exteriorize himself, does not ex-press himself, does not speak: speech is already a prosthesis. Any exit outside of oneself is a denaturalization; to the extent that our ills place us outside of ourselves, they "are of our own making . . . and we might have avoided them nearly all by adhering to that simple, uniform and solitary manner of life which nature prescribed" (Rousseau 1973, 56).

The Second Origin

Why was what nature prescribed no longer heeded? Nature is equilibrium, and original man finds himself in harmony with nature and with animals. It is on account of their natural confidence in this equilibrium that "Negroes and savages are so little afraid of the wild beasts they may meet in the woods . . . armed only with bows and arrows; but *no one has ever heard of one of them being devoured by wild beasts*" (Rousseau 1973, 55). Here we have the maieutic Carib. He is *almost* naked. Armed *only* with a bow and arrow. The whole problem obviously being these two adverbs: what supplement, what separation do they indicate? "Almost," "only," but enough for there to be already a question of a "creature," however close it may be to the origin. In what distancing was this proximity that is also a distance, this separation of two adverbs, able to consist? And how did this *Ent-fernung* manage to operate?

In the original equilibrium to which the Carib is still quite close, the weaknesses of man, which are not due to civilization and to technics, are sheer balance and naturalness, they do not threaten man in his nature, they are natural infirmities: infancy, old age, and death. They are *almost nothing* since they do not trouble the general equilibrium. And *death itself*, an essential moment of the fiction, plays practically no role therein; the elderly of the origin pass away (rather than die) "without others perceiving that they are no more, and almost without perceiving it themselves" (Rousseau 1973, 56). Still the adverb "almost" seems this time to affect the origin itself. There follows a long and classic demonstration concerning medicine, as always the paradigm of human artifice. As with writing in Plato—that it must supplement faulty memory only helps to weaken it even more—medicine really only results in the secondary, uncontrolled, and disastrous effects of its medications. The history of civilizations thus becomes that of illnesses, a nemesis which is that of reason in history, and "I venture to say that a state of reflection is one contrary to nature and that the man who meditates is a depraved animal" (56). And since one knows that savages "are troubled with hardly any disorders, save wounds and old age, we are tempted to believe that, in following the history of civil society, we shall be telling also that of human sickness" (56). Almost.

As for the Carib, he has no need of these remedies, which are ills worse than those they are supposed to cure, and, sick or wounded, the men in the state of nature have no other "surgical assistance than that of time" (Rousseau 1973, 57). It is the integrity of original force that is here contaminated, amputated, poisoned, exhausted by "remedies."[13]

This is an accident, taking place after nature, after the origin, as a second origin, drawing man away from what the origin originally prescribed. This accident is the origin of remedies, prostheses, drugs—the origin of this fall and second origin. It is an exterior accident, which does not come from the nature of man: it happens to him and denaturalizes him. We should not believe, as our ethnocentrism will incline us to, that it is

> so great a misfortune to these primitive men, nor so great an obstacle to their preservation, that they go naked, have no dwellings, and lack all the superfluities which we think are necessary. . . . The man who first made himself clothes or a dwelling was furnishing himself with things *hardly necessary*; for he had until then done without them, and there is no reason why he should not have been able to put up in manhood with the same kind of life as had been his in infancy. (Rousseau 1973, 58)

These artifices and prostheses are, if not unnecessary, *hardly so. Almost* accidental and inessential, if not completely useless. Adverbs of this sort can never be totally eliminated, not even in fiction, which suggests that the fall might very well have always already begun. The fall is when one can no longer be satisfied with what one is in one's original nakedness, which, far from being a weakness, is the sign of force itself. The first man to have indulged in the apparent power of prostheses, obliged to do so by an accident in nature, took the road down to his fall, and led his descendants down the same. This is what must be repaired; this is the illness, carried by remedies, that must be repaired. "Obliged by an accident," this first man did not strictly speaking commit a fault: that would be contradictory to the thesis of original man "whole and entire about one." Since he needs nothing but what is strictly necessary, the evil cannot originate in himself. This said, Rousseau then begins a new moment of the analysis and opens another episode of his narrative.

The Interior of the Deviation: Possibility

"Hitherto I have considered merely the physical man; let us now take a view of him on his metaphysical and moral side" (Rousseau 1973, 59). This will require a differentiation between humanity and animality—difficult to recognize, even though it would seem at first sight obvious and perfectly classic: "I see nothing in any animal but an ingenious machine, to which nature hath given senses to wind itself up, and to guard itself, to a certain degree, against anything that might tend to disorder or destroy it" (59). This is a self-regulating machine whose activity, completely given up to protection against destruction, is guided by an instinct of conservation that is but the will of nature itself, in contradistinction to man, who is a free agent: "I see exactly the same things in the human machine," namely the five senses serving the instinct of conservation, "with this difference, that in the operations of the brute, nature is the sole agent, whereas man has some share in his own operations, in his character as a free agent" (59). The animal machine "chooses by instinct" and the human machine by "an act of the will: hence the brute cannot deviate from the rule prescribed to it, even when it would be advantageous for it to do so; and, on the contrary, man frequently deviates from such rules to his own prejudice" (59). The possibility of such a deviation is thus inscribed on the inside of the origin itself. The man of pure nature had no reason to deviate from the origin. But he nevertheless had the possibility: if this had not been the case, the providential accident would have had no effect on him. If the deviation *qua* exteriorization is to take place, there must be an interior before the deviation, which must also be the possibility of a deviation from the interior, the possibility of an afterward in the before, a between-the-two.

The advantage of freedom—(the possibility) of a deviation with respect to an instinct but not yet a deviation with respect to the instinct of conservation, a deviation within the instinct of conservation—is expressed negatively on the subject of animality: it might be advantageous for the brute to deviate from the rule, but it cannot do so. "Thus a pigeon would be starved to death by the sight of a dish of the choicest meats, and a cat on a heap of fruit or grain; though it is certain that either might find nourishment in the foods which it thus rejects with disdain, did it think of trying them" (Rousseau 1973, 59). Here then is the weakness of the brute with respect to man; just as he was able to adapt himself to all situations by imitating animals and by taking on their instincts, so too does he nourish himself with everything that nature offers as edible. This is at least the discourse we would expect for the constitution of the antithesis. But Rousseau says something else again, stressing on the contrary the perversity for man of such a possibility of deviation, which often, most often, represents a prejudice: "Hence it is that dissolute men run into excesses which bring on fevers and death; because the mind depraves the senses, and the will continues to speak when nature is silent" (59). The presentation of human freedom is thus negative, for at issue here is man after the fall, not the man of pure nature. In this case, freedom would indeed have been an advantage: it would have allowed man to partake of fruit in the absence of meat, of meat where there was no fruit, of grain in the absence of both meat and fruit. For Rousseau, this is a positive possibility for as long as man's will remains within the limits of his proximity to himself, that is, within those of his immediate and real needs with regard to the necessities of his conservation. His will could not have remained for long within these limits owing to the deviation that occurred accidentally in nature. When man's natural possibility of deviation from nature deviates from what nature stipulates with respect to equilibrium, nature itself has then deviated. The possibility of deviation thus becomes a negative deviation. But the positive one does not itself have the possibility of deviating from itself.

When this possibility, retained, deferred, maintained in equilibrium at the origin as long as it remains contained in its essence, becomes actual, it is *spirit.* "Nature lays her commands on every animal, and the brute obeys her voice. Man receives the same impulsion, but at the same time knows himself at liberty to acquiesce or resist: and it is particularly in his consciousness of this liberty that the spirituality of his soul is displayed" (Rousseau 1973, 60). The *act* of this liberty, the *perfectibility,* as the specificity of man, immediately reverses itself into default, "the faculty which, by the help of circumstances, gradually develops all the rest of our faculties" (60).

Spirit, proper to man, his nature, his being, his origin, is nevertheless what will upset the state of pure nature—a concatenation that is perfectly homogenous with the "paradox of power [*puissance*]" examined in the third section of this chapter. Technics, as the power of man, is what destroys in its actualization that of which it is the power. But if this comparison is valid, this would mean that power, that is, technics, is in the origin, is the origin as the possibility of deviation *qua* the absence of origin. This reversal will obviously not have taken place of itself, but "by the help of circumstances" that are themselves the fall. The origin is the origin only insofar as it opposed the fall as a possibility by deferring it, whereas the fall is the realization of the origin, its becoming-real, its passage into actuality (the actualization of the power it is), being simultaneously, by the same token, its derealization, its disappearance or its oblivion—and a differentiation erasing original equality. This is presented as a fatality, that of circumstances that cannot be circumvented. Spirit, perfectibility, is less the possibility of raising oneself as that of falling, or that of rising only to fall from higher up—it is an illusion: the process that perfectibility is first of all a becoming-idiotic:

> Why is man alone liable to grow into an idiot? Is it not because he returns, in this, to his primitive state; and because, while the brute, which has acquired nothing and has therefore nothing to lose, still retains the force of instinct, man, who loses, by age or accident, all that his perfectibility had enabled him to gain, falls by this means lower than the brutes themselves? . . . It is this faculty, which, successively producing in different ages his discoveries and his errors, his vices and his virtues, makes him at length a tyrant both over himself and over nature. (Rousseau 1973, 60)

Perfectibility is this power whose actualization is negative. Perfectibility is already there, indubitably, with freedom. But it is only there virtually. Perfectibility is *tantamount* to an originary freedom inasmuch as the latter is virtual perfectibility, but *only* virtual. This freedom is *almost* perfectibility, but *only this almost.* It must in no case be conflated with *actual* perfectibility. The act of freedom is its loss. The origin is in-action. As long as perfectibility remains virtual, freedom remains originary and *man, a quasi-animal.* The only initial difference between man and animals is that man is inclined to mimic them all; he has no particular instinct, and by this very fact, he can, endowed with en enigmatic adroitness (Rousseau 1973, 54), appropriate every animal instinct. "Savage man, left by nature solely to the direction of instinct, or rather indemnified for *what he may lack* by faculties capable at first of supplying its place, and afterwards of raising him much above it, must accordingly *begin* with *purely* animal functions" (60, my emphasis). Only the animal is present at the origin of humanity. There is no difference between man (in his essence) and animal, no essential difference between man and animal, unless it be an inactual possibility. When there is a difference, man is no longer, and this is his denaturalization, that is, the naturalization of the animal. Man is his disappearance in the denaturalization of his essence. Appearing, he disappears: his essence defaults [*son essence se fait défaut*]. By accident. During the conquest of mobility. Man is this accident of automobility caused by a default of essence [*une panne d'essence*, a "lack of fuel," an "empty tank"].

Man will mimic the instincts of animals to supplement the instinct he lacks without, however, ever adding anything. This mimetic-animal *freedom* (freedom *qua* the latitude that the absence of instinct, *determined* and *proper* to man, is), which is a guarantee of equilibrium as long as it not become perfectibility, has nothing to do with the ingenuity of reason, although Rousseau does speak of adroitness, of the singular capacity of man, *qua* his *metis,* corresponding to a lack or default of originary essence and determination. How shall we interpret this lack or this originary default, this lack-of ... found before the fall, before the realization of the default that is the fall? How shall we interpret this lack and this default which are neither lack nor default, almost not a lack and almost not a default, since we are in the origin, in original equilibrium in which being does not default itself [*ne se fait pas défaut à lui-même*]? As after the fact [*après coup*].

Originary freedom is virtually what the fall is in actuality, and the passage from virtuality to actuality is that from freedom to reason. Freedom is the inscription in originary man of the possibility of the fall and of disequilibrium, and reason, the (de)realization of that possibility. "Seeing and feeling must be his first condition, which would be common to him and all other animals. To will, and not to will, to desire and to fear, must be the first, and *almost* the only operations of his soul, till new circumstances occasion new developments of his faculties" (Rousseau 1973, 61).

Difference Is Reason, Reason Is Death, Death Is Its Anticipation

As long as the savage is not in the disequilibrium of freedom, as long as his perfectibility remains virtual and does not perturb the originary play between nature and his own nature, as long as his virtuality does not become real, that is *technical, he does not have the feeling of death and does not anticipate*: he is not *in time*. After this actualization of perfectibility, he is in time, and he is not only *in*, he practically *is* time, *qua* outside. This time he then is, this outside is also his death, his own death or the death of what is proper to him, his falling off [*dépérissement*], his denaturalization. The passage into death constitutes reason and passion by originarily binding them (reason, against the philosophical tradition, is like passion: dependency and lack of autonomy): freedom becomes perfectibility when passion replaces need or when need transforms into passion, overwhelming itself, becoming unbalanced, which is only possible when reason extends our horizon beyond what is immediately there at hand and develops our capacities for anticipation, or rather, develops itself as a capacity of anticipation.

> Whatever moralists may hold, the human understanding is greatly indebted to the passions, which, it is universally allowed, are also much indebted to

> the understanding. It is by the activity of the passions that our reason is improved; for we desire knowledge only because we wish to enjoy; and it is impossible to conceive any reason why a person who has neither fears nor desires should give himself the trouble of reasoning. The passions, again, originate in our wants, and their progress depends on that of our knowledge; for we cannot desire or fear anything, except from the idea we have of it, or from the simple impulse of nature. Now savage man, being destitute of every species of enlightenment, can have no passions save those of the latter kind: his desires never go beyond his physical wants. The only goods he recognizes in the universe are food, a female, and sleep: the only evils he fears are pain and hunger. (Rousseau 1973, 61)

The passions are the principle of the negative dynamic in which the perfecting of reason consists, reason being knowledge in general *qua* alteration, knowledge of the other *qua* suffering from the other. But if the development of reason is in need of the passions, passions in turn suppose reason, *qua* the dynamic principle of the extension of wants, of disequilibrium and of distancing from self: a movement toward what is not immediately at hand.[14]

Because he does not have reason, the only things savage man fears and desires are impulses from nature, inscribed in its equilibrium, and they are never due to passion. Passion *qua* the extension beyond what is at hand is the development of reason *qua* anticipation of a possible that, by nature, is not immediately there, but that can be feared and desired as *capable of* taking place.[15] *This can only be, in the first instance, the development of a fear,* not only the fear of pain, but *a form of knowledge* that original man does not possess: a knowledge of death, the anxiety, melancholy, and misanthropy of the *atrabilious man.* If the original man shares with the animal the instinct of conservation—perhaps his sole instinct, combined with pity, that other original instinct—this instinct of conservation is above all not the feeling of mortality. The savage man does not fear death. If that were the case, he would not be "whole and entire about one," he would be irremediably split with himself, affected with an absence in himself, of a default of origin. Original man in equilibrium with nature does not fear death; he fears only pain.

To what extent can he nevertheless be at once free and subject to the instinct of conservation? Does freedom not imply a relation to the end that on the contrary would be the actual possibility of eluding the instinct of conservation? What would freedom be if it were not already defined, and not only almost, as the relation to death *qua* the possibility of disobedience to the instinct of conservation, to the will of nature? In the preference given to the endurance of death over the loss of freedom, there is anticipation; possibility is essentially an opening out onto the future, one that precisely must not affect Rousseau's concept of original humanity, for this would mean affection from without and by prostheses. The original man passes away "almost without perceiving it" himself.

"I say pain, and not death: for no animal can know what it is to die" (Rousseau 1973, 61). Original man is animal: he does not fear death, and the proof of this is that "no animal can know what it is to die." To this Rousseau adds, in order to confirm that this deviation—as regards virtual man empowered with the enigmatic freedom that deviates from no equilibrium, who is only slightly capable of assuming, receiving, and developing the consequences of a foreign disequilibrium—is not yet a deviation: "the knowledge of death and its terrors being one of the first acquisitions made by man in departing from an animal state." Original man has no relation to time, no imagination:

> But who does not see . . . that everything seems to remove from savage man both the temptation and the means of changing his condition? His imagination paints no pictures; his heart makes no demands on him. His few wants are so readily supplied, and he is so far from having the knowledge which is needful to make him want more, that he can have neither foresight nor curiosity. (Rousseau 1973, 62)

Everything is already identically the same for original and savage man, who has no idea of the other, of this Other that time immediately and essentially is. Savage man will never have had any future, and this is perhaps why Rousseau had to specify that "he perhaps never did exist," as "religion commands us to believe." If philosophy is this wonder in which being is considered in its being, the savage as such, who is never surprised over anything, since nothing ever happens, is thus not a philosopher and has no need of being one, nor of considering, in being, what is: nothing is happening, nothing is in becoming, and being is not concealed, forgotten; the fall has not yet taken place. Everything immediately is, without detours and therefore without the detour of philosophy. "His soul, which nothing disturbs, is wholly wrapped up in the feeling of its present existence, without any idea of the future, however near at hand" (Rousseau 1973, 62). An idea of the future near at hand would in fact immediately imply an idea of the most removed of futures: as soon as there is an idea of the future, it must be of the whole future and of the possibility, infinite in its essence, of leaving the now, and just as much of infinite freedom. "And his projects, as limited as his views, hardly extend to the close of day" (62). While he has "no idea of the future," he nevertheless has projects, a kind of idea of an immediate future, although this is impossible without the whole future coming along in its stead, the whole future or the future *qua* the whole and *qua* nothing, as this overcoming of the whole that the possible is, as this wholly-other that is the absence of the whole. The origin is decidedly nothing but the almost of the origin, but here the almost is untenable, as in Rousseau's example: "*Such, even at present*, is the extent of the native Caribbean's foresight: he will improvidently sell you his cottonbed in the morning, and come crying in the evening to buy it again, not having foreseen he would want it again the next night (61, my emphasis). This Carib is in his own right almost outside of time, but *only almost*—he is *nevertheless* in time. Rousseau was never able to give an example of an original man originarily outside of time, for this would be a man before creation—a nonexistent man who would yet be the only natural man, the only man truly himself, true to himself. The essence of man that is not time, *that is* technics: here this is manifestly the *same* question.

"Bridging So Great a Gap"

We have arrived at a decisive point of the narrative: death, time, their originary absence and their arrival *qua* the fall itself, the appearance of man as his disappearance, the realization of his possibility *qua* his derealization—it is here, then, in the double of the technical and the human, or rather in the double question of technics and the human, that *the relation between anthropology and technics* appears as a *thanatology*.

Everything happens in one stroke at the moment when, the accident arriving, originary man slips over into mortality. This is a new artifice for naming and describing the improbable passage into mortality that becomes this commonplace where appearance is disappearance, the nearest, the farthest, the least accessible because the most immediate, the incomparable squarely within a horizon of differences, inequalities, jealousies, and comparisons.

The end of the first part of the *Discourse* speaks to everything original man is not, and how inaccessible it all remains for him without the intervention of providence; how everything he is not arrives in a single stroke, being in fact a whole, the "effects" of a selfsame "cause." Nothing could have brought man to these states after nature (work, language, society, love, the family) without divine intervention; God is the first intervenor setting off this series of primary and secondary causes and effects in which the effect set off by the cause derealizes it by the same token, as negative power: the paradox of technology and all its countereffects are the accomplishment of a divine will (to intervention). The abyss thereby opened up under the origin is thus the "great gap," the departure taking place in all its effects from within the accident, provoking the vertigo of death, in which what lets itself be endured can never be endured to the end, leaving no place for proof. The accident, or the following series of accidents that will cover over the fault, will have to be described. But first of all the extremities between which a chasm deepens will have to be opposed. Original man, who is not mortal, does not anticipate, nor speak, nor work, and has neither skills nor knowledge. In order to approach this mortality, to enter into the knowledge that comes with it, to be able to light these lights and in the first place that light that fire itself is, to come around to time, circumstances were necessary—circumstances without which man would never have been able to "bridge so great a gap." How was man able to discover fire? This is an enigma that can be solved with the hypothesis of a concatenation of hazards, individual discoveries, which remain quite improbable, but let us nonetheless consider them as obtaining: not able to communicate, without either language or society, original man will have invented this use of fire only for himself, and the invention will have been lost with his disappearance. For there is no language; neither is there any transmissibility: "How often must they have let it out before they acquired the art of reproducing it, and how often may not such a secret have died with him who had discovered it!" (Rousseau 1973, 63).

Supposing this man possessed of the light and enlightenment he is nonetheless deprived of, he could not transmit them: there is no memory of this originary humanity, which no more works than it accumulates or transmits knowledge—there is no way to imagine what incentive could have been found. And even if original man had desired such things, he would not have had the capacity to obtain them since he had no foresight, whereas agriculture is that art requiring so much foresight. Let us suppose nevertheless that the instruments and knowledge necessary to agriculture had been miraculously generated. On the one hand, labor would be necessary for cultivating fields, but man had no need of that, everything being close at hand, short of imagining a natural calamity, but also, on the other hand, a society would be necessary to protect the fruit of this work, and laws that would abolish that state of nature so sweet to those who live there that they themselves have no desire to leave it, a state that is the law, the law of total unbinding [*déliaison*]:

> What progress could be made by mankind, while dispersed in the woods among other animals? and how far could men improve or mutually enlighten one another, when, having no fixed habitation, and no need of one another's assistance, the same persons hardly met twice in their lives, and perhaps then, without knowing one another or speaking together? (Rousseau 1973, 64)

It is in the aporia of the origin of language that the chasm deepens: what will have come first, language for the foundation of society, or society for a decision on language? The cumbersomeness of the gesture, which can only designate objects in an ostensible mode, providing they be seen, will call phonation to its destiny as the language and institution of signs:

> Such an institution could only be made by common consent, and must have been effected in a manner not very easy for men whose gross organs had not been accustomed to any such exercise. It is also in itself still more difficult to conceive, since such a common agreement must have had motives, and it seems that speech must needs have existed before its use could be established. (Rousseau 1973, 67)

This fractioning out of Rousseau's fiction can only at once express and ignore the fact that since language is thought, since the will-to-say is the saying, language is the institution of society, and society is the institution of language. It must be shown that everything occurs in one stroke, through the fall, and by the same token, a principle antecedence must be established: first the simple origin, then the accident that comes to encounter it, setting in motion a process whose consequences must then be presented as a succession of effects implying one another. But what appears as well, simultaneously, is the impossibility of such a successive process.

This difficulty is all the greater given the presence of will in speech, the latter being not only expression but the occurrence of will itself: original man does not desire anything as long as he does not place himself outside of himself through expression. And yet, if the origin comes before the fall, gesture will have had to precede speech: it cannot accompany it. Everything will have come together, and yet there will have been a genesis of the whole. This is a ghastly logic of deviation in the face of which one is better off relying on the hypothesis of providential intervention:

> I am so aghast at the increasing difficulties which present themselves, and so well convinced of the almost demonstrable impossibility that languages should owe their original institution to merely human means, that I leave, to anyone who will undertake it, the discussion of the difficult problem: which was the more necessary, the existence of society to the invention of language, or the invention of language to the establishment of society. (Rousseau 1973, 70)

The intervention and its effects establish men in relation to one another, making them leave this nondependency that the state of nature is, which has nothing to do with the law of the strongest. There is force only in the relation of two forces, and there is no relation of forces without a relation; and the state of nature is precisely the absence of relation. But there is "another principle which has escaped Hobbes, which . . . tempers the ardor with which he pursues his own welfare, by an innate repugnance at seeing a fellow-creature suffer" (Rousseau 1973, 73). Compassion, which is the voice of nature, which even animals themselves "sometimes give evident proofs of it," is a virtue "so much the more universal and useful to mankind, as it comes before any kind of reflection" (73). Even tyrants are its subjects.

Is not pity, however, projection into the other, affection by the other? How is one to identify with another without an identification with his alterity, without a differentiation by the other. Original compassion is nevertheless identification rather than alteration and differentiation; it is this identification that is not yet alteration, for it is the voice of the origin in which the other is still the same. It is the feeling of original community in the very absence of all relation, before all relation (of identification *qua* the reduction of the other), despite this absence of all relation; it is the feeling of the community that the common absence of all relation is. Reason identifies by marking the difference, by comparing; reason is simultaneously differentiating, altering, and disrupting. With reason man can retreat, keeping at a distance from his fellow men and establishing them as others, precisely, and not as identical. "It is reason that engenders *amour-propre,* and reflection that confirms it; it is reason which turns man's mind back upon itself, and divides him from everything that could disturb or afflict him" (Rousseau 1973, 75). There is an essential coldness to reasoning; reason is insulation, but in question here is a poor insulation, in society and in dependency, determined by them, insulation that has nothing to do with the self-sufficient solitude of the origin. A factical isolation, depending on others as well as on particular interests—isolation in particularization and in difference. Proper isolation is not ruled by particular interest: original man has none; his wants are so elementary and natural that everyone's are the same; none are particularized. Undoubtedly each man, insofar as he is ruled by the instinct of self-conservation, appears as having to oppose himself to the other, to oppose his own interest to that of his fellow man. Undoubtedly, he might thus disrupt the equilibrium of the pure identity of all, the pure equality of wants: there is certainly an original love of self, which, left to itself, might be the beginning of inequality. But it is precisely this original self-love that compassion comes to balance and, by that very fact, to protect in its original warmth. It is compassion that wards off particularization; it is as original as the instinct of conservation, and the "combination of these two principles" characterizes the purity of the original state.

There is then a community of the originally isolated in the original absence of all relation. The men of the origin have no commerce with one another in that all relation immediately becomes a relation of force; the identification in the purity of all relation, combined with the instinct of conservation, is the elevation of the latter above the individual, at the level of the species: "It is then certain that compassion is a natural feeling which, by moderating the activity of love of self in each individual, contributes to the preservation of the whole species" (Rousseau 1973, 76). As such, compassion is the law of equilibrium, the Law as Equilibrium, the law before the disequilibrium that reason will be: "It is this compassion that hurries us without reflection to the relief of those who are in distress: it is this which in a state of nature supplies the place of laws, morals, and virtues, with the advantage that none are tempted to disobey its gentle voice" (76). This feeling, this gentle voice, are still, luckily, heard in society, and this is the only reason for hoping anew for the refoundation of law: "But what is generosity, clemency, or humanity but compassion applied to the weak, to the guilty, or to mankind in general?"

(75). After the accident, compassion will make itself heard again as the voice of nature in the law of men, as passion without passion balancing the passions of cold reason. A warmth of the origin comes to temper the ardor of the passion engendered by the coldness of calculation, that of this dispassionate reason which, by this very fact, gives birth both to passions for particular interests and to the dry and reasoned isolation of what only concerns oneself [*le quant-à-soi*].

Raised to the level of the species, however, the instinct of conservation is always, and above all, not the feeling of death. It is indeed in the imminence of the death of the other, and through it, in the fore-sight of the mortality of the species, that compassion can be endured, death being but the absolute wrong done to the other, and all wrongdoing to the other always being the mortification of this other. All suffering at seeing the other suffer is but projection, the anticipation of his elementary fragility, of the essential peril in which he finds himself, out of which and in which he is encountered. This is why Rousseau speaks of dead animals and of graves when he wishes to demonstrate that this feeling is so universal that "even brutes sometimes give evident proofs of it": "One animal never passes by the dead body of another of its species without disquiet: some even give their fellows a sort of burial" (Rousseau 1973, 74). Fundamentally, this is what compassion always means. And it is again such mortification of the other that compassion will elude by discouraging a robust savage from "robbing a weak child or a feeble old man of the sustenance they may have with pain and difficulty acquired" (76). Thus, these men of pure nature, who pass away almost without noticing it, and animals themselves would suffer from (in the knowledge or the feeling of) death in the imminence of the death of the other, who, moreover, is not yet other. This movement, this impulse, this spontaneity preceding all reflection do seem to transgress the instinct of conservation. And yet, the feeling of compassion must be before the feeling of death. The feeling of death is already the covering-over of compassion as an original feeling, since compassion is immediacy, whereas the feeling of death is anticipation, mediacy, concern, projection of a singular and particularizable future, differentiation and inequality in the fall, in time: original man, it must here be repeated, does not project, remains close to his now, devoid of memory, thus of a past as well as of a future, which is why he is not even rancorous: the feeling of revenge does not affect him, "unless perhaps mechanically and on the spot, as a dog will sometimes bite the stone which is thrown at him" (76).

Rousseau will give another example of this differentiation after death: love makes manifest the perversion of the original feeling into preference, as a particular interest shown to another, and not to one's fellow men in their indifferent equality. Love is an interested and particular passion, which risks bringing "destruction to the human race," making possible the opposite of that for which it seems to exist: "a terrible passion that braves danger, surmounts all obstacles, and in its transports seems calculated to bring destruction on the human race which it is really destined to preserve" (Rousseau 1973, 77). This paradox in which, after the fall, everything may reverse itself into its opposite also applies, and even in the first instance, to human laws that exist precisely to contain such possible reversals, affected here with the radical default accruing to remedies in general: "the more violent the passions are, the more are laws necessary to keep them under restraint; but . . . we should do well to inquire if these evils did not spring up with the laws themselves" (77). As for love, it is passion when a moral affection replaces the physical impulse it first of all is, and whose origin is nature; a passion in which what was destined to reproduce the species becomes a factor of destruction. This passion is unknown to original man—or almost: this feeling

> must be for him almost non-existent: . . . He follows solely the character nature has implanted in him, and not tastes which could never have acquired; so that every woman equally answers his purpose.
>
> . . . The imagination, which causes such ravages among us, never speaks to the heart of savages, who quietly await the impulses of nature, yield to them involuntarily, with more pleasure than ardor, and, their wants once satisfied, lose the desire. (Rousseau 1973, 78)

Since original man has neither imagination nor future, nor for all that a memory or a past, he is almost without love, almost without desire. Concentrating (on an object), not being lost (with the want), desire is the memory of desire.

Everything will thus have come with the feeling of death: death itself, labor, education, language, society, love. *Homo oeconomicus, faber, laborans, sapiens*: the logical, reasonable, or speaking animal, the politico-social animal, the desiring animal, all that traditional philosophy has always used to qualify the human race, from Plato to Aristotle to Marx and Freud—this all comes only after this accident by which man enters into the disastrous feeling of death, into melancholy.

There would, therefore, never have been original inequality, no natural inequality, and nature itself is not amorous nor thereby affected by preference.[16]

Again the Second Origin

Everything that will come afterward could have quite easily been named technics: anticipation as concern (*Besorgen*) in the gap that originarily deepens between present, past, and future and in which the now is constituted. This plunge into the temporality of the artifice, into the artifice of temporality, into becoming as it appears here, detached from being and having thoroughly corrupted it, this is the accidental passage from virtual perfectibility to actual perfectibility:

> Having shown that human *perfectibility*, the social virtues, and the other faculties which natural man potentially possessed, *could never develop of themselves*, but must require the fortuitous concurrence of many foreign causes that might never arise, and without which he would have remained forever in his primitive conditions, I must now collect and consider the different accidents which may have improved the human understanding while depraving the species, and made man wicked while making him sociable; so as to bring him and the world from that distant period to the point at which we now behold them. (Rousseau 1973, 81, my emphasis)

This accidentality is witness both to the *quasi*-impossibility of explaining a second origin and to the fact that this second origin will have ended up being the *origin itself* while being but an *absence* of origin. It witnesses the impossibility of recognizing, designating, and conceiving of any kind of beginning. Now, we will encounter this problem again, in all its difficulty, however draped in the prestige of science, in the paleontological discourse of Leroi-Gourhan. Rousseau's exigency that the second origin be considered only as providential accidentality will make no more inroads than scientific discourse into the aporia of the "appallingly ancient" that the question of time is. However, paleontology will profoundly affect the anthropological a priori governing at the profoundest level the most authentically philosophical questionings: "there may perhaps never have been a humanity," "perhaps we are already no longer humans": such will indeed be the possibilities that *Gesture and Speech* will keep us from ignoring.

Rousseau's narrative of the origin shows us through antithesis how everything of the order of what is usually considered specifically human is immediately and irremediably linked to an absence of property [*impropriété*], to a process of "supplementation," of prosthetization or exteriorization, in which nothing is any longer immediately at hand, where everything is found mediated and instrumentalized, technicized, unbalanced. This process would lead today to something inhuman, or superhuman, tearing the human away from everything that, hitherto, seemed to define him (language, work, society, reason, love and desire and everything deriving thereof, even a certain feeling of death and a certain relation to time: to all of this we shall return), a process by which the realization or the "actualization" of the power of man seems to be as well the derealization of man, his disappearance in the movement of a becoming that is *no longer his own.* Rousseau will not, therefore, have been mistaken; he will have been right, *almost,* for this narrative has set us face to face with the problem: an attempt at thinking *in a single movement* (the origin) of technics and (the "origin") of the human—technology and anthropology—presupposes a radical conversion of one's point of view. The question will be that of thinking the relation of being and time as a *technological relation,* if it is true that this relation only develops in the "originary" horizon of technics—which is just as much an absence of origin.

§ 3 Who? What? The Invention of the Human

The Différance of the Human

The invention *of* the human: without our needing to become complacent with the double genitive, its ambiguity signals a question that breaks down into two: "Who" or "what" does the inventing? "Who" or "what" is invented? The ambiguity of the subject, and in the same move the ambiguity of the object of the verb "invent," translates nothing else but the very sense of the verb.

The relation binding the "who" and the "what" is invention. Apparently, the "who" and the "what" are named respectively: the human, and the technical. Nevertheless, the ambiguity of the genitive imposes at least the following question: what if the "who" were the technical? and the "what" the human? Or yet again must one not proceed down a path beyond or below every difference between a *who* and a *what*?

To enter these questions, we shall focus on the passage into the human leading from the Zinjanthropian to the Neanthropian. This ground breaking [*frayage*], which is that of corticalization, is also effected in stone, in the course of the slow evolution of techniques of stonecutting. An evolution so slow—it still occurs at the rhythm of "genetic drift"—that one can hardly imagine the human as its operator, that is, as its inventor; rather, one much more readily imagines the human as what is invented.

The emergence of this being—producer, constructor, if not conceiver—begins then in a process of neurological evolution. However, on the one hand, it is no longer strictly a matter of a zoological phenomenon: the most archaic technical evolution is already no longer "genetically programmed"; on the other hand, beyond the Neanthropian, this process continues as pure technological evolution, the organization of the cortex being genetically stabilized. How are we to understand this second rupture? What is at stake *between* these first two coups of the "origin"? What epigenetic question does that open up?

One must first ask what mirage of the cortex is experienced [*s'éprouve*], as pathbreaking, in the hardness of flint; what plasticity of gray matter corresponds to the flake of mineral matter; what proto-stage of the mirror is thus installed. One must then ask what the closure of the cortical evolution of the human implies from the vantage of a general history of life, the closure of the cortical evolution of the human, and therefore *the pursuit of the evolution of the living by other means than life*—which is what the history of technics consists in, from the first flaked pebbles to today, a history that is also the history of humanity—a statement that will lead us to the unusual concept of "epiphylogenesis."

This investigation will question the possibilities we have of thinking the temporality that arrives in the passage from the Zinjanthropian to the Neanthropian. We shall seek to show thereby that our most profound question is that of the technological rooting of all relation to time—a rooting that quite singularly plays itself out again against the horizon of our most contemporary technology: speed. Leroi-Gourhan broaches this question with the problem of anticipation implied in all acts of fabrication from the first knapped flint tool.

We are considering a passage: the passage to what is called the human. Its "birth," if there is one. Why should we question the "birth" of the human? First of all because we have unceasingly, since Hegel, questioned its end (Derrida 1982, 120–21). Even the recent attempts to restore a pre-Hegelian thought of the human are determined by the thoughts of its end: they can only respond to that end, without introducing anything new. For the end of the human cannot be investigated without investigating its origin, just as questioning death is questioning birth in a mirror. To ask the question of the birth of the human is to pose the question of the "birth of death" or of the relation to death. But at stake here will be the attempt to think, instead of the birth of the human *qua* entity relating to its end, rather its invention or even its embryonic fabrication or conception, and to attempt this independently of all anthropologism, even if this would mean considering with the utmost seriousness this other question: "And if we already were no longer humans?" For if nothing supports our saying that what is called the human is finished today, we may in any case set down as a principle that what begins must finish. And since Darwin we have known that the human, if it exists, has begun, even though we are unable to think how it began. This is the reason why it is so difficult for us to think how it might end. But the fact of not being able to think how it began or how it might end does not prevent the fact that it began and will end. Indeed, one may even think it may have already ended.

This analysis based on the work of Leroi-Gourhan will also allow for a dialogue with Jacques Derrida around the concept of différance, as this concept describes the process of life of which the human is a singular case, but only a case. What is in question is not emptying the human of all specificity but radically challenging the border between the animal and the human. Such an aim encounters problems, to be set out in volume two of this work, that can be compared to those met in (at least) the relativization of the specificity of alphabetic linear writing. It is a case of the same reasoning starting with different names: (1) if the privilege granted to linear writing by Hegel and Rousseau is logocentric, (2) if metaphysics is logocentric and vice versa, (3) if all metaphysics are humanist and vice versa, (4) then all humanisms are logocentric. To privilege alphabetic writing is to privilege man: "phono-logocentrism" is always anthropo-logocentrism, whatever philosophy may say on the subject in general. To oppose speech to writing is always also to oppose man to animal in opposing him in the same stroke to the technical. However, it must not be forgotten that if grammatology is not "one of the sciences of man, [this is] because it asks first, as its characteristic question, the question of the name of man" (Derrida 1974, 83). How does grammatology pose this question? By calling man (or his unity) into question, and by forging the concept of différance, which is nothing else than the history of life. If grammatology thinks the *graphie*, and if in so doing it thinks the name of man, this is accomplished by elaborating a concept of différance that calls on the paleoanthropology of Leroi-Gourhan and does so to the extent that Leroi-Gourhan describes "the unity of man and the human adventure [no longer] by the simple possibility of the *graphie* in general, [but] rather as a stage or an articulation in the history of life—of what I have called differance—as the history of the *grammē*," while calling on the notion of program (Derrida 1974, 84).

> It must of course be understood in the cybernetic sense, but cybernetics is itself intelligible only in terms of a history of the possibilities of the trace as the unity of a double movement of protention and retention. This movement goes far beyond the possibilities of "intentional consciousness." It is an emergence that makes the *grammē* appear *as such* (that is to say according to a new structure of nonpresence) and undoubtedly makes possible *the emergence of the systems of writing in the narrow sense.* (Derrida 1974, 84)

The *grammē* structures all levels of the living and beyond, the pursuit of life by means other than life, "since 'genetic inscription' . . . up to the passage beyond alphabetic writing to the orders of the *logos* and of a certain *Homo sapiens.*" And it must be thought from out of the process of the "freeing of memory" described by Leroi-Gourhan: "an exteriorization always already begun but always larger than the trace which, beginning from the elementary programmes of so-called 'instinctive' behavior up to the constitution of electronic card indexes and reading machines, enlarges differance and the possibility of putting in reserve" (Derrida 1974, 84).

In other words, Leroi-Gourhan's anthropology can be thought from within an essentially non-anthropocentric concept that does not take for granted the usual divides between animality and humanity. Derrida bases his own thought of différance as a general history of life, that is, as a general history of the *grammē*, on the concept of program insofar as it can be found on both sides of such divides. Since the *grammē* is older than the specifically human written forms, and because the letter is nothing without it, the conceptual unity that différance is contests the opposition animal/human and, in the same move, the opposition nature/culture. "Intentional consciousness" finds the origin of its possibility before the human; it is nothing else but "the emergence that has the *grammē* appearing *as such.*" *We are left with the question of determining what the conditions of such an emergence of the "grammē as such" are, and the consequences as to the general history of life and/or of the grammē. This will be our question.* The history of the *grammē* is that of electronic files and reading machines as well—a history of technics—which is the invention of the human. As object as well as subject. The technical inventing the human, the human inventing the technical. Technics as inventive as well as invented. This hypothesis destroys the traditional thought of technics, from Plato to Heidegger and beyond.

Différance is the history of life in general, in which an articulation is produced, a stage of différance out of which emerges the possibility of making the *grammē* as such, that is, "consciousness," appear. The task here will be to specify this stage. We shall refer to a double rupture in the history of life—of what comes to pass or what passes, between two blows, two coups received by différance in general from a specific différance: the Zinjanthropian and the Neanthropian are the names of these two coups. What takes place here, the place of this event, is the passage from the genetic to the nongenetic. Derrida here refers, without quoting them, to two texts of Leroi-Gourhan (1993, 221 and 228), from which other consequences will be drawn in the second volume of this work. The passage from the genetic to the nongenetic is the appearance of a new type of *grammē* and/or program. If the issue is no longer that of founding *anthropos* in the pure origin of itself, the origin of its type must still be found. This means that a typology of *grammēs* and programs must be constructed. As Paul Ricoeur suggests, cultural codes, like genetic codes,

> are "programs" of behavior; like them, they confer form, order, and direction on life. But unlike genetic codes, cultural codes have been constructed in the collapsed zones of genetic regulation, and can prolong their efficiency only through a total reorganization of the coding system. Customs, mores, and everything Hegel put under the heading of ethical substance, of *Sittlichkeit*, preceding all reflective *Moralität*, thus takes up the relay from genetic codes. (Ricoeur 1983, 93)

The whole question is thinking the highly paradoxical possibility of such a relay or passage; this possibility is the unthinkable question of an absolute past, of an inconceivable present, which can only be an infinite abyss, a collapse Ricoeur says. The first man to have died, "or rather believed to be dead," is the man of the first present, of the first temporal ecstasis of the past, present, and future; a past that was never present gives rise to a present linking onto no past present. We shall take up this abyssal question again as the paradox of exteriorization in Leroi-Gourhan. And we will see how paleontology allows the question of time to be taken up differently. The concept of différance, and of a rupture in différance, is an attempt at "conceiving" this passage.

Différance means both differentiation and deferral, a spacing of time and a temporalization of space:

> The verb *différer* . . . has two meaning which seem quite distinct. . . . In this sense the Latin *differre* is not simply a translation of the Greek *diapherein*, . . .

> the distribution of meaning in the Greek *diapherein* does not comport one of the two motifs of the Latin *differre*, to wit, the action of putting off until later, of taking into account, of taking account of time and of the forces of an operation that implies an economical calculation, a detour, a delay, a relay, a reserve, a representation—concepts that I would summarize here in a word I have never used but that could be inscribed in this chain: *temporization. Différer* in this sense is to temporize, to take recourse, consciously or unconsciously, in the temporal and temporizing mediation of a detour that suspends the accomplishment or fulfillment of "desire" . . . this temporization is also temporalization and spacing, the becoming time of space and the becoming-space of time. . . . The other sense of *différer* is the more common and identifiable one: to be not identical, to be other, discernible, etc. When dealing with differen(ts)(ds), a word that can be written with a final ts or a final ds, as you will, whether it is a question of dissimilar otherness or of allergic and polemical otherness, an interval, a *spacing*, must be produced between the other elements, and be produced with a certain perseverance in repetition. (Derrida 1982, 7–8)

All of this points primarily to life in general: there is time from the moment there is life, whereas Derrida also writes, just before the Leroi-Gourhan quotation, that "the trace is the differance that opens appearing and the signification (articulating) the living onto the non-living in general, (which is) the origin of all repetition" (Derrida 1974, 65). To articulate the living onto the nonliving, is that not already a gesture from after the rupture when you are already no longer in pure *phusis*? There is something of an indecision around différance: it is the history of life in general, but this history is (only) given (as) (dating from) after the rupture, whereas the rupture is, if not nothing, then at least much less than what the classic divide between humanity and animality signifies. The whole problem is that of the economy of life in general, and the sense of death as the economy of life once the rupture has taken place: life is, after the rupture, the economy of death. The question of différance is death. This *after* is

> culture as nature different and deferred, differing-deferring; all the others of *phusis*—*tekhnē, nomos, thesis,* society, freedom, history, mind, etc.—as *phusis* different and deferred, or as phusis differing and deferring. *Phusis in différance.* (Derrida 1982, 17)

Now phusis as life was already différance. There is an indecision, a passage remaining to be thought. At issue is the specificity of the temporality of life in which life is inscription in the nonliving, spacing, temporalization, differentiation, and deferral by, of, and in the nonliving, in the dead. To think the articulation is also to think the birth of the relation we name with the verb "to exist"; this is to think anticipation.

What Heidegger calls the already there, constitutive of the temporality of Dasein, is this past that I never lived but that is nevertheless my past, without which I never would have had any past of my own. Such a structure of inheritance and transmission, which is the very ground of facticity itself since tradition can always conceal from me the sense of the origin that it alone can transmit to me, presupposes that the phenomenon of life *qua* Dasein becomes singular in the history of the living to the extent that, for Dasein, the epigenetic layer of life, far from being lost with the living when it dies, conserves and sediments itself, passes itself down in "the order of survival" [*survivance*] and to posterity as a gift as well as a debt, that is, as a destiny. This is not a "program" in the *quasi*-determinist biological sense, but a cipher in which the whole of Dasein's existence is caught; this epigenetic sedimentation, a memorization of what has come to pass, is what is called the past, what we shall name the *epiphylogenesis* of man, meaning the conservation, accumulation, and sedimentation of successive epigeneses, mutually articulated. Epiphylogenesis is a break with pure life, in that in the latter, epigenesis is precisely what is not conserved ("the programme cannot receive lessons from experience" [Jacob 1974, 11]) even if this is not without effect on the genetic selection in which evolution consists (these questions have at any rate to be put in the perspective of the relation phenotype/genotype as embryology sets it forth, thereby giving a new place to epigenesis)[1]—but this effect can therefore only transmit itself genetically, precisely; epi-*phylo*-genesis also in the sense in which, just as the embryo recapitulates each stage of evolution, each branch of the shrub of which it is the most recent bud, epigenesis must be recapitulated to take place. This is the very ideal of *mathēsis* (an analogy to be handled all the more prudently as the concept of embryonic recapitulation is itself a metaphor). Epiphylogenesis bestows its identity upon the human individual: the accents of his speech, the style of his approach, the force of his gesture, the unity of his world. This concept would be that of an archaeology of reflexivity.

This is what Heidegger called the historical [*l'historial*]. We come now to Heidegger after having opened up the questions of the temporality of différance *qua* the movement of life in general because there is in Heidegger an opposition between the time of technical measurement and concern, which is the loss of time, and authentic time, which is proper to Dasein—wrenched from the technical horizon of concern. Now if it is true that only epigenetic sedimentation can be the already-there, this is only possible when the transmission allowing for the sediments is of an absolutely technical, nonliving essence: made possible by the organized albeit inorganic matter that the trace always is—be it a matter of tool or of writing—let us say one of an *organon* in general.

The ambiguity of the invention of the human, that which holds together the *who* and the *what*, binding them while keeping them apart, is différance undermining the authentic/inauthentic divide. We shall look into this at the very moment of its passage, from *phusis in différance* (life in general) to the différance of this différance. Différance is neither the *who* nor the *what*, but their co-possibility, the movement of their mutual coming-to-be, of their coming into convention. The *who* is nothing without the *what*, and conversely. Différance is below and beyond the *who* and the *what*; it poses them together, a composition engendering the illusion of an opposition. The passage is a mirage: the passage of the cortex into flint, like a mirror proto-stage. This proto-mirage is the paradoxical and aporetic beginning of "exteriorization." It is accomplished between the Zinjanthropian and the Neanthropian, for hundreds of thousands of years in the course of which the work in flint begins, the meeting of matter whereby the cortex reflects itself. Reflecting itself, like a mirrored psyche, an archaeo- or paleontological mode of reflexivity, somber, buried, freeing itself slowly from the shadows like a statue out of a block of marble. The paradox is to have to speak of an exteriorization without a preceding interior: the interior is constituted in exteriorization.

Hominization is for Leroi-Gourhan a rupture in the movement of freeing (or mobilization) characteristic of life. This rupture happens suddenly, in the form of a process of exteriorization which, from the point of view of paleontology, means that the appearance of the human is the appearance of the technical. Leroi-Gourhan specifies this as the appearance of language. The movement inherent in this process of exteriorization is paradoxical: Leroi-Gourhan in fact says that it is the tool, that is, *tekhnē*, that invents the human, not the human who invents the technical. Or again: the human invents himself in the technical by inventing the tool—by becoming exteriorized techno-logically. But here the human is the interior: there is no exteriorization that does not point to a movement from interior to exterior. Nevertheless, the interior is inverted in this movement; it can therefore not precede it. Interior and exterior are consequently constituted in a movement that invents both one and the other: a moment in which they invent each other respectively, as if there were a technological maieutic of what is called humanity. The interior and the exterior are the same thing, the inside is the outside, since man (the interior) is essentially defined by the tool (the exterior). However, this double constitution is also that of an opposition between the interior and the exterior—or one that produces an illusion of succession. Where does this illusion come from? To anticipate the next section, let us say that it comes from an originary forgetting, *ēpimētheia* as delay, the fault of Epimetheus. This becomes meaningful only in the melancholy of Prometheus, as anticipation of death, where the facticity of the already-there that equipment is for the person born into the world signifies the end: this is a Promethean structure of being-for-death, a structure in which concern is not the simple covering-over of *Eigenlichkeit.* This is the question of time.

Leroi-Gourhan attempts to resolve this paradox by positing that the technics of the Zinjanthropian is still a quasi-zoology. And yet it is already no longer anything of the kind, otherwise one could not speak of exteriorization. This is why there is an intermediary period, between the Zinjanthropian who is already a man, and the Neanthropian opening onto the human that we are—if we are still human: this partition calls into question the unity of the human. Between the two is set up the definition of a cortex that, after the Neanthropian, will no longer evolve. It is in this period that the coupling cortex/flint, living matter / inert matter, will be elaborated, when a double plasticity will be woven, where the hardness of mineral matter will both inform and be informed in the fluidity of "spiritual" immateriality (which is still matter, a mode of being, differing and deferring, of matter), work that is still genetic, but that is already governed by epigenesis as epiphylogenesis, that is, by an epigenesis that the flint support conserves. Flint is the first reflective memory, the first mirror.

At the dawn of hominization, that is, of corticalization, the epiphylogenetic vector becomes flint as that which conserves the epigenesis; the process of corticalization operates as a reflection of this conservation, which is already, in itself, a reflection.

Everything Begins with the Feet

Leroi-Gourhan questions the empirical-transcendental divide from which Rousseau's philosophical anthropology derives. But the more Leroi-Gourhan, by planting the roots of the technical tendency into an older, deeper zoological dynamic, tries to solve the resulting paradoxes, the more he will himself encounter them in turn. Once again, this thought will run up against technology as thanatology and temporality, and hence will not be able to avoid the schema of a second origin producing itself incomprehensibly, if not providentially.

Having stressed that the disquiet of origin seems attested quite early on in the human, Leroi-Gourhan states the bottom line of his thesis through a critique of Rousseau. The so simple and so evident idea of supposing the original human's "conformation to have been at all times what it appears to be to us today, that he has always walked on two legs, and made use of his hands as we do" (Rousseau 1973, 52), is a "cerebralist theory" since the hands are empty and the body naked. The "end" in this theory is totally constituted from the origin, and becoming as such is ignored. The originary attributes have nothing to do with technicity itself, which only occurs with the fall, coming only afterward. The essence of natural man that arrives in one stroke as it is today but without technology, before culture, before deferred nature, is not constituted by his history. Leroi-Gourhan will demonstrate the opposite, first by establishing an essential link between the upright skeleton, technics, language, and society, and next by approaching technology as a singular zoological reality.

It is nevertheless the case that he effaces the very enigma of Rousseau's narrative: the duplicity of (the question of) the origin, the transcendental necessity of affirming a first origin that the second will come to accomplish in derealizing it. The fact that this internal necessity is not criticized explicitly, nor even evoked, is obviously not a case of pure negligence: the aporia constituting this necessity will never be actually assumed by the paleontologist, who will then repeat the artifice—while resituating it. He nevertheless thereby opens the question of the possibility—of time—in an approach quite thoroughly emancipated from an anthropocentric comprehension of technological dynamics and allowing the constitution of temporality to be apprehended from the standpoint of the emergence of memory elaborated and conserved by the organization of the inorganic. What was in Rousseau the first origin as the immediate availability [*mise à portée*] of the hand becomes originary distancing, manipulation as a new form of mobilization, exteriorization—that is, an absolute default of origin as well as the disquiet over the very possibility of an assignable beginning. This thought which thus opens the ultimate possibility of a pursuit of technological differentiation—pursuit of life by means other than those of life—by the renunciation of humanity itself. Becoming may then be fully thought, if not fully endured, as the actualization of power [*puissance*].

The human is not a spiritual miracle that would suddenly belong to an already given body, in which the "mental" would be grafted onto the "animal": the human does not descend from the monkey. The human body, even the most archaic of bodies, is functionally different from that of primates: in question is another branch of the tree of evolution. The psychic has its roots in a specific general physiological organization; it is first of all a state of the body—but it is not that alone.

In the eighteenth century the evolutionist point of view comes into prominence with Carl Linnaeus, along with the idea of zoological continuity with the work of Louis Daubenton, who studied "the position of the occipital foramen in humans and animals." The comparison between the chipped flint tool and the human is made by John Frere in 1800. Charles Darwin publishes *The Origin of Species by Means of Natural Selection* in 1859, in which "humans can only be understood as part of a terrestrial totality. . . . Conventional wisdom links the name of Darwin to the expression 'the human being is descended from the monkey'" (Leroi-Gourhan 1993, 8). By affirming the opposite, Leroi-Gourhan can show that the hominid anatomo-systematic, the general economy of its mechanical and motor system, is such that early on the specific elements of the human, the erect position and a new organization of the anterior field, are called forth, whose logical consequences are technicity and the forms of sociability they immediately imply. The human is an originary psycho-physical complex the substance of which is to be understood in terms of the dynamic of the skeleton, following a line of evolution embedded in the most remote past.

The Neanderthal brainpan is discovered in 1856, the "turning point in human paleontology. . . . The image of the ape-man comes into clear focus; he has a name . . . : Anthropopithecus (or Homosimian)." But "the error was that of drawing a straight line linking *Homo sapiens*, via the Neanderthalians, with the impressive anthropoid foursome of modern times—the gorilla, the chimpanzee, the orangutan, and the gibbon" (Leroi-Gourhan 1993, 10–11). The determining archaeological element is the Zinjanthropian, discovered in 1959, "accompanied by his stone implements . . . a man with a very small brain, not a super-anthropoid with a large brainpan. . . . This finding necessitates a revision of the concept of the human being" (18) because the direct consequence is that the human did not begin with the brain, but with the feet, and that in the general dynamic thereby inaugurated—anthropological as well as indissociably technological—"to some extent cerebral development is a secondary criterion." Erect posture determines a new system of relations between these two poles of the "anterior field": the "freeing" of the hand during locomotion is also that of the face from its grasping functions. The hand will necessarily call for tools, movable organs; the tools of the hand will necessarily call for the language of the face. The brain obviously plays a role, but it is no longer directive: it is but a partial element of a total apparatus, even if the evolution of the apparatus tends toward the deployment of the cerebral cortex.

The acquisition of an erect posture, one of "the solutions to a biological problem as old as the vertebrates themselves," is inscribed in the series of living beings, and as the logical term of their evolution, from which the hand-face linkage in the anterior field must be thought, with primordial consequence that "tools for the hand, language for the face, are twin poles of the same apparatus," itself determined by a specific cerebral organization (Leroi-Gourhan 1993, 20). We shall attempt to show that this specificity resides in a unique coupling with the outside *qua* epiphylogenetic vector, that is, *qua* the "truth" of the inside.

Advance and Delay

If paleontology thus ends up with the statement that the hand frees speech, language becomes indissociable from technicity and prostheticity: it must be thought with them, like them, in them, or from the same origin as theirs: from within their mutual essence.

By inscribing his description of hominization in the very long history of the living animal, Leroi-Gourhan shows how all the elements quite anciently come into play for the emergence of a general system of a certain function that remains unique: the human, that is, technology, "exuded" by the skeleton. There is no sudden and miraculous rise of a totally constituted human: technics, which is the synthesis of the different criteria of humanity, which is the very criterion, can only be understood in a zoological perspective, even if it is impossible to remain solely within this perspective, which is not without epistemological problems. Leroi-Gourhan will stay *almost* within this perspective, but never exclusively.

General zoological evolution is understood from the standpoint of the concept of "liberation," of which the freedom of the hand and all its consequences are but individual cases; and an essential idea is here introduced for us, readers of Rousseau: "To what a striking degree the urge to conquer time and space, our dominant trait, is also characteristic of all the [animal] witnesses selected to illustrate the ascent of the human being. It is possible to regard mobility as the significant feature of evolution toward the human state" (Leroi-Gourhan 1993, 26). Mobility, rather than intelligence, is the "significant feature," unless intelligence is intelligible only as a type of mobility. What is specific to the human is the movement of putting itself outside the range of its own hand, locking onto the animal process of "liberation": "the brain was not the cause of developments in locomotor adaptation but their beneficiary" (26). The hand never has anything within its range. Prostheticity, here a consequence of the freedom of the hand, is a putting-outside-the-self that is also a putting-out-of-range-of-oneself. Pursuing the "process of liberation," the installation of this techno-logical complex nevertheless brings on a rupture.

The conquest of mobility, *qua* supernatural mobility, *qua* speed, is more significant than intelligence—or rather, intelligence is but a type of mobility, a singular relation of space and time, which must be thought from the standpoint of speed, as its decompositions, and not conversely (speed as the result of their conjunction). It would be necessary, moreover, to analyze the relation of différance to speed: différance is itself also a conjunction of space and time more originary than their separation. It is in this sense, then, that différance will, perhaps, have to be thought *as* speed.[2]

At the end of the process of mobilization, which is also that of "liberation," and with liberation becoming "exteriorization," a particular type of cortical organization of the brain appears on the scene by which evolution takes on "an extra-organic sense." Is the sense "spirit"? For the moment the only issue is the appearance of technics, which is liberation when it becomes exteriorization, but which must be thought from out of the extremely remote biological past in which the anterior field is structured. The role of the brain can only be understood according to the most ancient tendencies of the functional system of living vertebrates. If its "role as a coordinator is . . . a primordial one whose function appears as the 'tenant' of the rest of the body, . . . there is no special relationship between the evolution of the brain and that of the body which that brain controls" (Leroi-Gourhan 1993, 37).

Six major stages in the evolution of vertebrates mark the general process of "liberation." The first four stages take place between 300 and 200 million years before us, and it is on the backdrop of this enormous anteriority that hominization must be understood. This situation—in which a general framework is quite largely anticipated without being, for all that, totally accomplished, that is, stabilized—

> is parallel to the precocity with which the anthropoid apes freed their hand and achieved erect posture long before their brain had reached the level of ours today. . . . The development of the nervous system follows in the wake of that of the body structure. Theriodont reptiles had the bodies of carnivorous mammals, but their brain was still no larger than a fountain-pen cap suspended inside an edifice whose entire inner space would be filled, two hundred million years later, by the brain of a dog. (Leroi-Gourhan 1993, 50)

At the end of the completion of the functional system, evolution continues by rupture and not by fulfillment [*remplissement*]. In the course of this fulfillment, the skeleton advances beyond the nervous system, as in the hypothesis that technics advances beyond society, an advance the terms of which were set out in the introduction to this work, and which would be a shift in the latter, as if life, considering the other means through which it is pursued, were a succession of modalities of relationships between a structural advance and delay, producers of differences by the play of tension in which they consist.

Mammals that only walk seem to lead to a definitive stabilization of the physiological system and to a hyper-specialization, what Simondon would have called a biological "hypertelia," whereas the graspers, orienting themselves, on the contrary, toward an ever more open functional indetermination, prepare the terrain for what will be in the human case technicity in the strong sense. The interpretation of this theme of indetermination, as we will meet it again in the myth of Prometheus, will lead in the following chapters to the properly philosophical formulation of a dynamic of the undetermined.

Skeleton, Equipment, and the Brain

The appearance of the tool, accomplishing the indetermination specified from the moment of the human as a process of exteriorization, must be brought into relation to the particular organization of the cortical zones of the brain. This organization sheds light upon the dialectical relation formed between the hand and the central nervous system: there is a direct link between nonspecialization and the development of the cortical zones of the brain.

With the advent of exteriorization, the body of the living individual is no longer only a body: it can only function with its tools. An understanding of the archaic anthropological system will only become possible with the simultaneous examination of the skeleton, the central nervous system, and equipment.

The set of hypotheses proposed retraces the possibilities of passage between three stages of archaic humanity: the Australanthropian, the Archanthropian, and the Neanthropian, in the course of which the cortical fan opens. Australanthropians are already humans—not so much "humans with monkeys faces as humans with a braincase that defies humanity. We were prepared to accept anything except to learn that it all began with the feet!" (Leroi-Gourhan 1993, 65). If the small size of the brain confirms its "delay," with the new bipolar organization of the anterior field, there is a corresponding cortical organization radically different from that of primates. If the being under scrutiny is a human, it is manifestly not endowed with all those faculties normally attributed to "humanity." This is the human of pure nature more than any other human: but are we still capable of detecting what we would call "human nature"? Do we not see, in this original human, that "human nature" consists only in its technicity, in its denaturalization?

The humanity of the Archanthropians "remains disconcerting. Their face is enormous and their braincase is appreciably smaller than ours" (Leroi-Gourhan 1993, 69). Lastly, if the volume of the Neanderthal brain may reach present-day volumes, "the relative proportions are not the same in Neanderthal man as in ourselves. The Paleoanthropian skull is dilated in its occipital part, the forehead remaining narrow and low" (71).

The determining question is the deployment of the cortical fan at the moment when the skeleton organization stabilizes. The cortex of graspers already contains "technical" zones in the sense that fabricating technicity obviously has its source in grasping (Leroi-Gourhan 1993, 80). However, technicity *qua* exteriorization implies an organic link between hand and face—between gesture and speech—which presupposes a shared competence, "zones of association" where the relations between cortical zones are redistributed. There is a contiguity of the territories of the face and the hand in the fourth area. This articulation of the motor areas of the anterior field is attested by the "neurological experiments [which] have demonstrated that the zones of association that surround the motor cortex of the face and hand are jointly involved in producing phonetic or graphic symbols" (88). From here, Derrida will draw the grammatological consequences, the arche-trace, older than the specification of two zones as well as the constitution of these zones of association, allowing the ensemble of the movement of exteriorization to be interpreted as différance (Derrida 1974, 84–87).

The unity of the human here becomes tenuous: one can hardly see any other permanence, in the vital phenomenon described from the Australopian to *Homo sapiens*, than the fact of technicity. The form of the trajectory continuing the starting point of denaturalization is what enables a sole phenomenon to be seen at work throughout millions of years. The continuity of the human would be due only to the permanence of "liberation" having become "process of exteriorization," without, at least up to now, the permanence of its necessity in the pursuit of movement being assured or demanded.

The fact remains that this techno-logical continuity also signifies that cortical organization as it is developed in the technical gesture as a process of exteriorization, must also have necessarily engendered language: starting with the Zinjanthropian, there must have been the possibility of speech.

Once the question of cortical organization has been established, and before the analyses of the three stages of archaic humanity by the comparison of their tools can begin, there one must face the problem posed for the determination of a species-related, that is, zoological character by the appearance of an element that can evidently not be considered as living, as a part of the body's anatomy, but that is no less essential to the definition of its zoology, an element itself invested with morphogenetic movement, caught in a play of evolutional constraints that then coincide with the zoological "liberation's" having become "exteriorization." With what kind of scientific apparatus must technics be apprehended: zoology, sociology, or another discipline? This problem will appear to motivate Leroi-Gourhan's retreat, when he restores the invention of the second origin.

The projection of the hand and its objects toward what is ever more out of their range first appears, at the level of the Australanthropian, as an actual "anatomical consequence, the only solution possible for a being whose hands and teeth had become completely useless as weapons" (Leroi-Gourhan 1993, 90). It is from this initially zoological understanding of technics that the question of its eventual originary autonomy can be opened up, as a question of its own phylogenetic movement. However, the conquest of this independence is here not yet effected, and we shall clearly see later what will have made it possible.

"We arrived at the concept as being a 'secretion' of the Anthropian's body and brain" (Leroi-Gourhan 1993, 91). Its body and brain are defined by the existence of the tool, and they thereby become indissociable. It would be artificial to consider them separately, and it will therefore be necessary to study technics and its evolution just as one would study the evolution of living organisms. The technical object in its evolution is at once inorganic matter, inert, and organization of matter. The latter must operate according to the constraints to which organisms are submitted. The idea of a sort of zoology or phylogenetics of technics as it has been developed here carries further the analyses of *Man and Matter.*

"Technical Consciousness" and Anticipation

The analysis conducted from the standpoint of tools becomes concretized in the case of the flaked pebbles of the Zinjanthropian pebble culture. If the "stereotypes" of the fabrication of tools evolve, however slowly, and do so in an ascending, ever more accelerated movement, this is due to the very fact of exteriorization *qua* emancipation with regard to the processes of genetic programming. It is from such a viewpoint and from the onset that once the Australanthropian stereotype has been recognized, the hypothesis of a "technical consciousness" must be entertained; and yet, from the Australanthropian up to the Neanderthalian, the evolution of stereotypes is so slow that its determinations still seem to derive from neurological, thus genetic characteristics of the individuals that make the tools, as if technics had not yet become totally autonomous with respect to the living: for thousands of years, the industry of archaic man "remained unchanged—conditioned, as it were, by the shape of his skull" (Leroi-Gourhan 1993, 92). If there is no consciousness in the sense of "creative consciousness," nor then in the sense of what is ordinarily called consciousness, if there can only be a technical consciousness that is nevertheless not the simple automatic or programmatic-genetic behavior of a fabricating animal, then there must be anticipation. "Technical consciousness" means anticipation without creative consciousness. Anticipation means the realization of a possibility that is not determined by a biological program. Now, at the same time, the movement of "exteriorization," if it seems to presuppose this anticipation, appears here to be of a strictly zoological origin, to the point of still being determined by the neurophysiological characteristics of the individual. When this determination will have completely ceased its action on technical evolution, Leroi-Gourhan will introduce a notion of spirituality: *a second origin.*

The very idea of the emergence of a forthrightly recognizable humanity must be challenged; the tracing of any simple boundary between humanity and animality must be seriously called into question. This position is in the end not so far removed from the fiction of a first origin in Rousseau, but it will lead Leroi-Gourhan, to the extent that he collapses the dynamism of archaic technical objects onto that of the cortex, to shift the aporia toward the second origin.

We are here confronted with the question of a passage that is not anthropological so much as it is techno-logical. Nevertheless, the issue is anticipation: rather than being that of the human or the technical, the question is what absolutely unites them, time as the emergence of the "*grammē* as such," différance when it differs and defers in a new regime, a double différance. But does the emergence of the "*grammē* as such" coincide with this doubling up of différance? Might the emergence not come later?

In the ultra-archaic period extending from the Zinjanthropian to Neanderthal man, the essential part of the process of transformation is the spreading of the cortical fan, which translates directly into the evolution of forms of equipment, meaning that in the final analysis, technological dynamism still remains strictly biological, even while it will have been necessary to introduce the hypothesis of a "technical consciousness" and thus a certain form of anticipation so as not to lose the initial hypothesis of a rupture (an exteriorization) effective from the Zinjanthropian onward. This theme of anticipation will issue in an opposition between technical and spiritual intelligence that will end up being the question of death for archaic humanity.

With flaked pebbles, there was only one gesture in the handling of the pebble (a blow struck at 90 degrees, to which corresponded *one* sharp edge and a technical consciousness). With the Archanthropian stereotype, the gesture is combined with others: "This [acquisition] was more than simply the addition of something new, for it implied a good deal of foresight on the part of the individual performing the sequence of technical operations" (Leroi-Gourhan 1993, 97). Anticipation was present from the start, from the first gesture, with somewhat less foresight. But what does this "good deal of foresight" mean? As soon as there is any sort of anticipation, in whatever "quantity," has not a qualitative threshold been surpassed that should first be described for itself before wishing or being able to measure it? If it is possible to measure this "thing," should one not know what is being measured?

Because it is affected with anticipation, because it is nothing but anticipation, a gesture is a gesture; and there can be no gesture without tools and artificial memory, prosthetic, outside of the body, and constitutive of its world. There is no anticipation, no time outside of this passage outside, of this putting-outside-of-self and of this alienation of the human and its memory that "exteriorization" is. *The question is the very ambiguity of the word "exteriorization"* and the hierarchy or the chronological, logical, and ontological preeminence that it immediately induces: if indeed one could speak of exteriorization, this would mean the presence of a preceding interiority. Now, this interiority is nothing outside of its exteriorization: the issue is therefore neither that of an interiority nor that of exteriority—but that of an originary complex in which the two terms, far from being opposed, compose with one another (and by the same token are posed, in a single stroke, in a single movement). Neither one precedes the other, neither is the origin of the other, the origin being then the coming into adequacy [*con-venance*] or the simultaneous arrival of the two—which are in truth the same considered from two different points of view. We shall later name this structure the *complex of Epimetheus*, and shall see that for Simondon it is a question of a transductive relation. A "prosthesis" does not supplement something, does not replace what would have been there before it and would have been lost: it is added. By pros-thesis, we understand (1) set in front, or spatialization (de-severance [*é-loignement*]); (2) set in advance, already there (past) and anticipation (foresight), that is, temporalization.

The prosthesis is not a mere extension of the human body; it is the constitution of this body *qua* "human" (the quotation marks belong to the constitution). It is not a "means" for the human but its end, and we know the essential equivocity of this expression: "the end of the human."

What is called "interiority" nevertheless indicates the problem of a potentiality of which "exteriorization" seems to be the act, that is, according to the Aristotelian theory, of which it is the truth, the sole truth. "Interiority" would be only the expectation, the call, or the promise of exteriorization—the tendency to exteriorization. Now, expectation means projection and future—anticipation. The whole problem, which thus becomes the distendedness of the past, the present, and the future, is caught in a circle in which the tool appears at one and the same time *qua* the result of anticipation, exteriorization, and *qua* the condition of all anticipation, anticipation appearing itself *qua* the interiorization of the originary fact of exteriorization. Exteriorization *qua* the act that is the horizon of anticipation, *qua* the gesture, is also an *Erinnerung*, the very moment of reflexivity, of the affection of self as a return to self. The problem remains that it does not seem that such a reflexivity may be manifestly characterized as a relation to the *grammē* as such.

Anticipation and everything it implies by way of engagement in the process of exteriorization, which was thus already there from the Australanthropian onward, receives confirmation in the next stage, the opening of latitudes in which it consists, and which perfectly coincide with the process of exteriorization:

> In the case of the Atlanthropians . . . to make a hand ax one has to choose the point on the surface of a lump of stone at which to split off the large flake whose cutting edge will be the blade of the future tool. Furthermore, a second operation has to be performed in order to reduce the initial flake to a shape that must be preexistent in the maker's mind. (Leroi-Gourhan 1993, 97)

It is the process of anticipation itself that becomes refined and complicated with technics, which is here the mirror of anticipation, the place of its recording and of its inscription as well as the surface of its reflection, of the reflection that time is, as if the human were reading and linking his future in the technical. But here two levels of the understanding of anticipation must be distinguished: the emergence of this possibility of anticipation, at the level of our analysis here, proceeds in a quasi-immobility in relation to another level, which would no longer be only *this* time of anticipation (which could be called the "operative" time) but would be a time of anticipation in which the form of anticipation itself undergoes transformation, is itself broadened out, and in which the human (be)comes (to) itself, becoming only what the technical becomes. There would be (1) anticipation insofar as without it, humans could not make tools, and (2) anticipation insofar as the fabrication of tools is not only repeated in the form of a stereotype, but evolves, is transformed, becomes differentiated.

But can these be separated? Where does the differentiation of the *what* come from? If we grant Leroi-Gourhan that there is a zoological dimension to the instrument, which explains the extreme slowness of its evolution at the beginning of the process of exteriorization, this in no way eliminates the question of how an evolution of instrumental stereotypes is possible. And if it seems obvious that this evolution is not only determined by that of the *who qua zoon*, by the *who qua* living, but also differentiated *as are all other living beings*, then the conclusion must be drawn that it is rather the evolution of the *what* that has a return effect of the *who* and governs to a certain extent its own differentiation: the *who* is not differentiated like the other living beings; it is differentiated by the nonliving (and a deferral of death by this differentiation in death), by organized but inorganic matter, the *what.* How else to explain the evolution of instrumental stereotypes, if not at the level of anticipation, since instrumentality is no more than quasi-zoological, regulated as it is in its production and its differentiation by the fact of "genetic collapse"? The question of technics is the question of time.

The issue is also that of the emergence of mortality, embedded in the very ancient ground of the instinct of conservation. If this instinct does not operate, does not produce differences, the rupture point is technicity: one can only speak rigorously of morality in the presence of exteriorization and prosthesis. But one must in all rigor speak of mortality as soon as there is exteriorization and prosthesis. Mortality, that is, anticipation (of the end), will have to be analyzed at two indissociable levels.

The Double Origin of Technical Differentiation

"Tools and skeletons evolved synchronously. We might say that with the Archanthropians, tools were still, *to a large extent*, a direct emanation of *species* behavior" (Leroi-Gourhan 1993, 97). This reference to a *specificity*, that is, to a strictly zoological character, is contradictory with what

Leroi-Gourhan will say in the second part of *Gesture and Speech*, where he will oppose the *specificity* of animal groups (as species) to the *ethnicity* of human groups, these two types of zoological groupings being governed, one by a *specific*, that is to say genetic, *differentiation*, the other by an *ethnic*, that is to say technico-socio-cultural *differentiation*. The species specific is here opposed to what we have called the epiphylogenetic.

These differentiations are opposed in the fact that in the first case the memory governing the group is internal to the organism, while in the second it is external. "Species specific" signifies "strictly zoological" by opposition to "ethnic," which means nongenetically programmed: since ethnic memory is external to the individual, it can evolve independently of genetic drift and is thus found to be in this sense temporal. Now the "specificity" Leroi-Gourhan is speaking about here has a decidedly more vague sense, and since it also lies at the origin of what will later be the ethnic differentiation of human groupings, it is therefore in no way opposed to differentiation.

The hypothesis of a "direct emanation of species behavior" stems from the fact that the stereotypes evolve with the rhythm of cortical organization—an evolution that remains at least codetermined by genetics. However, cortical evolution might well itself be codetermined by exteriorization, by the nongenetic character of the tool. There would be a double emergence of cortex and flint, a convention of the two, an arche-determination that would surpass them, would be the double work of a double différance abysmally mirrored [*s'abîmant en miroir*]. The whole problem will be to exhume the complex (transductive) dynamic of this "Epimethean complex." Saying "to a large extent" is a way of avoiding or forgetting this problem, of allowing its stakes to go unnoticed, of consequently reintroducing spirituality.

Differentiation is only possible inasmuch as the memory of the group, when human, is "external." But from the moment it is external, group memory is no longer species specific, for from that moment it is technological, the technical and the logical (or linked to "language") being only two aspects of the same property, as Leroi-Gourhan writes elsewhere. Ethnic differentiation in this sense (as species specific) can only be originary in the human, in principle, even if no trace of it can be found (Leroi-Gourhan 1993, 141), if only because *there is a possibility of language from the moment that there is a possibility of the tool, and a language cannot be conceived that is not immediately an idiomatic differentiation*, the ethnic differentiation of which it is perhaps but a case. As soon as there is exteriorization, and even if it must certainly have had a species-specific origin in which it is still caught, we are precisely no longer simply in the specific, but in the process of a differentiation between (human) groups governed by techno-logical and idiomatic, if not "ethnic," "laws." The fact that we do not see the differences, that we are not able to identify them, does not mean that they are nonexistent. Genetic differentiation still continues. The problem is, then, to know how these two levels of differentiation are articulated.

The idea of ethnic difference as the proper trait of humanity in the totality of the living is a tenuous one. Perhaps we see appearing today a humanity in which ethnic differentiation is on the way out on account of deterritorialization, supposing ethnicity to be of territorial essence. It seems to us more prudent to speak of idiomatic differentiation, whatever the level at which it operates: individual or group (ethnic, but also technical, etc.), and not only language-related differentiation.

Leroi-Gourhan opposes two sorts of intelligence, technical and nontechnical. He affords himself this distinction not only because of the problem he has in thinking anticipation (of which the idiomatic is but another name), but also because he had stated in *Man and Matter* that there were *de facto universal technical types, factual technical universals*, tendencies cutting through the diversity of cultures and imposing themselves in a process similar to that of Simondon's concretization. As a result, the technical differentiation effected through these tendencies is no longer cultural in the ethnic sense, but still is in the nonnatural sense. Does not this differentiation, however, remain idiomatic in origin?

If Leroi-Gourhan does not focus on the problem posed here by the approximate use of the phrase "species specific," as if it were not a problem for him, the reason is that he will himself reintroduce everything he had elsewhere helped to drive out, namely an *opposition between the spiritual and the moral*, on the one hand, and the *technicomaterial or technophysical*, on the other. He will end up saying: technological evolution is *essentially* of zoological origin, and *elsewhere* there is a "nontechnical," reflexive and symbolic "intelligence." Where will this intelligence come from? Why was it not playing any role in the anticipation that all exteriorization presupposes?

"To a large extent" ("tools were still, to a large extent, a direct emanation of species behavior") means: up to a certain point, not entirely—yet in truth, one should say: no longer at all. What governs exteriorization *qua* evolution (as differentiation) is not species specific because anticipation is the measure, that is, the limit, of what Leroi-Gourhan called a "large extent." To be sure, this new form of evolution still has genetic consequences, is still counterconditioned by these consequences, but the genetic no longer governs: Leroi-Gourhan uses this expression ("to a large extent") to designate what we have called codetermination. If he does not wish to say that it is no longer at all a question of specific determination (although the zoological evolution of the cortex yet has this role), this is also because he refuses to place the origin of human evolution in human creativity, that is, in a creative "consciousness."

His reasoning must be refused when it comes down to giving to the anticipation of archaic humans only an operative role and then rediscovering a nontechnological element in the human, a "creative consciousness," and all the implications thereof, at a more evolved "level" of humanity, as if Leroi-Gourhan himself ended up admitting that archaic humans will finally not have been fully human, and thus not humans at all. If this is the meaning of his contestation of the unity of the human, then, since it issues in a determination of two types of humanity on the basis of a quite traditional opposition between technics and intellect, it cannot be accepted. From the absence of unity in the human, it would be better to conclude instead that the human can only be defined negatively, by the trait of this technical inhumanity that allows it to be differentiated without, however, permitting its identification. This impossibility of anything but a phantasmatic identification is "the mirror stage."

The opposition between the two levels of anticipation leads Leroi-Gourhan to posit that before *Homo sapiens*, the human had only technical intelligence at his disposal—technical, as opposed to reflective, individual, spiritual, essentially nontechnical intelligence, the passage from *Homo faber* to *Homo sapiens* being linked to cortical deployment. This is a strange approach, to assign a determining role—so severely criticized earlier—to the brain. It is all the more strange if lithic equipment is an "extension of the skeleton"; if the skeleton has always been in advance upon the nervous system, equipment should, quite on the contrary, determine the cortical fulfillment rather than be determined by it.

From the Zinjanthropian to Neanderthal man, a cortical differentiation as well as a lithic differentiation is effected, extending from the flaked pebble and the laurel leaves of the Neanderthalians to the biface. There is with the Neanderthalian a second rupture. We submit that between these two ruptures, cortex and equipment are differentiated *together, in one and the same movement.* The issue is that of a singular process of structural coupling[3] in *exteriorization* that we are calling an *instrumental maieutics,* a "mirror proto-stage" in the course of which the differentiation of the cortex is determined by the tool just as much as that of the tool by the cortex: a mirror effect whereby one, looking at itself in the other, is both deformed and formed in the process [*l'un se regardant dans l'autre qui le déforme s'y forme*].

Instrumental Maieutics

Exteriorization means that genetic memory and its transformation do not coincide with the memory of the stereotype and its transformation. It seems obvious that the memory of the stereotype is influenced by the transformations of genetic memory. It is no less the case that another memory is set up. The question then becomes: *where* is the memory of the stereotype kept, if not *in the material trace of the stereotype in which the preexisting tool itself consists, repeated, duplicated by its "maker" and guiding the latter much more than being guided by him or her*? In this sense, the archaic cortex and equipment are codetermined in a structural coupling of a particular sort. The issue is to know the kind of repetition at work in the duplication of stereotypes down through generations of archaic humans, how it is distinguished from genetic duplication, in what way differences play and are inscribed in the duplication, and where they come from. But it is certainly not because the technological is the guide here that one must conclude with the specific or the zoological. In the process and in its evolution, the human undoubtedly remains the agent of differentiation, even though it is guided by the very thing it differentiates, even though it discovers itself and becomes differentiated in that process, in short, is invented or finds its image there, its *imago,* being here neither a phantasm nor a simulacrum—as it always is when describing technics. Yet can one then measure what is therefore said of the human, of (the absence of) its unity and its essence?

It is undoubtedly a question of an "unconscious" process, analogous from this point of view to a zoological process. But the issue is not just one of analogy. Leroi-Gourhan attests to this fact when he ends up acknowledging that in this process "individual intelligence . . . certainly played some part" (1993, 97).

Reading these contradictorily approximate remarks, one feels unavoidably that the issue has been extremely simplified—as though the alternative were between individual intelligence and zoological determination. The question must be asked: what type of anticipation does a projection-exteriorization of the lithic type, as memory support, make possible? For there is a history of techno-logical possibilities of anticipation—which is the history of the different mirror stages in which humanity reflects itself, and this is how that reflection takes place. This is the whole question of time, apprehended on the basis of the techno-logical problematic of artificial memory, always the memory of the human *qua* already-there. The already-there is the pre-given horizon of time, as the past that is mine but that I have nevertheless not lived, to which my sole access is through the traces left of that past. This means that there is no already-there, and therefore no relation to time, without artificial memory supports. The memory of the existence of the generations that preceded me, and without which I would be nothing, is bequeathed on such supports. This is the memory of past experience, of past epigeneses that are not lost, contrary to what occurs in a strictly biological species. The epiphylogenetic structure makes the already-there and its appropriation possible, as reappropriated expropriation, a maieutics of "exappropriation": flint, the object of work and of the project of anticipation, is also what will keep the memory of this experience, of this epigenesis—time being the process of modification of the industrial stereotype, the repetitive anticipation of the stereotype being only the arche-form of this temporality, a form certainly embryonic and privative of anticipation, but nonetheless the only form in which anticipation is effected. A very embryonic temporality: the already-there of the Zinjanthropian perhaps comes down to this pebble that is clenched in his hand—and that is his poor world. But this is already no longer the poverty of the world of which Heidegger speaks in another context.

Neglecting the crucial nature of these questions, Leroi-Gourhan reintroduces the very metaphysical notion of *Homo faber*, in a movement that can be found again, for example, in Georges Bataille (1979), a notion opposed to that of *Homo sapiens*. This opposition between technicity and intellect is, however, contradicted by the role given later to writing, as technics, in the constitution of thought.

The neurotechnological dimension indubitably present in the dynamic of the process should be studied as a particular aspect of a thoroughly singular apparatus of memorization, which neither classic zoology nor classic sociology is able to come to terms with, and in which one sees to what type of prosthetic supports of anticipation the given neurophysiological supports correspond, without overestimating or misunderstanding the importance of this question (as Leroi-Gourhan himself stresses elsewhere). Either the Zinjanthropian is nothing but a prehominid who cannot anticipate, that is, who is not in time and who in no case accomplishes its future since it has none, no more than does "the man of pure nature"; or else the human is human from the Zinjanthropian onward, in which case there is technico-intellectual intelligence as such in a single stroke. The latter means that there is anticipation in the full sense of the term, just as there is idiomatic differentiation (if not yet ethnic differentiation), and no longer simply species-specific differentiation ("individual intelligence" means nothing else than the possibility of such idiomatic differentiation).

Always and Again the Second Origin

The Neanderthalian skull is an expansion of anticipatory capacities. Extension or expansion of capacities here means: the increase in performances of foresight, in the efficiency of anticipation, and not "greater" anticipation, for access to anticipation is not quantifiable. Only efficiency is. Access to anticipation is access to the possible. The efficiency of access to the possible does not so much reside in the organization of the cortex itself as in this organization inasmuch as it is reflected in the flint mirror, opening it onto such efficiency, measured by Leroi-Gourhan in the centimeters of cutting edge obtained per kilo of flint.

Continuing at this Neanderthalian stage his description of the evolution of lithic industry, Leroi-Gourhan underscores a refinement of anticipatory possibilities, still linked to cortical becoming, and especially sensitive in the case of the Levalloiso-Mousterian prototype, for which "extraction of the point required at least six series of operations performed in strict sequence, each series being conditional upon the others and presupposing a rigorous plan" (Leroi-Gourhan 1993, 100). This foresight allows for a much greater exploitation of matter since the initial lump, for all its status as tool, becomes the source of tools (with the intermediary stages).

Clarifying here the relation between "technical intelligence" and the organization of the cerebral cortex, and adding that this Neanderthalian neurological equipment is, for technical intelligence, identical to our own, Leroi-Gourhan introduces his thesis of a "not strictly technical intelligence" and its correlate: a consciousness no longer "technical."[4] One wonders whence such a consciousness emerges, and what it means as an event in technological evolution understood as an essential process of exteriorization. Leroi-Gourhan himself is from the start critical of, as if to free himself from, the shortcuts that religious as well as rationalist thinking afford themselves to explain the emergence of "consciousness" (the miraculous artifice is just as suitable to rationalist determinism, which, *qua* teleology, places the human at the end of an ascension, and *qua* an anthropocentrism, leaves the central status of the human inexplicable and unexplained—even if it this status is no longer that of a creature made in God's image but that of "life becoming conscious of itself," or that of its "opposition to nature," etc.). But what is Leroi-Gourhan's strategy here? The issue is less that of criticizing the miracle thesis than that of showing the humanity of the human before religiosity, even if it is not the fully human (not a *Homo sapiens* but a *Homo faber*), and this is exactly what the miraculous solution enables theologians to avoid thinking, since they inscribe the criteria of humanity within religiosity. However, the question remains whether Leroi-Gourhan may not be satisfied here with a new artifice for the problem's solution—precisely that of the opposition *faber/sapiens*, or *technics/spirituality*. For the second "passage" is at bottom that of access to this "nontechnical intelligence," to which Leroi-Gourhan himself unreservedly subscribes, but which he then fails to question: everything he has been able to tell us by way of "an explanation" of technical intelligence brings no light to the question of the emergence of the so-called "nontechnical" intelligence. In the same stroke, an enigmatic second origin must have taken place. The whole purchase gained by the analysis of "exteriorization" for the understanding of the rise of the technical, which establishes that its rise is not the fruit of a creative intelligence, is lost again with the restoration of a nontechnical intelligence that is considered creative.

The critique of Rousseau consisted in saying that the human is not a spiritual miracle that would be added to a previously given body of the primate. Now, with the second origin, something is "added" to the technological: the *symbolic*, or the *faculty of symbolization*, without an understanding of its provenance. We know the origin of the technological supplement because it has no need of the spiritual, simply extending the evolutional tendency by other means, following phyletic lines embedded in the deepest organizational transformations of vertebrates. The tendency will only pursue this extension beyond the second origin, without ever depending on what the origin adds to it. Without any relation, consequently, with technical intelligence, which derives finally and exclusively from the zoological movement—the spirit—the truly intellectual intelligence, "reflective intellectuality," "not related to mere survival," *freed from the instinct of conservation.* This is the real exteriorization, if one can thus express the actual exit from the profoundly *natural* movement that the technical tendency essentially remains:

> [With] the Paleoanthropians . . . we witness the first upsurge of *new aptitudes of the brain* that both counterbalance and stimulate technicity. . . . The *reflective intelligence,* which not only grasps the *relationship between different phenomena* but is capable of *externalizing a symbolic representation* of that relationship, was the ultimate acquisition of the vertebrates. It cannot be conceived of before the anthropoid age. . . . This all happens, *on the plane of "gratuitous" intellectual operations,* as if the gradual development of the frontal and prefrontal areas entailed a *progressively growing faculty for symbolization.* (Leroi-Gourhan 1993, 107, my emphasis)

Rousseau went astray in thinking that technical exteriorization was an exit from the movement of pure nature, for in making tools, the man of pure nature adds nothing, or rather, he pursues a tendential movement of additions and new organizations which is that of pure nature. But as in Rousseau, in Leroi-Gourhan *Homo faber* is fundamentally only an animal. Technological organization only pursues the zoological work. The *veritable gap* is in the uprise of "gratuitous" reflective intelligence, of this "activity that surpasses technical motricity" and that frees itself of the zoological by avoiding the constraint of the pure instinct of conservation. There is a *technical reflexivity,* completely given over to survival behavior, and a *symbolic reflexivity,* purified of the *quasi-instinctive* useful finality governing technical evolution. It is clear that the spiritual only comes *after* the technical, just like the grave. How is such a great interval bridged? Here again, the leap corresponds to the acquisition of a new stage of cortical organization.

The hitch in such a logic is of the same nature as what Leroi-Gourhan discovers in Rousseau. What the latter sees coming to be added to the physical was already there before the first origin: technical exteriorization was but the pursuit of the very movement of life. Now, exactly the same can be said on the subject of the "second origin": there is no such origin because technical differentiation presupposes full-fledged anticipation, at once operative and dynamic, from the Australanthropian onward, and such anticipation can only be a relation to death, which means that symbolic intellectuality must equally be already there. Reflective intellectuality is not added to technical intelligence. It was already its ground. By taking on new forms, forms with which we are familiar, it only pursues itself in new prosthetic configurations (to the nature of which we shall return later). Certainly, the installation of this apparatus presupposes a "coming to fruition," takes "time" just as the opening of the cortical fan did not take place in a day. What is important is to recognize the threshold from which anticipation and reflexivity deploy themselves, rather than to evaluate the "rate of fulfillment": this threshold is beyond all doubt "exteriorization," which must not be understood as a rupture with nature but rather as a new organization of life—life organizing the inorganic and organizing itself therein by that very fact. *Nature must be understood differently, and the greatest vigilance with respect to oppositions is called for—even if—and nothing is more difficult—the contestation of oppositions must not eliminate the genetics of differences.* How is the *evolution* of techniques to be imagined without a play, without a degree of latitude—a precise degree, however minute—in the general behavioral stereotypes that implement the instinct of conservation? Leroi-Gourhan himself said as much in conceding awkwardly that "individual intelligence . . . certainly plays some role" in the morphogenesis of stereotypes. A distinction should perhaps be made here between anticipation for survival and anticipation *qua* the production of difference, or *qua* the productive repetition of a divergence. There is certainly a kind of "privative" form of anticipation. But this is only possible to the extent that the possibility of an anticipation in the full sense of the term is already opened up (as productive of difference, as "différance differed and deferred," as a rupture in life in general *qua* différance, but not with life), a possibility that is opened however minutely, in a darkness as black as one will, but that is already the possibility of a divergence and therefore something of a projection of a "symbolic" type rather than of a type of "survival behavior." In this respect, the Rousseauist thematic of perfectibility, already inscribing the aporia of the fall in the center of pure origin, was much more subtle than the reasoning of the anthropologist. And that Leroi-Gourhan thought he could leave it aside is all the more surprising given that in the second volume of *Gesture and Speech* he anticipates the pursuit of exteriorization as an actual derealization (for example, as a regress of the hand)[5] and at the same time as an "exteriorization" of the "nervous system," a projection initiated on the basis of an analysis of writing that, already at the end of volume one, totally linked the realization of reflexivity, *qua* rationality and philosophy, to the linear process of the (technical) recording of traces.

To clarify the meaning of "symbolic" is to introduce the question of mortality:

> Archaeological evidence of such activity—which goes beyond technical motor function— . . . [is] the earliest of an aesthetic or religious character, [and] can be classified in two groups as reactions to death and reactions to shapes of an unusual or unexpected kind.[6]

This unique and incontestable relation to death, through the body of the deceased itself, in which the incommensurability (of the body) of the other is manifested in its passage to the state of a corpse that cannot be left simply to decompose, *is linked by Leroi-Gourhan here again to a state of cortex development.* A few archaeological elements witness a symbolic activity, quite rare but incontestable, whereby the status of *the last Paleoanthropians was "transitional . . . in what we regard as the sphere of human thought proper"* (Leroi-Gourhan 1993, 112, my emphasis). These are the humans that "invite us to the opening of a new world, that of symbolic thought." This new reference to cortical development, which offers no explanation but is given as a fact concealing that pre-sapian technical development, remaining completely determined by the zoological, remains itself and in the same stroke unexplained; this final state of cortex development opens "a new world," which is also the opening of a language already our own.

The Language of the Almost Human

The prehominids (*Homo faber*) would not necessarily have had the feeling of death, yet it was immediately necessary to form the hypothesis that they could speak. They already speak, without anticipating, for all that, their own end. They already speak, without, however, having access to the symbolism opposed to simple technical intelligence. This statement or affirmation is all the more strange since no language exists that is not already symbolic, as Leroi-Gourhan himself will say. He is strangely obliged here, at a moment when he has specified the nature of the second origin, to go back prior to it, to the age of the language of the "prehominids," which he will limit to a simple *play of technical symbols.* As if a symbol could be "simply technical."

The question of language is above all a question of the "neuromotor organization and the quality of cerebral projections. The answer to the problem of language does not lie in the mandible but in the brain" (Leroi-Gourhan 1993, 112). This returns to the question of the symbol, but in a different sense than previously. Against apparently everything that has been argued so far, developing, albeit in a perfectly provisional analysis, what he had already affirmed at the beginning, that is, "the hand frees speech," Leroi-Gourhan now maintains that *there is symbolization with the advent of exteriorization* by repeating that there is language with the advent of technics, and therefore that technical activity and symbolic activity are indissociable:

> *Humans . . . can make tools as well as symbols, both of which derive from the same process, or, rather, draw upon the same basic equipment in the brain.* This leads us back to conclude, not only that language is as characteristic of humans as are tools, but also that both are the expression of the same intrinsically human property. (Leroi-Gourhan 1993, 113, my emphasis)

This far-ranging affirmation is immediately challenged by what then follows: In what respect are these symbols not those of nontechnical intelligence? In the respect that the issue here is not "technical language." There is a "technical language" just as there is a "technical intelligence" and a "technical consciousness": "technical progress has gone hand in hand with progress in the development of technical language symbols" (Leroi-Gourhan 1993, 114). This "organic link" between equipment and language "appears to be strong enough to justify crediting the Australopithecinae and the Archanthropians with language at a level corresponding to that of their tools" (114), and to their technical intelligence, which is in no way dependent on the existence of a "nontechnical intelligence." In short, language is the product of the zoological evolution of forms. Now, just as anticipation, relation to the future, is immediately relation to all future, to the possible *qua* the in-finity of possibility, is not language immediately all language—and perhaps the fruit of an intelligence belonging to what Leroi-Gourhan calls reflective intellectuality, "spirituality"?

What do expressions such as "technical language symbols" mean; to what extent do they not necessarily call for (or not themselves consist in) "nontechnical" symbols? For Leroi-Gourhan, this means: a language that would only express concrete situations (a fable very close to the ideas developed by Rousseau in his *Essay on the Origin of Language*, and more generally, by most philosophical genetic accounts of language). But we know, furthermore, and have known for quite some time, that there is language only when it is constituted by signs that are not simply signals, as Leroi-Gourhan will concede. Now a sign that is not a signal is a symbol designating a generality, a conceptual class, always already an "abstraction," and not a unique and singular referent—for in that case there would have to be as many signs as there are realities to designate; we would have an infinity of signs; and there would simply no longer be this general and abstract economy in which language consists and which allows it to name, in an indefinite combination of a finite ensemble of signs, an infinite reality. All language, being essentially finite and able nevertheless to account for an a priori indefinite and *quasi*-infinite reality, is necessarily and immediately the implementation of a process of abstraction and generalization. A "concrete language" is therefore a contradictory concept. What is more, Leroi-Gourhan's very remarks tend toward this conclusion. Such a process (the appearance of language) is only possible, once again, from the advent of a capacity of anticipation, which is also the capacity of putting-in-reserve, of memorization *qua* the possibility of being affected by a *past that lasts*—and this is why the word, like the tool, "is preserved to be used on later occasions":

> The operations involved in making a tool anticipate the occasions for its use and . . . the tool is preserved to be used on later occasions. The same is true of the difference between signal and word, the permanence of a concept being comparable to that of a tool although its nature is not the same. (Leroi-Gourhan 1993, 114)

"The material situation triggering" (114) the behavior of the great apes, precisely because it remains in essence and for all time "concrete," immune from the attack of distension, is never susceptible in any way of giving rise to language or technics, which would suppose an originary entry into "abstraction," into the apprehension of a generality, again, however minute it may be: the simple fact that a word lasts, and serves for the designation of different concrete situations while remaining the same word, means that all words are immediately generalizations.[7] (Like all concern *qua* the horizon of utensility, all enunciation presupposes an already-there that is also and always a still-there.) Now, how are these analyses to be reconciled with the hypothesis of two stages in archaic language, one that only expresses "concrete situations" and is thus found stymied on the threshold of access to generality and to abstraction, and the other, with the Neanderthalians, in which "the exteriorization of nonconcrete symbols took place"? When the splintering of the unity of the human appeared *qua* the consequence of exteriorization, we understood that the definition of the human was not in the unity of its originary "interiority" but in the work of the outside as a process of differentiation. Now it turns out that for Leroi-Gourhan this also, indeed above all, meant that there is a "prehominid" humanity that is not a full-fledged humanity: an almost human humanity in opposition to which the unity of present-day humanity can be described *qua* a spiritual being.

The relation between technics and language is established with the concept of operating sequence, on the use of which the following passage, reviewing the entire hypothesis, must be quoted *in extenso*:

> Technics involves both gestures and tools, sequentially organized by means of a "syntax" that imparts both fixity and flexibility to the series of operations involved. This operating sequence is suggested by memory and comes into being as a product of the brain and the physical environment. If we pursue the *parallel with language*, we find a similar process taking place. On the basis of what we know of techniques from pebble culture to Acheulean industry, we could adopt the hypothesis of a language whose complexity and wealth of concept corresponded approximately to the level of those techniques. The language of Zinjanthropus, with his single series of technical actions and small number of operating sequences, would then have had a complexity and wealth of symbols scarcely greater than that of the gorilla's vocal signals, but, unlike the latter, *it would have been composed of already available and not totally determined symbols.* The operating sequences of the Archanthropians with their doubles series of actions and their five or six different tool forms were already much more complex, and the language we may credit them with was considerably richer, though probably still limited to expressing concrete situations. . . . The exteriorization of nonconcrete symbols took place with the Neanderthalians, and technical concepts were thenceforth overtaken by

> concepts of which we have only manual operating evidence—burial, dyes, curious objects. This evidence, however, is sufficient to establish with certainty that thought was being applied to areas beyond that of purely vital technical motor function. (Leroi-Gourhan 1993, 114–15, my emphasis)

Is it possible to say simultaneously that there are available but not totally determined symbols and that they are linked to the expression of concrete situations? This would be to maintain the contradiction that there is first the possibility of generalization (of indetermination), and that this generalization is not a generalization, since it remains caught in a particularity opposed to the generality. Now, either this particularity is determined as particular against a horizon of generality, against the backdrop of which it outlines itself—and in this case the generality is already there and language is already general—or else there is simply no expression, no situation nor any particularity. Expression is the possibility of generalization, that is, of anticipation *qua* intellectualization. The symbol is always already an "intellectual," "general" symbol, and never simply the "technical symbol" of a merely technical language—and it is always with such adverbs that thought deals offhandedly with its limits. Moreover, all operating sequences, *qua* combinatories, already presuppose such a possibility.

This new opposition between technical and concrete language, on the one hand, and nontechnical language in general, on the other, is parallel to the idea of restrained anticipation that governed the above analysis of tool fabrication and its evolution, as well as to the resulting opposition between technical and reflective intelligence and spiritual and individual intelligence. All of this being perfectly coherent, but, *as with Rousseau, under the sway of "almost" and of "merely,"* is articulated around the idea that with the Neanderthalians a qualitative threshold is crossed, a second origin is stamped, and the origin of this origin is merely cortical. But this explains almost nothing, indeed nothing at all.

With the advent of the second origin, there would be a direct link between spiritual symbolization *qua* the possibility of generalization and inhumation. This symbol, constituted in the relation to death, will also be the emergence of purely cultural differentiation. The point in opposing *Homo sapiens* and *Homo faber* is to show that paltry prehominid language does not yet contain the possibility of idiomatic differentiation, while the "Neanderthalians' language probably differed only slightly from language as we know it today" (Leroi-Gourhan 1993, 115). If one postulates the nonabstraction of prehominid language as attached to the concreteness of situations, its indifferentiation is lost in the same move. Such a language, not being produced as a process of individuation, is without play or latitude, without any possibility of signification: it is a mute language; it says nothing. It is similar to those tools that would be put to no use, for the use of tools is already essentially the variation of possible usage of the tools, and unquestionably an element of differentiation of the tools themselves. The idiomaticity of language and the evolutional dynamic of tools at the second level of anticipation derive from the same possibility—the very possibility that Leroi-Gourhan refuses to accord the "prehominids." But this totally contradicts what *Gesture and Speech* will establish in its second volume.

Memories of the Rupture

Only when the following has been granted can instinct and intelligence be differentiated:

> The problem of grouping would dominate the question of what is animal and what is human. Society, whether animal or human, would be seen as maintained within a body of "traditions" whose basis is neither instinctive nor intellectual but, to varying degrees, zoological and sociological at one and the same time. (Leroi-Gourhan 1993, 221)

This means that the rupture in which exteriorization consists must be understood as the emergence of a new organization of memory, as the appearance of new memory supports:

> If it is true to say that the species is the characteristic form of animal grouping and the ethnic group of human grouping, then a particular form of memory must correspond to each body of traditions. (221)

It is by freeing itself from genetic inscription that memory at once pursues the process of liberation and inscribes thereupon the mark of a rupture—on stones, walls, books, machines, madeleines, and all forms of supports, from the tattooed body itself to instrumentalized genetic memories, dis-organized, made inert [*inertifiées*] as it were, then reorganized, manipulated, stored, rationalized, and exploited by the life industries named "biotechnologies," including the holographic memories that the information-processing industry is planning. An inscription of memory through rupture, the inscription of the rupture in memory. The rupture is but the memory of the rupture, is but the effects of the traces it engenders.

A question of memories combining themselves with programs, modes of programming:

> What is at issue . . . is not the contrast between instinct and intelligence but only the opposition of two modes of programming, one of which {—the insect mode—} involves a maximum of genetic predetermination and the other—the human mode—apparently none at all. (Leroi-Gourhan 1993, 222)

From this it must not be understood that programmatics would be determining for the animal while exteriorization would issue in the suspension, as well as the indetermination, of programs. If the theme of indetermination returns here, it is under the condition of a new "mode of programming." For it to be understood, three types of nonhuman living beings must be distinguished, whence, from type to type, extended possibilities of choice appear: the ant "chooses" more than the worm; the vertebrate "chooses" more than the ant. In each case, a superior level is set up while an identical behavioral ground is conserved at the inferior level, and above all, in each of these cases the possibilities of "choice" are not truly choices: they are genetic selections of possible responses inscribed in the patrimony as virtual memory, and actualized in individuals as phenotypic imprints bringing on the encounter of somatic plasticity with the actual vital milieu. From the worm to the vertebrate a certain "latitude of maneuver" of memory comes to the fore, witnessed by possibilities of conditioning and training. An individual memory is then constituted, registering past "experience" (the adaptation of the individual), overdetermined by the nonspecific [unrelated to species] hereditary genetic capital responsible for the irregular efficiency of the various lineages of a species, the whole being subjected to the pressure of natural selection. This mnemo-instinctive apparatus exists in humans to the extent that the human is also animal, and "a significant part of human activity is instinctual" (Leroi-Gourhan 1993, 224).

On the backdrop of this instinctive layer, the first constitutive layer of humanity, one must distinguish intelligence, which presupposes the existence of language at two superior levels. These three levels are the

> species-related, socioethnic, and individual. At the species-related level, human technical intelligence is connected with the degree of development of

> the nervous system and the genetic programming of individual aptitudes. . . . At the socioethnic level, human intelligence behaves in a wholly particular and unique manner in that, transcending both individual and species-related limits, it creates a collective organism with astonishingly rapid evolutional properties. For the individual, the degree of socioethnic constraint is as imperative as the zoological constraint that causes one to be born *Homo sapiens*, but the terms of the former are different from those of the latter to the extent that, under certain conditions, they admit of the possibility of a certain degree of individual liberation.
>
> At the individual level, the human species is equally unique because, having received from the human cerebral apparatus the ability to compare between situations translated into symbols, the individual is capable of freeing him or herself symbolically from both genetic and socioethnic bonds. (Leroi-Gourhan 1993, 227)

These three layers inseparably form the ground of memories from which the "technical behavior of humans" becomes possible. Yet here a certain ambiguity remains: if the second level undoubtedly and directly concerns the technical possibilities of the human, this is less evident for the third, which seems to target mainly symbolic activity. If it is granted that the true symbol is spiritual, and if the question here concerns only the symbol (the second origin), the third level will no longer concern symbolic activity proper. The issue, on the contrary, is symbolic activity, insofar as it accompanies technical activity from the very beginning: "technics and language being two aspects of the same property" (the process of exteriorization) (114). This individual level will therefore become that of differentiation in general—of the symbol as well as of tools, which moreover does not presuppose a creative consciousness, for no linguist has ever denied that speech is engendered at the individual level of diachronic-idiomatic variation, nor ever contested the Saussurian affirmation that the diachronico-idiomatic drift of languages escapes the will of individuals effecting it.

The "socioethnic" constraints are for the human grouping (the ethnic group) this new "modality of programming," constituting *qua* program something of a social analog of the genetic constraints of the animal grouping (the species)—but only an analogue, for whereas the animal is not able to free itself from genetic constraints, the human individual, with regard to socioethnic constraints, constantly can, although only up to a certain point. This modality of programming of, and by, memory, the consequence of the passage from liberation to exteriorization, concretizes its new possibilities at the individual level, reinserting them, when they are totally realized, into the socioethnic level. The ensemble of the process, which describes idiomatic differentiation, derives from anticipation, and it is in the exappropriation of the relation between ethnic constraints and their idiomatic appropriation—being also the more or less slow transformation of the rules in which they consist—that the evolution of ethnic cultures and their differentiation are effected. "Rapid and continuous evolution could apparently be achieved only by breaking the link between species and memory, an exclusively human solution" (Leroi-Gourhan 1993, 228). After exteriorization, the process of differentiation then undergoes an essential shift from the level of the species to that of the individual, who is undetermined in its behavioral possibilities, if not in its zoological limits and in the already-there of the world in which it lives, from which it inherits, to which it must answer, and which it appropriates by altering it:

> Individuals at birth are faced with a body of traditions that belong to their ethnic group; a dialogue takes place, from childhood, between the individual and the social organism. Tradition is as biologically indispensable to the human species as genetic conditioning is to insect societies. Ethnic survival relies on routine; the dialogue taking place produces a balance between routine and progress, routine symbolizing the capital required for the group's survival and progress the input of individual innovations toward a better survival. (Leroi-Gourhan 1993, 228–29)

What is tradition's situation today? If it is essential to survival, how shall we survive? Must new forms of "tradition" be thought up?

Idiomatic Indifference

The question is time, becoming *qua* the bringing into play of the nonprogrammed, the im-probable, and destiny *qua* nonpredestination. The temporality of the human, which marks it off among the other living beings, presupposes exteriorization and prostheticity: there is time only because memory is "artificial," becoming constituted as already-there *since* [from the point of: *depuis*] its "having been placed outside of the species." And this "since" must be taken literally: inheriting the name "human" is inheriting the entire past already there, everything that has taken place, since the "appallingly ancient." This is where two "origins" are marked, where a division is inscribed between two "coups": the "Zinjanthropian" and the "Neanderthal." With the second "coup," according to Leroi-Goürhan, society makes its appearance:

> From the moment of the disappearance of the prefrontal ridge, a characteristically human evolution led to the birth of a technical world that drew its resources outside the confines of genetic evolution. From the emergence of *Homo sapiens*, the constitution of an apparatus of social memory dominates all problems of human evolution. (1993, 229)

What are our objections to all this? On the whole, nothing. Everything, if the problem is posed in terms of anticipation. There is anticipation from the Zinjanthropian onward, even if the latter is only realized under conditions of cerebral incompletion: there is already confrontation or reflection, but in such technical and cerebral conditions as remain today profoundly alien to us—and it is the very strangeness of the reflexivity that is here given over to be experienced. In theory the progress of the cortical fan excludes neither that archaic technical evolution already supposes the exteriorization of memory—in the tool itself, but also in language—nor that it supposes an already generalizing symbolization, full-fledged anticipation, albeit in a mode essentially veiled for us. The opposition between technical and nontechnical intelligence is practical for descriptive purposes, but superficial. Contrary to what is proposed here by Leroi-Gourhan, for whom society is established only at the end of corticalization, the human is social from the moment of the Zinjanthropian, even if this socialization does not present the forms with which we are familiar. It is indeed from the Zinjanthropian onward that "the placing-outside of the zoological species of ethnic memory" takes place. If this were not the case, nothing would be understandable, and all the initial hypotheses would have to be given up in a return to Rousseau.

The power of these hypotheses resides in the relations they establish between the skeleton, the brain, and tools. Their limit is in not allowing the intellectual to be thought—and therefore the process of sociotechnical differentiation in general, as being itself as well the direct product of exteriorization. Leroi-Gourhan, moreover, contests this bipartition in the last passage we shall quote. Having established that the Neanthropian stage is that of the development of prefrontal areas—the prefrontal cortex appears as "one of the principal elements of individual personality, and most neurologists believe that it plays a predominant role in controlling operations and in the powers of foresight and lucid consciousness"—he adds that concerning "the role of the prefrontal cortex as an instrument of affective regulation, before [it] was achieved, there could be no question of intelligence or thought in the fully human sense," which can only mean: such as we know it. Indeed,

> some development of the prefrontal areas may no doubt have occurred even in the most primitive Anthropians. . . . In accepting the postulate that in the case of the Australanthropians and Archanthropians, the development of techniques more or less kept pace with that of the skull, we allowed for the possibility of individual creative intelligence manifesting itself. (Leroi-Gourhan 1993, 131)

In truth, this "role of individual intelligence" has remained essentially overlooked, it has never been thoroughly "taken account of," and the question remains inadequately posed in this form: the issue is less intelligence than anticipation. Individual intelligence is not the essential question. On the basis of these specifications, which blur a too distinct boundary between the different stages of the archaic human, Leroi-Gourhan introduces his major thesis on the last stage—the preponderant role played by society: "The fact that emerges most clearly, once the freeing of the forebrain has taken place, is the importance assumed by the social group as opposed to the zoological species" (Leroi-Gourhan 1993, 131). Must this mean that society was not there before? Certainly not. That there is a dynamic in which preponderances shift is obvious. But that boundaries should be marked off in this dynamic is less satisfactory. Everything is there in a single stroke. Everything is differentiated in one coup, together. It is the *inorganic organization of memory* that constitutes the essential element, the first coup, engendering all the others and being transformed in transforming all the others in its wake. In this complex, the brain has in fact only a secondary role, in no case a preponderant one. It is one of the instances involved in the total transformation of the landscape in which the organization of the inorganic consists. It is that transformation's organic consequence. But not its cause. Furthermore, the issue is one not of a cause but of a *coup*, whose dynamic development is marked simultaneously on tools, on the cortex, on the group, and on the territories that it impregnates, occupies, or cuts across. Depending on whether one sees the boundaries or decodes the slow, mixed, apparently contradictory movements, stratified tendencies penetrating into one another, one's observations split into divergent paths.

Once corticalization is achieved, technical differentiation will totally depend upon social differentiation, and no longer on zoological differentiation at all—although its movement of development and differentiation is pursued as if it were a matter of zoological drift, since its evolution remains phylogenetic in appearance, idiomatically totally indifferent. But, in truth, technical differentiation was already social, temporal, and generalizing before the end of corticalization.

We meet once again with all of Rousseau's arguments: before, there would have been no or practically no reason (spiritual intelligence), no language (spiritual symbols), no society (ethnic groupings)—all of the attributes by which philosophy had hitherto identified humanity. Everything comes afterward, through the fall, from the coup bridging so great an interval.

The Already-There, Différance, Epiphylogenesis

To question the birth of the human is to question the birth of death, as we said at the beginning. Let us see again why by recapitulating.

At issue was thinking the "invention of the human" by setting ourselves in the very ambiguity of this expression, and thereby beginning a reflection on the concept of différance: différance is the history of life in general, in which an articulation is produced (where art, artifice, the article of the name, and the article of death resonate),[8] which is a stage of différance, and which had to be specified. The rupture is the passage from a genetic différance to a nongenetic différance, a "*phusis* differing and deferring." In order to approach the question of time as it has been set up, we anticipated the development of a concept, that of epiphylogenesis.

The "paradox of exteriorization" led us to say that the human and the tool invent each other, that there is something like a technical maieutics. Consequently, the vector of epiphylogenetics, at the dawn of hominization, is flint. The process of corticalization is achieved as a process of reflection upon this conservation of experience, upon this constitution of the past that the flint is *qua* the registering of what has come to pass, a conservation that is itself already, *qua* trace, a reflection.

The aporias that the question of anticipation open up are the very ones that constitute the paradox of exteriorization: a delay that is also an advance, the structure of the *après-coup* in which it can never be determined whether the cortex makes the flint possible or the reverse. The interior should precede the exterior, but in fact it is constituted by the latter, which therefore precedes it. Unless they are said to precede each other, to be the same thing considered from two different but already derived points of view. We are left then with the question of movement, whatever point of view is taken on the subject (at once exterior-ization and interior-ization): its provenance and its principle.

We have encountered the need to distinguish two levels in the understanding of anticipation: operative anticipation, and anticipation *qua* the differentiation of stereotypes as well as of the very form of anticipation. It is at the second level, always already implied in the first, that the question of movement arises: it is a matter of knowing the provenance of differentiation. From the Zinjanthropian to the Neanderthal, cortex and tools are differentiated together, in one and the same movement. It is a question of a singular process of structural coupling in "exteriorization," an instrumental maieutics, a "mirror proto-stage" in which the differentiation of the cortex is determined by the tool as much as that of the tool by the cortex, a mirror effect in which one, informing itself of the other, is both seen and deformed in the process, and is thus transformed. It is straightaway this couple that forms the original dynamic in a transductive relation.

The question remains whether there is an acceptable biological explanation of such a phenomenon. We must put forward here the hypothesis of an absolutely new genetic process of selection. Far from being simply determined by cortex evolution, the evolution of knapped flint determines in turn the process of corticalization. Such a hypothesis involves an attempt at elaborating a concept of artificial selection: the selection of mutations exerted at the cortical level in the context of a relation to the original milieu, mediated by the technical apparatus constituting the system of defense and predation and informing simultaneously the process of individual adaptation and the evolution of the entire species, which does not imply a heredity of acquired characteristics, even if that illusion ensues.

The point is to focus on the originality of the epigenetic process that is put in place from the moment of the appearance of tools, insofar as they are conserved in their form beyond the individuals producing or using them. (The appearance of these tools, an actual nonliving yet vital memory, organized but inorganic matter, supposes, *qua* the vector and accumulator of past epigeneses, a singular epigenetic plasticity of the cerebral structure.) In nonartificial life, nontechnical, nonarticulated by the différance of différance, all summation of epigenetic events is lost for specific memory with the loss of the individual who was their support. In the case at hand, life conserves and accumulates these events. This conservation determines the relation to the milieu and *the whole process of selection of mutations,* notably those taking place at the cortical level. Consequently, the hypothesis can be formulated that here, in apparent contradiction of the laws of molecular biology, *epigenesis exerts a powerful countereffect on the reproduction of the species, channeling or conditioning an essential part of the drive of selection.* In this case, the individual develops out of three memories: genetic memory; memory of the central nervous system (epigenetic); and techno-logical memory (language and technics are here amalgamated in the process of exteriorization).

The stereotype is as much the result as the condition of its production, both the support of the memory of operational sequences that produces it, conserving the trace of past epigenetic events that accumulate as lessons of experience, and the result of the transmission of these operational sequences by the very existence of the product as an archetype. Such is epiphylogenesis. Three types of memory should thus be distinguished, to clarify while slightly modifying Leroi-Gourhan's hypothesis of the three layers. The three types are genetic memory, epigenetic memory, and epiphylogenetic memory.

Epipylogenesis, a recapitulating, dynamic, and morphogenetic (*phylogenetic*) accumulation of individual experience (*epi*), designates the appearance of a new relation between the organism and its environment, which is also a new state of matter. If the individual is organic organized matter, then its relation to its environment (to matter in general, organic or inorganic), when it is a question of a *who,* is mediated by the organized but inorganic matter of the *organon,* the tool with its instructive role (its role *qua* instrument), the *what.* It is in this sense that the *what* invents the *who* just as much as it is invented by it.

The *Who* and the *What*

The genetic/epigenetic relation is a dimension of différance *qua* the history of life. The question then is that of a specification of différance differing and deferred, of the possibility of such specification, if it is true that Leroi-Gourhan's major point consists in putting into question a clear break between the animal and the human. His way of broaching this problem brings him back, in the final analysis, to the heart of a simple opposition, albeit one shifted to the also quite traditional level of *faber/sapiens.* He is brought back in the same stroke (the coup of the second origin) to the metaphysics of an opposition between the inside and the outside, the before and the after, of the animal human and the spiritual human, and so on. We are trying to preserve and to broach the aporetic impossibility of simply opposing the interior to the exterior in speaking of an instrumental maieutics that alone permits an understanding of how tools do not derive from a creation or from a consciousness present to itself, master of matter, but pursue a process engaged long before the rupture yet nevertheless constitute a rupture—a new organization of différance, a différance of différance. Now, if the central concept is in fact that of epiphylogenetic memory, allowing for both *the contestation of oppositions and the description and preservation of differentiations,* it does not seem to us to have any equivalent in grammatological deconstructions. We shall develop this question further on the level of linear writing. Without such a concept, it seems to us impossible to specify the différance, differing and deferring, with respect to différance in general *qua* the history of life in general, or to say what the human is or is not. We are left with the ambiguity of the invention of the human, that is, of the subject of the verb "to invent," that which holds together the *who* and the *what,* as being that which binds them while separating them; this is, then, différance—this double movement, this intersection of reflection, this reflecting whereby the *who* and the *what* are constituted as the *twin faces of the same phenomenon.*

Leroi-Gourhan misses the thematic of difference and deferral by opposing technical intelligence (*qua* the process of restrained anticipation) to the symbolic or "faculty of symbolization" *qua* the fruit of an intelligence "of a nature not related to mere survival," consisting in the complete emancipation from still *quasi*-instinctive finalities that corresponds to the movement of technics and that is an opening onto the feeling of death. In the same stroke, this coup of the second origin will have allowed the analysis of a new "différantial" dynamic to be avoided. This dynamic, in place since the Zinjanthropian, sees the opening of the feeling of death linked to a state of (late) cortex development. And in the same stroke, this opening is also that of a language already our own. Now, this question of language derives entirely from the "epiphylogenetic" level. There never was a "concrete language"; to express a situation is always to abstract it. The incoherent "nonabstraction" of "prehominid" language is nevertheless coherent with the incoherent idea that it does not express the slightest possibility of idiomatic differentiation (resulting from the point of view developed on all pre-Neanderthalian tools). But at the beginning of the second part of *Gesture and Speech*, the exteriorization of memory (the "transfer of ethnic memory outside the zoological species") implies an idiomatic "dialectic"—whereby "rapid and continuous evolution could apparently be achieved only by breaking the link between species and memory (an exclusively human solution)," a "dialogical" exchange between the individual and society (1993, 228). This analysis may, setting aside certain shifts, however essential they may be, bring us back to the Heideggerian problematic of time.

The questions posed by our reflection on technics and on its dynamic in the paleoanthropological domain in fact spring up again directly into the existential analytic (of "being-for-the-end")—and into all philosophy. Up to a certain point, it is with a similar gesture that Leroi-Gourhan separates and finally opposes, on the one hand, technicity, and on the other, the relation to death and thus "reflective" intelligence, while Heidegger opposes the time of calculation (the inauthentic time of measurement, the attempt to "determine the undetermined") and authentic time as relation to death. Starting with the critical analysis of the material proposed by Leroi-Gourhan, we can conversely imagine an existential analytic of time, an analytic of the temporal being that is Dasein, of the *who* that would be an analytic of the *prostheticity* whereby he exists and becomes embodied—of prostheticity *qua* being his already-there, or of his *already-there qua* being *essentially* prosthetic (accidental), never manifesting itself other than as a *what*—and that opens up its relation to time, far from being its denaturalization. Of this analysis, one could say that it is Heidegger's own, under the name of *facticity*. However, we shall show in the next section that this is not the case.

PART II

The Fault of Epimetheus

Introduction

At the end of the first chapter, we ended with the following question: How is the techno-logical dynamic, agent of technical epochs and organizations, articulated with the operatorlike, anthropo-logical dynamic of anticipation? How, in other words, is technicity to be constituted in terms of technological phenomenology? At the end of the last chapter this question then became: How is temporality itself constituted in terms of technicity? How is the temporality of the *who* constituted in the actuality of the *what*? We ask the question taking the operative validity of the concept of "epiphylogenesis" to be established.

If there is a temporal arche-structure—constituted in the "already there" nature of the horizon of prostheses as anticipation of the end, in the movement of exteriorization, on "collapsed zones of genetic sequencing"—then on the basis of this collapse:

1. Nothing can be said of temporalization that does not relate to the ephiphylogenetic structure put in place each time, and each time in an original way, by the already-there, in other words by the memory supports that organize successive epochs of humanity: that is, technics—the supplement is elementary, or rather elementary supplementarity *is* (the relation to) time (différance).

2. This kind of analysis presupposes an elucidation of the possibility of anticipation (of the possibility of possibility). Such an elucidation is the very object of existential analytic, which should accordingly be *interpreted in terms of the question of prostheticity.*

The above step could not be taken by jumping abruptly from anthropology to phenomenology; the initial questions are quite different from this sort of approach. We will first read various occurrences of the myth of Prometheus and Epimetheus, where an originary bond is presented that is formed between prostheticity (Prometheus, god of technics); anticipation (Prometheus, god of foresight); mortality (Prometheus, giver to mortals of *elpis*—both worry concerning the end and ignorance of the end); forgetting (the fault of Epimetheus); and reflexivity, or the "comprehension of being," as delay and deferred reaction [*après-coup*] (*ēpimētheia*, or knowledge that arises from the accumulation of experience through the mediation of past faults). From the perspective of this myth, "exteriorization" will immediately call forth socialization, considered as the relation to death or as anticipation.

§ 1 Prometheus's Liver

"What then?" I exclaimed with curiosity.
"*Who then*? you should ask!" Thus spoke Dionysus.
—Nietzsche

Any being is a *who* (existence) or a *what* (presence-at-hand in the broadest sense). {What is} the connection between these two modes of the characters of being?
—Heidegger

The Forgetting of the Forgetful

In the Greek mythology of technics, two ideas, *promētheia* and *ēpimētheia*, which stem from the name of gods, are handed down to everyday language. These ideas are organized into elements of what one might call a quasi- "existential analytic," which would have coherence in an essentially tragic, pre-Platonic, prephilosophical and premetaphysical domain—that is, in a domain where the tragic is still experienced in terms of (the astonishment at the fact that there is) technicity. This mythology falls into contradiction with metaphysics. We have seen this type of contradiction at work in Leroi-Gourhan, where he is forced to resort to the coup of a second origin and separate the moments of exteriorization and society in order to save spirit (from technical animality), all the while tying these moments back together again when distinguishing specific difference and ethnic difference. Leroi-Gourhan appears to say that exteriorization precedes socialization, but then he proceeds to identify them. In the same move, he remains ambiguous concerning the relation between language and technics, both maintaining that the one implies the other and returning to a metaphysical position with the hypothesis that true (spiritual) language can become free of (the) motricity (of technicity).

If one holds to the first hypothesis, according to which language and technics are bound to each other as two aspects of one and the same human attribute, this anthropology confronts metaphysics head-on, since metaphysics is constituted through the very formation of an opposition between *logos* and *tekhnē*, *phusis* and *nomos*, the intelligible and the sensible, asters and disasters, haps and mishaps. Thus, for metaphysics: (1) *tekhnē*, the field of artifacts, is the possibility of the arbitrary and of the worst *hubris*, of the violence of man against *phusis* when he considers himself a god; and (2) the *logos*, the site of *alētheia*, is also the *metron*, in the attention that it brings to the "as such" of a being (to its *phusis*).

The tragic Greek understanding of technics is, however, quite different. It does not oppose two worlds. It composes *topoi* that are constitutive of mortality, being at mortality's limits: on the one hand, immortal, on the other hand, living without knowledge of death (animality); in the gap between these two there is technical life—that is, dying. Tragic *anthropogony* is thus a *thanatology* that is configured in two moves [*coups*], the doubling-up of Prometheus by Epimetheus.

Epimetheus is not simply the forgetful one, the figure of essential witlessness that makes up all experience (since what happens, what has passed, must, as past, be ruminated); he is also the one who is forgotten. The forgotten of metaphysics. The forgotten of thought. And the forgotten of forgetting when thought thinks itself *as* forgetting. Whenever Prometheus is spoken of, this figure of forgetting is forgotten, which, like the truth of forgetting, always arrives too late: Epimetheus. It is astounding that this figure of deferred reaction, of the *après-coup*, of return through the failure of experience, of *ēpimētheia*, giving its name to thought as such, not only is *not* at the center of the phenomenological thinking of finitude but is starkly excluded from it.

The figure of Prometheus (to be found, for example, in Heidegger's Rectorate Discourse [Heidegger 1985]) *makes no sense by itself.* It is only consistent through its doubling by Epimetheus, who in turn doubles up on himself—first, in committing the fault of forgetting, which amounts to witlessness, distractedness, imbecility, and idiocy, and ... second, in reflecting upon it, in a re-turn that is always too late. This is the very quality of reflectivity, knowledge, wisdom, and of the quite different figure of remembering, that of experience. Everyday Greek language roots reflective knowledge in *ēpimētheia*, namely, in the essential technicity that makes up (the condition of) finitude. The absence of these figures in the existential analytic of Heidegger is both striking and rigorously necessary. For, on the one hand, the intertwining of the two figures of *promētheia* and *ēpimētheia* yields the major elements of the structure of temporality, described as being-toward-the-end, while, on the other hand, the originary, irreducible rooting of this relation in technicity, which the two figures *taken together* signify, undermines any possibility of placing in opposition authentic time and the time of calculation and concern.

Thanatology: Nothing Present-at-Hand

The question we have so far been pursuing now takes a decisive tack: any residual hint of the anthropological is abandoned in the fact that techno-logy becomes properly speaking a thanato-logy. In the Platonic dialogue of his name, Protagoras narrates the myth of Prometheus and Epimetheus in the following terms:

> Once upon a time, there existed gods but no mortal creatures. When the appointed time came for these also to be born, the gods formed them within the earth out of a mixture of earth and fire and the substances which are compounded from earth and fire. And when they were ready to bring them to the light, they charged Prometheus and Epimetheus with the task of equipping them and allotting suitable powers {*dunameis*} to each kind. Now Epimetheus begged Prometheus to allow him to do the distribution himself—"and when I have done it," he said, "you can review it." So he persuaded him and set to work. In his allotment he gave to some creatures strength without speed, and equipped the weaker kinds with speed. Some he armed with weapons, while to the unarmed he gave some other faculty and so contrived means for their preservation. To those that he endowed with smallness, he granted winged flight or a dwelling underground; to those which he increased in stature, their size itself was a protection. *Thus he made his whole distribution on a principle of compensation, being careful by these devices that no species should be destroyed.* . . . Now Epimetheus was not a particularly clever person, and before he realized it he had used up all the available powers on the brute beasts, and being left with the human race {*non-aloga*} on his hands unprovided for, did not know what to do with them. While he was puzzling about this, Prometheus came to inspect the work, and found the other animals well off for everything, but man naked, unshod, unbedded, and unarmed, and already the appointed day had come, when man too was to emerge from within the earth into the daylight. Prometheus therefore, being at a loss to provide any means of salvation for man, stole from Hephaestus and Athena the gift of skill in the arts {*ten enteknen sophian*}, together with fire—for without fire there was no means {*amekhanon*} for anyone to possess or use this skill—and bestowed it on man. In this way man acquired sufficient resources to keep himself alive, but he had no political wisdom {*sophia*}. This art was in the keeping of Zeus. . . . Through this gift man had the means of life, but

> Prometheus, so the story says, thanks to Epimetheus, had later on to stand his trial for theft.
>
> Since, then, man had a share in the portion of the gods, in the first place because of his divine kinship he alone among living creatures believed in gods, and set to work to erect altars, and images of them. Secondly, by the art which they possessed, men soon discovered articulate speech {*phonen*} and names {*onomata*}, and invented houses and clothes and shoes and bedding and got food from the earth. (Plato 1961, *Protagoras*, 320d–322a, my emphasis)

It is immediately by deviating from the equilibrium of animals, from tranquillity—a departure engendered by the fault of Epimetheus—that mortals occur. Before the deviation, there is nothing. Then the accidental event happens, the fault of Epimetheus: to have forgotten humans. Humans are the forgotten ones. Humans only occur through their being forgotten; they only appear in disappearing.

Fruit of a double fault—an act of forgetting, then of theft—they are naked like small, premature animals, without fur and means of defense, in advance of themselves, *as* advance, and also as delay (no qualities are left, everything has already been distributed). They do not yet possess the art of the political, which will be made necessary by their prematureness, directly ensuing from the technical. But this "not yet" does not imply that there will be two steps to their emergence, a time of a full origin, followed by a fall: there will have been nothing at the origin but the fault, a fault that is nothing but the de-fault of origin or the origin as de-fault [*le défaut d'origine ou l'origine comme défaut*]. There will have been no appearance except through disappearance. Everything will have taken place at the same time, in the same step.

By referring first to Jean-Pierre Vernant's reading of the poems of Hesiod, the *Theogony* and *Works and Days*, we shall have the means to interpret this first part of the Protagorean version of the myth, since the versions of Hesiod continue to inspire Protagoras's account. If the myth in the *Theogony* evokes a golden age in which humans banqueted next to the gods, this means that humans had not yet occurred, since nothing had yet occurred, the golden age lying prior to the time in which something could occur.

> {The golden age} does not oppose a state of nature to a civilized state; it erases all differences between them, presenting civilized foods as the spontaneous product of nature bestowed upon men without their having to lift a

finger, the food already cultivated, harvested, stored, cooked, and ready to be consumed. (Vernant 1979, 70)

Thus the deviation, if there is one, is not in relation to nature but in relation to the divine. Again this means that the real issue here concerns *the relation of mortals to immortality,* that *this anthropogony is in the first instance a thanatology.* Anthropogony only acquires meaning in theogony, the conflict between the Olympians and the Titans, which continues, in an underhanded way, with the struggle between Zeus and Prometheus. It is in this sense that humans participate in the divine, on the basis of the double fault, particularly that of the theft of fire, erecting altars to the gods *qua* those who are immortal. It is a religion entirely made up of trepidation at the condition of technicity (its power, implying equally the powerlessness of mortals). Before the fault, nothing had happened. The fault takes place, and everything disappears: humans, in their condition of mortality, issue from a deceitful lot given by Prometheus, to the detriment of Zeus and to the apparent benefit of humanity, whose sacrificial practices in the Greek city recall the consequences. Mortals come to be through their very disappearance, a disappearance inherent to their condition, that of dying. It is here that all divine gifts collapse upon themselves, turning into their opposite:

> The good lot that mortals congratulate themselves on (just as they congratulate themselves on the "beautiful bane" granted them by Zeus in the form of Woman) turns out in fact to be a bad lot. The trap, set by the Titan to fool Zeus, turning back against Prometheus, ends up closing upon mankind; the fire itself, the fire stolen by Prometheus, is not, despite its advantages, a gift less ambiguous than the first female creature, also attributed with powers of dangerous seduction. (41)
>
> The narrative procedure that consists in setting up a Zeus who is totally foreseeing, then showing him on two occasions surprised and fooled until his victorious counterattack, aims to unveil progressively to the reader during the course of a story in dramatic form the deceptive character of the Promethean gifts, whose ambiguous benefits turn finally against their beneficiaries. (70)

It is the theogonic dispute that lends its meaning to anthropogony, itself nothing other than a thanatology: theogony both defines im-mortals and characterizes, in antithesis, mortality.

As food rite, the sacrifice "revives the memory of the former companionship at table when, intermingled, men and gods made merry day after day at common table" (Vernant 1979, 43). This golden age, as we have seen, is not, however, an origin. It is a limit, irremediably lost, a condition both forgotten and unforgettable, since it is re-evoked and recalled antithetically by the counterimage of the Immortals, always present in their distance, a proximity nevertheless forever withdrawn, and thus, for mortals, an infinite regret in which the eternal melancholy of the *genos anthropos* is configured:

> In and through the ritual of sacrifice the distance separating mortal from immortal is opened up and perpetuated: . . . the unchanging youth of the Olympians . . . and the ephemeral form of existence that humans must henceforth assume in order to become themselves. (47)

Through sacrifice mortals are put in their place: *between* the beasts and the gods, in this in-between (between appearing and disappearing) resulting from a deviation. It is not a matter of recalling a state of nature, nor of claiming what "human nature" ought to have been; there was no fall, but a fault, no hap nor mishap, but mortality.

> For Hesiod, bringing to light the condition of humanity consists not in defining a "human nature" of which he has no idea, but in unveiling, through the narrative of the founding of the sacrifice, all the implications, immediate or distant, of this cult that regards the very status of humans, that is, the place assigned to them. (81)

The Hesiodic myth allows us to understand how the question of the community—which becomes the question of politics (ending up, in the Protagorean version, with the sending of Hermes)—is indissociable from the cult of sacrifice: the political community is solely constituted in the memory of the original sacrifice, that is, *indissociable from the Promethean fault.* It can also be seen in this context that religion and the *polis* are indissociably understood in ancient Greece in terms of mortality *qua* the originary departure from all origins, that is, *qua* technicity—an ambiguous, stolen, all too human reflection of power/potential [*puissance*]. Humans,

> like all mortal creatures, like beasts, . . . are on a different level to the gods, standing to one side, strangers to the divine sphere. Singular, however, among mortal creatures, and unlike the beasts, their mode of existence implies a con-

> stant reference to, a particular relation with the supernatural Powers. There is no city, no human life that does not set up a relation to the divine world through an organized cult, establishing thereby something like a community with it. It is this ambiguity concerning the human condition, both separate from and close to the divine, outside it and in relation to it, that Prometheus assumes in his own manner within the divine sphere itself. (49)

In other words, the duplicity of power/potential derives from the sphere of Immortals itself. And when it is carried out—an act that constitutes the fault of Prometheus, failing to stem Olympian omnipotence—it means a fall [*une déchéance*] (quite similar to the one that Heidegger's existential analytic will attempt to think) which the sacrifice recalls and whose acceptance of the fact mortals affirm in the practice of the cult. The failure of Prometheus

> does not simply turn the sacrificial rite into an act that symbolizes the complete segregation of the two races (mortal and immortal); it confers upon this separation the character of an irremediable and justified fall, one whose validity, each time by sacrificing in Promethean mode they engage in communication with the superior powers, mortals must recognize. (50)

This fall, dying, is the origin of *ēris* ("spirit of competition, jealousy, quarrelsomeness"), which takes root in the divine world itself and eternally brings to bear upon mortals the threat of dispersion, of ever-imminent war, of *stasis*. It is the political necessity for a community that always remains ready to conquer. It is the property of *ēris* which ties the condition of mortals to the genesis of Immortals; it is through *ēris* that Vernant makes the link between the *Theogony* and the pseudo-anthropogony that is the thanatology narrated in *Works and Days*:

> The drama of *ēris*, which in the *Theogony* through the intervention of the gods is directed toward and touches human beings, is matched in the *Works* by something played out directly on Boeotian soil between Hesiod and his brother Perses. (Vernant 1979, 54)

While, however, divine *ēris* is clear, unequivocal, its outcome brooking no doubt—Zeus will vanquish Prometheus, who will suffer punishment (the meaning of which we must analyze in a moment)—human *ēris* is ambiguous, like every characteristic particular to mortality, these quasi-"existentiales" proceeding from the fault of Prometheus. Complexity and duplicity will also come to form the irreducible characteristics of politics, in which conflict *qua competition* forms the dynamic factor of the community: emulation as much as the imminence of destruction, which speech will defer.

It is in these terms that *promētheia* can be seen to determine mortality, giving to ancient Greek religion and politics, as well to the tragic, their entire meaning. Mortality *is promētheia*, and ever since Zeus realized that he was being duped by Prometheus, "human existence [has been] how we see it: entirely prey to the twofold struggle, unceasingly torn between," on the one hand, the good *ēris*, which is made up of competitive emulation at work, and, on the other, fratricidal war (between Perses and Hesiod, between members of the same city, between cities) (Vernant 1979, 57). In this respect, it is somewhat astonishing to note the total neglect and forgetting of this Promethean origin, which has almost come to form the core of modern and contemporary philosophical analyses of Greek politics and religion, when Vernant has shown with utter clarity that "if the life of human beings, contrary to that of the gods, cannot shirk *ēris*, it is because *the mortal condition finds its origin and its raison d'être in the* ēris *that set Prometheus against Zeus*" (57, my emphasis).

Prometheus attempted to mislead Zeus, as a result of which there emerged the human condition. But the truth of the appearance of humanity is to be found in its disappearing: such is the vengeance of Zeus. The golden age is succeeded by a period of ills in which humans no longer dispose of anything ready to hand, no longer have anything, that is, to put in their mouth, now irremediably bent to the yoke of *ponos*, the labor that must be spent in payment for the lack of origin, for corn to appear. For, from now on, *bios* remains hidden in the belly of the earth, disappearing yet again and forever, like mortals themselves, while the obligation to work, to *handle instruments*, will reappear over and over again for these same mortals, until, grown old through *care*, they at last pass away.[1]

Outside Itself

We can now return to the first moment of the Protagorean version of the myth. There was the first fault, Epimetheus's forgetting, then the second fault, Prometheus's theft, as a result of which appeared the disappearing nudity of mortals, the advance of their prematureness that is their eternal delay. If they do not yet possess the art of the political, called for by their de-fault of origin, and arising from their technicity, it is because their condition must take root, firstly, in the memory of the Titanic conflict in Olympia, a memory in the sacrifice *out of which* they come to *speech*. Speech, and later politics, proceed from this memorial participation in the divine, and thus from this theft. From out of this memory, in this speech, they come to *invent*.

Religion, speech, politics, invention—each is but an effect of the default of origin. The essential is the accident, the absence of quality. The political question, the question of the community, only makes sense if one starts from the community of a de-fault or of the imminent de-fault of community. Religion, sacrifice, the altar only make sense with *this* political question, which originates in Prometheus's stamp. Speech will only make sense in terms of the meaning that *this* sacrifice saves.

Man invents, discovers, finds (*eurisko*), imagines (*mēkhanē*), and realizes what he imagines: prostheses, expedients. A pros-thesis is what is placed in front, that is, what is outside, outside what it is placed in front of. However, if what is outside constitutes the very being of what it lies outside of, then this being is *outside itself*. The being of humankind is to be outside itself. In order to make up for the fault of Epimetheus, Prometheus gives humans the present of putting them outside themselves.

Humankind, we might say, puts into effect what it imagines because it is endowed with reason, with *logos*—that is, also with language. Or should we rather say that it is because it realizes what it imagines—as we said a moment ago, because it lies outside itself—that humanity is endowed with reason, that is, with language? Is it *tekhnē* that arises from *logos*, or the reverse? Or rather, is it not that *logos* and *tekhnē* are modalities of the same being-outside-oneself?

Discovery, insight, invention, imagination are all, according to the narrative of the myth, characteristic of a *de-fault*. Animals are already marked by a de-fault (in relation to being as it is and as it endures through change, and in relation to the gods): they perish. One must understand "de-fault" here *in relation to what is*, that is, a flaw in being. And yet, whereas animals are positively endowed with qualities, it is *tekhnē* that forms the lot of humans, and *tekhnē* is prosthetic; that is, it is entirely artifice. The qualities of animals make up a sort of nature, in any case a positive gift of the gods: a predestination. The gift made to humanity is not positive: it is there to compensate. Humanity is without qualities, without predestination: it must invent, realize, produce qualities, and nothing indicates that, once produced, these qualities will bring about humanity, that they will become *its* qualities; for they may rather become those of technics.

Prometheus robs Hephaestus and Athena. By pursuing Athena, Hephaestus becomes the father of the Athenians. Here arms, tools, and instruments of war play a large role: Athena rose from the head of Zeus clad in arms, delivered by the patron god of handicraft with an axe. Athena is in turn pursued by Hephaestus when she orders arms from him: in this manner the craftsman's sperm is spilt on the earth, constituting the myth of Athenian autochthony, a myth that will be important to us later.[2] Origin, war, politics: with each it is a matter of instruments. From these gods who handle instruments is stolen the "creative genius of the arts" (which translates *ten entekhnen sophian*: it is, again, a matter of *sophia* and *tekhnē*).

Sophia and *tekhnē* are nothing without fire, with all that this connotes of *duplicity*, given that it concerns the fire stolen by Prometheus. Fire, in the hands of mortals, is a power of divine origin through whose mediation, in sacrifice, the mortals put themselves in the place of the gods. Fire is not, however, the power *of* mortals, it is not their property; it is much more a domestic power that, when escaping the technical mastery of this domesticity, reveals its wild violence, disclosing the powerlessness of mortals, only appearing in their hands, yet again, through disappearing.[3]

The role that fire plays here must be given a temporal sense: anticipation, care, conservation, and so on, in a succession of mistakes set in play by the originary double fault. The duplicity of fire, symbol of the duplicity of mortal "power," is nothing but the effect of an originary doubling-up: Prometheus's fault, origin of the de-fault in being for mortals of the human species, is the doubling-up of a fault: the fault of Epimetheus is compensated for by another fault, which inevitably engenders the de-fault.

In this duplicity, mediating through sacrifice, "voices" (*phonen*) and "parts of discourses" (*onomata*) are heard. Language, the *logos* as language, occurs (it too in disappearing, it too two-faced, always capable of meaning the opposite of what is intended) through technics, through the theft of fire and the "arts" (*tekhnai*). The *logos, qua* religion, *qua* politics, is (on the basis of the fault) wholly technical, fruit of an originary incompleteness of technical being. This technicity and incompleteness of technical being stem from the gods themselves, who are expert in technics. This constitutes the incompleteness of theogony, characterized first by Epimetheus, "whose wisdom was incomplete": a god who is not exactly wise, not truly wise, or rather, wise without being wise—wise after the event.

Animals are perishable; humanity is mortal. There is a difference, and this difference is marked in the text by the reference to the cult of the gods. Humanity, *qua* mortal, "has a share in the portion of the gods" (Plato 1961, *Protagoras*, 322a). Its mortality appears through its relation to immortals for whom it erects temples and fashions images. It is only then (*epeita*) on the basis of this partaking that it acquires "the art of emitting sounds and swiftly articulating nouns" (322a). Once this difference with beings deprived of reason or *logos*, *aloga* (unable to mimic immortals because not partaking of their lot) is made, the unqualifiable race will have become *logoin*, logical, endowed (but through default) with *logos*. To partake of the lot of immortals means to endure one's mortality by the fact of being in (privative) relation with immortality. The unqualifiable race speaks from out of its "disqualification," from out of its mortality; it only speaks its mortality, its disappearance, for the divine defines itself in relation to death, and not death in relation to the divine. It is true that one says "the gods, *oï theoï*," but what bestows content upon this notion of "god" is the im-mortality of god; it is death that defines the divide between those who are divine and those who only partake of the divine, a divide that relates and separates them at one and the same time.

In the *Theogony*, it is Prometheus who commits the first fault, trying to deceive Zeus about the sacrificial beast, and giving him bones while keeping the meat back for humans, for which Zeus will take revenge by depriving humans of fire. Prometheus also commits the second fault, proceeding to steal the fire of which Zeus deprived mortals in order to take his revenge, and from there, Zeus will again take his revenge by sending humans Pandora. There are two faults, then, and there are two acts of vengeance. As for Epimetheus, his fault will be to accept the gift from Zeus, the beautiful bane in the form of Pandora. Zeus's second act of vengeance is the mark of *sexual difference*, the very mark that in Rousseau produces discord, the speaking of many tongues and inequality. The sending of difference is the sending of a being covered in artifice and resplendent, deceptive finery, what is also called *kosmos*, still spoken of and seen in cosmetics, a decorous set of ornaments worked on by the handicapped god Hephaestus. This difference, more than any other, places the *andres* in a calamitous state, outside themselves, left exhausted.

Birth and Uncertainty

The originary duplicity, the doubling-up of the first act, inside this act, in one act—for there were never two origins, there is no origin at all, there is only the duplicity of an originary flaw—this act, then, of doubling-up also constitutes the duplicity of a "contractuality" that will forever fall short, of a compromise pregnant with all possible betrayals, of a promise never kept:

> What has become of the difference [between Prometheus and Zeus] from which humans draw their status? It is . . . the result neither of crude violence nor of a reciprocal agreement. It is not imposed by force, although it is not decided in common either. . . . The open war that divides Titans and Olympians is replaced by a muffled conflict, a test of duplicity and scheming. . . . *This uncertain and oblique procedure responds to the equivocal character of the status of humans in the relations that both unite them to the gods and separate them therefrom.* (Vernant 1979, 47–49, my emphasis)

The duplicity is evident on a daily basis in the very existence of the *anthropoi* who, through Pandora, figuring the arrival of birth as the mirror of death, become *andres,* forever associated with women, "destined to the double fatality of begetting and death." And this is the fault, again, of Epimetheus. Labor—that is, technics—and generation in sexual difference are stamped with the same mark: that of the vengeance of Zeus, disappearance.[4]

The "ultimate meaning" of what occurs with Pandora is the jar, and the meaning of the jar is *elpis*: anticipation, time. In other words, *temporality is thought here not only in terms of mortality but also in terms of birth qua sexual differentiation.*

The theme of *elpis,* expectation, takes us to the profoundest part in Hesiod of the theme of prosthetic mortality, an analysis of which was made at the end of our reading of Leroi-Gourhan. There the theme was considered in terms of a new modality of programming—exteriorization—and as the staking-out, if not of the unprogrammable, at least of the improbable or of the open and undetermined, which is the future thought in terms of anticipation without predestination, or deferred différance—themes we will come across again in our further reading of the myth of Protagoras. It should be stressed that it is precisely here that Epimetheus, absent from Hesiod's version, enters the picture.

Elpis designates firstly expectation, conjecture, presumption, and foresight. The noun thus implies as much hope as its opposite, fear. *Elpis* is shut up in Pandora's jar together with the ills that Zeus has stored up for mortals. It is consequently most often also considered as an ill. Vernant, whom we must quote at length here, questions this reading:

> *Elpis*, as long as it is not specified as fear or as trust, is neutral: it can refer to a good or an ill. A question thus arises: if, by placing Elpis in the jar (of Pandora) in company with all ills, Hesiod completely assimilated it, making it into the anxious expectation of ill in order to avoid ambiguity, ought he not to have named it *Phobos* in preference to *Elpis*? But there is something more serious going on here. As soon as one turns *Elpis* into the expectation of ill, it is seen as the "ultimate ill," "the worst among them": more awful than misfortune itself is the anticipation of misfortune, its presence in the mind of man even before it is assailed by it {a phenomenon undoubtedly symbolized by Prometheus's consumed liver}. In our understanding, *Elpis* portrays a radical dimension of uncertainty; whether it be expectation of good or of ill, its meaning is never stable, never definite. It does not carry the value of *pronoia*, of prescience; being of the order of conjecture, always implying credulity, it oscillates between the dreams of the presumptuous and the terrors of the timorous. Returning to the Hesiodic context, we would say that Elpis is not less foreign to *promētheia*, foresight, than to *ēpimētheia*, comprehension after the event {or rather, that it is the tension between the two, their *stricture*}. Through his *mētis*, Prometheus represents, in the misfortunes that strike him, the hero of prescience: "I know in advance all events to come. For me no misfortune happens unexpectedly." This complete certainty the Titan has of the sufferings that are marked for him constitutes in a certain sense the opposite of the uncertain Elpis that humans share. . . . In a passage of *Prometheus Bound* . . . , the Titan enumerates the qualities he has bestowed on man: "I stopped mortals from foreseeing death." "What cure did you discover for that ill?," the chorus asks. "I sowed in them blind hopes," Prometheus replies. It is not the foreseeing of ill, the foreknowledge of death, which carries the name here of *elpis*; on the contrary, *elpis*, housed among humans, as is Pandora, constitutes through her very blindness the antidote to foresight. She is not a cure for death, which has none, since, whatever one does, death is inscribed in the course of human life. Finding her place within the very seat of mortal life, *elpis* can balance out the consciousness of death with lack of knowledge of the moment when and the manner in which death will come and take this life. (Vernant 1979, 125–26)

Thus, in the anticipation, always already hidden, of their end—the knot that binds together *promētheia* and *ēpimētheia*[5]—the temporality of mortals is set up. As in the Heideggerian existential analytic, this knowledge of the end, which is also a nonknowing, forms the primordial situation out of which each person conducts himself or herself. *Elpis* could be seen as (the relation) to the indeterminate,[6] that is (the anticipation of) the future, and as such, "the essential phenomenon of time."

Epimetheus: The Idiot

To endure the fault of Epimetheus, doubled up by that of Prometheus, is to descend into a primordial knowledge of death unknown to *aloga*. It is true that at the beginning of the story Protagoras designates by the expression *thnēta gēnē* not only those whom we are here calling mortals but also those who perish, animals that are *aloga*. And yet, the *non-aloga* will become, after the event, *nonimmortals*, and not simply those who are engendered, a trait that they share with animals. *Between* god and beast, neither beast nor god, neither immortal nor prone to perish, sacrificial beings, mortals are also and for the same reasons nascent, bestowing meaning, and "active." In *elpis*, which is being-toward-death, in *elpis* alone, but there necessarily from the moment that *bios* and all properties have been hidden while the ills have been scattered, a technical *activity* that characterizes all humanity as such, that is, all mortality, can plunge out of control. To be active can mean nothing but to be mortal. Activity is to be thought in terms of (the différance of) absolute inactivity. This being-toward-death, ecstasis, being-outside-oneself, in expectation, hope or fear, configures a particular mode of being of mortals *among themselves*, a being-together that does not come into existence before Epimetheus's act of forgetting (beings that are *aloga*, simply engendered without birth, are not "together"). Technics, art, facticity can harbor madness: the prosthesis is a danger, that of artifacts, and artifacts can destroy what gathers within an effective and active being-together. Being-together is constantly threatened by its own activity. Animals are in essence not in danger, unless with mortals: if they perish individually, their species do not destroy themselves. Mortals, because they are prosthetic in their very being, are self-destructive.

Hence prostheses, when visible, frighten or fascinate, as *marks* of mortality: the knife that the *mageiros*, butcher and sacrificial killer, is reluctant to use and that he flings from himself as soon as the animal has been killed (Détienne 1979), the wooden leg, the nineteenth-century steam engine, the set of dentures at the bottom of a glass, the television hallucinating intimacy, the robot on the automated factory floor, the computer chess-champion, translating machines ... There is nothing but prostheses: my glasses, my shoes, the pen, the diary, or the money in my pocket; and because they are frightening, their visibility is reduced. There are all kinds of strategies—blind ones, moreover—to do so. And yet, from the beginning there is a constitutive blindness and forgetting that is the mark of Epimetheus—that is, of différance in the fact of being technical, as doubling-up (deferred différance). *Ēpimētheia* constitutes this carelessness, this primordial idiocy, source of finite singularity and freedom, as a result of which it is possible to act and possible for something to occur, to take place. To have a past is to be fallible: nothing can happen to the infallible; no difference can affect it. *Ēpimētheia* is also the carefulness that comes too late to reflect upon its passive mode, this very reflexivity lingering in the empirical, that is strewn with accumulated errors. The horizon of this careless care is the facticity that is always already there, having always already preceded the mortal who, whatever he or she does, arrives too late, inheriting all the faults of his or her ancestry, starting with the originary de-fault of origin.

Facticity is felt in the life of the group, in its *coming together as one* [*faire corps*] through default (atomization) or through excess (herding), both as its origin and as its threat: a political question emerges here. And this is where Protagoras resumes his story of the myth at the point where we left off. It is where the question of prostheses arises in the most basic terms for a "race" that is not predestined to be what it is, that is "unqualifiable" because "without qualities," and the question is that of a hermeneutic and Promethean condition, the condition of mortals. Who are mortals? They are those who do not come together as one immediately, who have to be brought together, who have to be, and who are less predatory than bellicose. In the same sense, in *Being and Time*, Dasein is marked by facticity, in which Da-sein is there not in the sense that being is given to it but in the sense of its having to be, which means: Dasein is time. All that it is given is a feeling of having-to-be, of a de-fault of being where at one and the same time a having-to-be and a failing-to-be are affirmed. In Heidegger, especially toward the end of his work, this question becomes that of technics. Indeed, Heidegger's question, put from the very beginning in terms of a hermeneutic, moves toward, and is already moving within, the Promethean question. And yet, the existential analytic and the Heideggerian question of time ignore the primordial sense of the Promethean/Epimethean figure that Vernant's reading has brought to light.

"The community of those who have no community"

The Protagorean version of the myth is articulated in a horizon that is novel when compared to that of Hesiod. The political question has since assumed the *form* of a question. The duplicity of language has here revealed itself, in the eyes of philosophy, in the form of writing, which not only concerns but constitutes as such all properly political practices, as Marcel Détienne (1981) has decisively shown. It is within this new horizon that the appearance of Hermes in the myth makes sense and that the *polis* tries to interpret citizenship as such—citizenship that is—according to the problematic at the end of the last part, when interrogating the articulation, after the "removal of ethnic memory from zoological species," between the "socio-ethnic" and "individual" levels recognized by Leroi-Gourhan[7]—a singular situation of idiomatic individuation and time: its *historical* site. The sending of Hermes also forms the (techno-logical) opening to the book of History.

After being "provided for" by Epimetheus,

> they lived at first in scattered groups {*sporadēs*}; there were no cities. Consequently they were devoured by wild beasts, since they were in every respect the weaker, and their technical skill, though a sufficient aid to their nurture, did not extend to making war on the beasts, for they had not the art {*tekhnē*} of politics, of which the art of war {*polēmikē*} is a part. They sought therefore to save themselves by coming together and founding fortified cities, but when they gathered in communities they injured one another for want of political skill {*ten politikhen tekhnen*}, and so scattered again and continued to be devoured. Zeus therefore, fearing the total destruction of our race, sent Hermes to impart to men the qualities of respect for others {*aido*: modesty, respect, shame; perhaps today one might say the feeling of finitude} and a sense of justice {*dikē*}, so as to bring order into our cities {*poleon kosmoi*} and create a bond of friendship and union {*philias sunagogoi*}. Hermes asked Zeus in what manner he was to bestow these gifts on men. "Shall I distribute these *tekhnai* as the arts were distributed—that is, on the principle that one trained doctor suffices for many laymen, and so with the other experts {*demiourgai*}? Shall I distribute justice and respect for their fellows {*aido*} in this way, or to

> all alike?" "To all," said Zeus; "let all have their share. There could never be cities if only a few men {*oligoi*} shared in these virtues, as in the arts {*tekhnai*}. Moreover, you must lay it down as my law that if anyone is incapable of acquiring his share of *aido* and *dikē* he shall be put to death as a plague to the city." (Plato 1961, *Protagoras*, 322b–d)

Thus the bad side of *ēris* makes its appearance. To contain it, another *tekhnē* is required, a *tekhnē* that will not be like the others because shared by all alike, just as writing, when the practice of it spreads throughout ancient Greece, forms a *tekhnē* that is no longer paradoxically (in principle if not in reality) the privilege of specialists. It is not the philosopher, the sophist says, who will lead the city, but the city itself through its coming-together. What brings this togetherness about is found in the feeling of shame, that is, of finitude, *aido*, such as it stems from the fault(s) of Prometheus/Epimetheus (Vernant 1979, 80). Politics is an art, a technics, imprinted in every mortal as the originary feeling of the divine coup of technicity itself—this, in the widest understanding of the term, that is, as the necessity of a différance, deferral as the imminence of the end of "the community of those who have no community"[8] but an art that presupposes a *praxis* of the letter. It is *in effects* (generating differences) the *feeling* of the de-fault of origin.

Hermes, the messenger-god of the gods, the god of sacrifice and hiding, of enigma and aporia, of interpretation and translation, Hermes the herald, brings *dikē* and *aido*, feelings that are also forms of knowledge [*savoirs*]—they are feelings and/or *hermeneutical* forms of knowledge. *Dikē* as well as *aido* must be *interpreted* and *translated*, beyond and through the disparity intrinsic to a race that lacks quality, like marks of this race's community given on the basis of its very de-fault of community. The meaning of *dikē* and *aido* is not given, is lacking—because the community of mortals is "the community of those who have no community," no essence, no quality. To have to partake of or share in *dikē* or *aido*, in knowledge of the de-fault, is not an "ought" and can only have meaning for those for whom one has to [*il faut*] decide, immersed as they are in activity. Each time, in every situation of decision, in every position of necessity [*falloir*] that opens up at the same time a flaw [*faille*], one has to invent their meaning in *hermēneia*—which is made up unquestionably of *promētheia* and *ēpimētheia*. *Hermēneia* signifies, in common language, expression and elocution, translation and interpretation.

Promētheia is the anticipation of the future, that is, of danger, foresight, prudence, and an essential disquiet: somebody who is *promethēs* is someone who is worried in advance. *Ēpimētheia* equally means prudence, being-sensible, a sort of wisdom, whereas Epimetheus himself is "the one who is not particularly sensible," the forgetful one, the bemused, the idiot, the unthinking one: this ambiguity forms the hollow of the gap [*le creux de l'écart*] in which thought alone can take place; and it comes to mind *after the event*, in delay, because preceded by a past that could never be anything but a failure and an act of forgetting. Prometheus and Epimetheus, inseparable, form together the reflection particular to mortals that partake of the divine lot: it is a reflection *qua* ecstasis, "in" time, that is, in mortality, which is anticipation and différance; it is reflection *as* time and time *as* reflection: in advance from the Promethean side as well as in delay from the side of Epimetheus—never at peace, which is the exclusive privilege of immortal beings.

In other words, *aido* and *dikē*, feelings that guarantee the safety of the gathering of mortals, are the very feelings of mortality that alone mortal beings have in common from default of quality, mortality itself ensuing from this de-fault, from their technicity. This gathering, which means here for Plato the city (*polis*), implies decision, and decision implies anticipation: *promētheia*, advance, whose truth is the return after the event, the delay, *ēpimētheia*; and insofar as it constitutes in one stroke (*ēris*) the possibility of the city and the possibility of its destruction (its impossibility), *promētheia* as advance *presupposes* hermeneutics (related itself to the technics of writing), which lies at the very basis of temporality.

The Liver

This is the meaning of Prometheus, chained to the rock, his liver consumed by the eagle sent from Zeus. Through this act of Olympian revenge, a primordial melancholy, vehicle of every phantasm, of every hypochondria, of every bilious misanthropy, will pre-cede as its possibility the hermeneutic community.

> With the fire that he put in their hands, Prometheus determined the type of food proper to mortal beings. . . . Like the immortal liver of the Titan, the hunger of men who perish is postponed from one day to the next, constant and recurrent, requiring food to be procured without end to maintain them

in the form of a precarious and short-lived life that is henceforth their lot. (Vernant 1979, 90)

Like hunger, the cold, labor, and basic cares return each day, never more than deferred. Just as the future is as inevitable as it is implacably undetermined, so Prometheus's liver, consumed by day and restored by night, is the Titan's *clock*[9]—become feast of the sacrifice, as much as his torment. It is the ceaseless process of différance in which time is constituted with that one coup of technicity that is the mark of mortality. "Why the liver?" It is an organic *mirror* in which divinatory hermeneutics is practiced, in which, during the sacrifice, divine messages are interpreted. And it is Hermes who, in Aeschylus, announces to Prometheus his punishment. Organ of all *humors*, of feelings of all situations, because it is the seat of the "feeling of situation," the liver is also, as a mirror of ceaseless mortality—which never *occurs*—of the body and the heart, the mirage of the spirit (*Gemüt*). A clock, its vesicle conceals those stones [*calculs*] that secrete black bile, *melas kholie*.

§ 2 Already There

> The connections between historical numeration, world time as calculated astronomically, and the temporality and historiality of Dasein need a more extensive investigation.
>
> —Heidegger

The Instrumental Condition

To determine *dikē* and *aido* within *hermēneia* does not imply of course arbitrarily determining their meaning; rather, it implies experiencing the question of their meaning. Mortals are immersed from the start, elementarily as it were, in a problem. To be is to be in the question of destiny *qua* nonpredestination, to be, that is, a *who*.

The who *and* the what, in their very conjunction, are the concern both of the present chapter and, especially, of the next. In the course of the lecture "The Concept of Time" (1924),[1] Heidegger, elaborating a phenomenological hermeneutics of Dasein *qua* a being that has to be, that is, a historial being immersed in *hermēneia*, sets up the articulation between the *who* and the *what* through the thematic of the clock. Despite this early articulation, the later existential analytic ends up discarding this possible conjunction, thereby ignoring the Epimethean (Promethean) meaning of any hermeneutics and leaving shrouded in ambiguity the question of the already-there, expressly set up in other respects *as* constitutive of Dasein: the facticity of Dasein ensues from its being *already there*, from the precedence of its past (the past of Dasein has always already preceded it). The analytic ends up dissolving the stones [*calculs*] of the liver: the prosthetic facticity of the already-there will have had no constitutive character, will never have taken part in the originarity of the phenomenon of time, indeed, and on the contrary, will have only figured as a destitution of the origin. At the same time, writing, as the mark of this technics, will be removed from the inauguration of the history of being, an inauguration that also forms the opening of the book of History in which the rights and duties of citizenship are laid down.[2]

We want to show that there is a techno-logical constitution (earlier than "chthonian") to epochal reflexivity. Plato only quotes Protagoras in order to oppose him. Opposition to the Sophists is constitutive of philosophy; the opposition turns around the question of technics, such as it finds specification in writing. Writing is already something like a language machine, producing a language of synthesis. But it is also in writing, insofar as writing opens up the space particular to political "publicity" and historical "temporality," that the *logos* becomes a question and acquires, strictly speaking, definition, distinguishing itself as reason from what is not yet rational. Now, writing is a technics. And we have seen in the story of Protagoras how *tekhnē* gives rise to the *polis.*

Whatever the shifts in Heidegger's successive accounts of this question—to begin with *Being and Time*, one major consequence of which is the highlighting of the ontological singularity of beings that are "ready-to-hand," tools, that is, the *what* (and the sign is itself a tool)—Heidegger's thought is fundamentally still inscribed in the traditional opposition between *tekhnē* and the *logos.* If he denounced, well after *Being and Time,* and in another vocabulary, analyses of technics that are conducted in terms of the categories "end" and "means," it was in order to uncover an *instrumental* conception of technics, an analysis in which he does not appear to put in question the determination itself of an instrument *as* a means. The metaphysical illusion from Plato onward that turns language into a means through which humans express themselves, rather than its being located as the site of their very constitution, is abundantly criticized by Heidegger. Yet it is the same error that induces consideration of an instrument as a means. Heidegger criticizes the instrumentalization of language, its "cybernetization" in terms of the elimination of idiomatic difference, as what "transforms language into an exchange of news[, with] the arts becoming regulated-regulating instruments of information" (Heidegger 1969a, 376), a theme that is taken up again and developed in *The Language of Tradition and Technical Language* [*Uberlieferte Sprache und technische Sprache*, 1989]. But if the instrumentalization of language is possible, this is because its instrumentality is inherent to it. The question is consequently one of knowing how an instrument should be understood, that is, as a being-ready-to-hand, as the what. It is a question not of struggling against the instrumentalization of language but of resisting the very reduction of an instrument to the rank of means. There is no point in looking to isolate a noninstrumental aspect to language; nothing of the kind exists. The issue is rather that of addressing the modalities of instrumentality as such, modalities that harbor the condition of idiomatic instrumentality as much as that of the condition of massive indifferentiation, together with all the multiple dimensions of what we might call, here, *the instrumental condition.*

Ēpimathēsis: Tradition

Through the recurrent themes of the *heritage* of tradition, on the one hand, and modern technics and calculation, on the other, the question of the idiom, as well as the opposition between *logos* and *tekhnē* articulating the terms of the question, prevails in the work of Heidegger, from *The Concept of Time* to "Time and Being."

Now, the fatality of heritage provides the profoundest meaning to the figure of Epimetheus. As the accumulation of faults and forgettings, as legacy and transmission, in the form of a knowing that is both reflexive and forgetful, *ēpimētheia* gives also the very meaning of tradition.

We have characterized this accumulation of individual experiences in forgetful error with the concept "epiphylogenesis." Without doubt, it is not by pure chance that the first three letters of the name of Epimetheus are to be found in the prefix of this neologism. What could the etymology of this name be? First is to be understood the etymology of the root found in pro-*mētheia*. "*Mētheia*" comes from *manthano*, which means to learn, to study, to teach oneself, to notice something or remark, to understand. The verb is also to be found in the term *mathēsis*, of which Heidegger says in *What Is a Thing?*:

> The mathematical is a fundamental position towards things, one in which our apprehension *pro-poses* things with regard to the way in which they are *already* given to us and must be so given. The mathematical constitutes therefore the fundamental presupposition of the knowledge of things. (Heidegger 1967b, 63)

So, what does the prefix *ēpi* stuck to the root *mētheia* mean? *Ēpi* carries the character of the accidentality and artificial factuality of something happening, arriving, a primordial "passibility" [*passibilité*]. With *matheia*, or *mathēsis*, we are dealing with something happening, that is from the first passed on, shared: knowledge *is* primordially. *Epimētheia* means heritage. Heritage is always *ēpimathēsis*.

Epimētheia would also mean then tradition-originating in a fault that is always *already there* and that is nothing but technicity. This understanding of the term is faithful to traditional historiality, which forms an existential trait of Dasein: Dasein, as "being-thrown," inherits the already-there that is its past, always having preceded it and from out of which it "is" this particular "who," child and grandchild of so and so, and so on—*its* past, which is not properly speaking *its* past since it did not "live" it. The temporal mode of being of Dasein is historiality, which "designates the constitution of the historizing-being of Dasein as such," and the meaning of this historizing is itself facticity. "In its factical being, any Dasein is as it already was, and it is 'what' it already was. It *is* its past, whether explicitly or not" (Heidegger 1967a, 20). One can understand the (awesome) sense of the adverb "already" here. If the mode of being (of Dasein's past) historicizes "from the future,"

> Dasein has grown up both *into* and *in* a traditional way of interpreting itself: in terms of this it understands itself proximally and, within a certain range, constantly. By this understanding, the possibilities of its being are disclosed and regulated. Its own past—and this always means the past of its "generation"—is not something which *follows along after* Dasein, but something which already goes ahead of it. (20)

This past of *mine* is only inherited insofar as it is not *my* past: it has to come "to be so." It will only be so after the event, *après coup* (in the after event of the "resolution").

If the Epimethean character of tradition originates in technicity, what, then, of tradition in the today of technological deterritorialization (what Heidegger would call "uprooting")? Does ethnic difference co-originate with technical difference, or does it only form a *modality* of an idiomatic difference that is essentially deterritorializable? This type of question haunts the whole of Heidegger's thinking, forms its ghost, most particularly with regard to his "political adventure." The reference to Prometheus in the Rectorate Discourse is the bitter index. The absence of the same figure in *An Introduction to Metaphysics*, where Antigone, that is, her father, Oedipus, is foregrounded, is a further mark of this forgetting—while the theme of uprooting informs all of *Being and Time*'s reflections.[3]

This way of introducing our reading of Heidegger could encourage one to think that Heidegger's political "fault" or "mistake," together with the metaphysical shortcomings of his thought in general, consisting in a "forgetful" understanding of the fault as such, and this despite the major theme of *Schuldigsein* (being-at-fault or in-debt), take place owing to a traditional metaphysical position toward technics. This would be wholly wrong, and we would wish to contribute to dissipating a misunderstanding that predominates in most interpretations of Heidegger: that, for example, of Jacques Rolland, who considers that for Heidegger the question is one of "escaping the hold of technics" (Rolland 1986, 170); that also of Marlène Zarader, who organizes her interpretation of the meaning of *Ereignis* on the basis of the question of modern technics and calculation.[4] In this interpretation Zarader simply confuses two concerns (technics and calculation), a confusion that leads her to write:

> The essence of man is circumscribed by Heidegger . . . like a homeland to be gained. It is only when man, concerned with such a conquest, will have reached or at least approached this proximity, which is his without him having ever inhabited it, that what *Sein und Zeit* calls "falling" will have been surmounted. (Zarader 1976, 124)

As if falling were "surmountable." This so-called reading of Heidegger has quite simply never read Heidegger, if we take the warning of paragraph 38 in the least seriously:

> We would . . . misunderstand the ontologico-existential structure of falling if we were to ascribe to it the sense of a bad and deplorable ontical property of which, perhaps, more advanced stages of human culture might be able to rid themselves. (Heidegger 1967a, 176)

The impertinence of Zarader's reading is patent. Dasein is "thrown," and this is what grounds its "mobility": it "exists factically." If Dasein has the possibility of understanding, this is because it has the possibility of falling. This existential structure is very close to a being-in-de-fault, to a being-through-de-fault—of the Promethean-Epimethean "stricture."

Hence Hubert Dreyfus is more correct than he believes to see in the philosophy of *Being and Time* a "technical phenomenology," even if Heidegger remains fundamentally ambiguous on this point and fails to carry this reflection to a conclusion:

> Opposing the Cartesian subject/object distinction in terms of an account of Dasein as a user of equipment becomes an ambiguous form of opposition, for it is no longer clear whether such an analysis offers a critique of technology in the form of a transcendental account of the pre-technological everyday understanding of equipment, or whether, under the guise of a transcendental account of everyday activity, such an analysis reflects a transition in the history of the way equipment *is* which prepares the way for technology. In other words, it is not clear whether *Being and Time* opposes technology or promotes it. (Dreyfus 1992, 175)

The allusion made here to "The End of Philosophy and the Task of Thinking" shows that Dreyfus misinterprets Heidegger in the same way that Rolland does. For it is never a question of such an alternative; it is not "the task of thinking" (Heidegger 1969a, 392) to "confront" technics—nor of course to promote it—but to "open oneself to it" (390–92). Heideggerian reflection on technics does not remain any the less ambiguous, an ambiguity found in concentrated form in the Epimethean question of the already-there. For us the question of technics was discussed under the thematic first of invention (Gille, Leroi-Gourhan), then of operative temporality (Simondon), then of being-within-reach (Rousseau), and finally of the prosthetic already-there in mortality (with the myth of Prometheus)—themes that all inform the work of Heidegger unremittingly, while the question of the already-there leads to and governs the theme of the historiality of Dasein, which "is *its* past," a structure that, after the "turning," is recast as that of the history of being. Now, if Epimetheus is a figure simultaneously of knowledge and of forgetting, then historiality, when it becomes the history of being, is itself the dehiscence of an originary knowledge that forgets itself: knowledge of the ontological difference forgetting itself in the différance that is the history of being.

These thematics are, if not all present, certainly imminent from the time of the lecture delivered by Heidegger in 1924, "The Concept of Time." In this chapter we will read the lecture in the light of the amendments made at the beginning of the second division of the first part of *Being and Time* ("Dasein and Temporality"), which exposits the thematic of being-toward-the-end. In the following chapter we will return in greater detail to the analytic of everydayness (first division) in order to expound the conditions in which the thematic of the already-there is taken up and set out, as well as to the theme of being-at-fault or in-debt

[*Schuldigsein*] developed in the beginning sections of the second division. We will finally read the last two sections, which elaborate the constitution of historiality.

Our interpretation aims at repercussions up to and including the last texts that might allow one to reopen the oldest philosophical questions as Heidegger's thought has bequeathed them to us, starting from his acts of forgetting and his mistakes in his very meditation upon forgetting and being-at-fault. We always understand the history of philosophy *qua* the most radical form of the *knowledge of the de-fault* as *a history of mistakes*, awkwardnesses, distortions, and sinister failings that *had to be*, or that *will have had to be* [*qu'il faut—ou qu'il aura fallu*]. Which is the meaning of every tradition that one inherits, willingly or not, but that one cannot efface.

The Unity of Knowledge and the Weight of the *What* Ready-to-Hand

"The following reflections are concerned with time," Heidegger writes at the beginning of *The Concept of Time*. In a reading of this text we are not simply concerned with the question of *phenomenological* time, such as it is to be distinguished from *cosmic* or physical time, but with the hypothesis of a *technological time* (the time of *what*), constitutive of the temporality of the *who*.

This question of time must be taken through the question of knowledge that issues directly from our "Epimethean" or "epiphylogenetic" problematic. The question of knowledge is omnipresent in Heidegger's work: it is the knowledge of the ontological difference that constitutes the privilege of Dasein. Tradition is one name for knowledge. In *The Concept of Time* Dasein has knowledge of a nonknowledge: that of the imminence of its radically indeterminate end. Tradition raises the question of the *transmission* of knowledge. Our hypothesis is that this transmission is determined by the explicitly technological forms recording forms of knowledge, by the conditions of *access* they provide—this is also true for the very inventor of a domain of knowledge.[5] We *raise* this question at a moment when, in the perspective of contemporary technics, the technologies of the elaboration, conservation, and transmission of forms of knowledge are undergoing radical transformation, profoundly affecting the order of knowledge itself. But what is knowledge as such [*le savoir*] if it is transformable in this way? Can one say that it has a "unity"?

Such a question on the state of "knowledge today" might appear a little too obvious, entering, indeed, into the immediacy of the present, in short as a truly topical question, one that informs many current debates. What form(s) of knowledge, however, are being spoken about? It is here that, perhaps, the topicality, the actuality or the *Gegenwart* must be put on reserve, deferred, made inactual or untimely. If one wishes to speak of knowledge [*le savoir*] from a reading of the "well-known" Heidegger, then it can only be a question of a knowing of the ontological difference. Knowledge, in any case, of *a* difference and, as we will say later, knowledge *as* différance, with Epimetheus, attached to the feet of Prometheus, figuring the return after the event that confuses foresight. Now, this difference in *The Concept of Time* is precisely not yet the ontological difference. In 1924 the question of time passes necessarily through such knowledge, such knowledge of a difference. But it is not yet a question of the ontological difference. Between what and what does this difference pass, or rather, between *what* and *whom*? We wish to privilege this text insofar, precisely, as it expounds the constitutive difference of knowledge, in an exemplary examination of the question, as the articulation and differentiation between a *who* and a *what*. The *who* is Dasein, named here still "now"; the *what* is the clock. The question of time is that of the relation between a *who* and a *what* such that it appears to be the knowledge of a différance. The question of the *what* could be said then to be constitutive of the initial Heideggerian reflection on temporality and will explicitly reappear in the conclusion to the first and only finished part of *Being and Time*. In paragraph 83, Heidegger asks why the understanding of being always ends up in a form of reification. He ends by leading us back to the question of the *weight* of the *what*—of a *what* that, as we shall see, could never have been the *what* that is at issue for us in these pages; but, it must be stressed, Heidegger opens up the possibility of thinking this latter *what* when he insists, in this last paragraph of his major work, on the difference between the present-at-hand and the ready-to-hand:

> Why does being get "conceived" "proximally" in terms of the present-at-hand *and not* in terms of the ready-to-hand, which lies *closer* to us? (Heidegger 1967a, 437)

In short, what we are aiming at under the "name" of *what* is called in Heidegger the "ready-to-hand."

The Durable Fixing of the Now

The being in proximity to the *who* who interrogates time, this *what* that is always already at its hand, is the clock. To think time in terms of time is to think it *first* in terms of the clock. "If we achieve clarity about what a clock is, then the kind of apprehension thriving in physics thereby becomes alive, and so does the manner in which time gets the opportunity to show itself" (Heidegger 1992, 2E).

The clock measures time (or change) by comparing the duration of an event "to identical sequences on the clock[,] and [it] can thereby be numerically determined," which it can only do as "a physical system in which an identical temporal sequence is constantly repeated" (Heidegger 1992, 4E). At the end of 24 hours, it is the first hour that returns. How could a clock mark anything beyond its 24 hours? Because it only functions for Dasein, a *who,* who collects or re-marks the return of the cycle. This marking only forms, however, the putting into play of another system, of which the clock forms one element. For what is important here is the installation of calendar inscriptions in general as well as the structure of datability that they presuppose. This structure includes the various installations for conserving traces, the entire setup of mnemotechnics,[6] and, finally, that of the "transmission of forms of knowledge." The calendar system itself is inscribed in the movement of the planets, within which lies the system of seasons, and where the name for climatic time finds its justification. An entire "programmatic" is set up—from starlight to what appears later in the text as *mortality.*

"What primarily the clock does in each case is not to indicate the how-long or how-much of time in its present flowing, but to determine the *durable fixing* of the now. . . . What is the now?" (Heidegger 1992, 5E, my emphasis). This, then, is the true question of time: the now—here the now in its ability *to be fixed,* to be inscribed, to be considered in its "as such." The question, in its form, reiterates the question in terms of which Hegel also found a system of durable fixing, writing. It is Augustine, however, to whom Heidegger directs his comments:

> What is this now, the time now as I look at my watch? . . . Am I the now? Is

> every other person the now? Then time would indeed be myself, and every other person would be time. (5E)

Does the fixing of the now give to the *who* a singular possibility of accessibility to self *as* now? And if the "now" that I *can* be is indeed invented in the now, in the clock, in the *what*, is not the *what* truly constitutive of this *who* in its possibility of now *as* now? Or rather does the clock only give the occasion for access to a *who* constituted elsewhere *as* now, before all clocks, before any determined *what*, in the very gap of the *what*? Heidegger's response is indeed the latter; it is, we are arguing, too quick:

> What is involved in the fact that human existence has already procured a clock prior to all pocket-watches and sundials? . . . Do I mean by the now myself? (5E)

As for "the natural clock of the alternation of day and night," what relation does the *who* entertain with it? Is this alternation, like the clock, a *what*? If so, should it not be considered as a *cosmological program*, one covered over today by the products of "program industries" (if we accept that present technological time, characterized by Paul Virilio as "false light" [*faux jour*], covers over the time of natural (day)light)? Paragraph 80 of *Being and Time* will analyze this covering-over as having always already taken place. The proxying [*pro-curation*] of a clock is the *hepatic* mark of *promētheia*, the liver consumed by day but restored by night. There is, then, something like the proxying of a clock *before* all historico-natural programmatic systems (from the day and the seasons to the real-time installations of global capitalist industry). This proxying would have always already called forth a *historial programmability*. It is something like the minimum program or the program from de-fault *qua* the programmatic, improbable, and impossible absence of any program. Its manifestation, however, articulated always upon a "datability," on a *what*, can be nothing but programmatic, can only be programmatic in all senses of this word. These are issues emerging for us in an "epoch" of the absence of epoch, or the epoch of program industries. And this, in a certain sense, is what the 1924 lecture brings to light.

"Am I the now?" Heidegger asks, and, in so saying, he makes the first step toward the lecture's true aim: the thesis that *time is Dasein*. And yet it is through the clock, in its stases, at its pace so to speak, that the lecture sets its course toward this aim. So, in what relation with programs, that is, with technics, is Dasein time? The rest of Heidegger's analysis concerns this originary relation, understood as withdrawal if not forgetting, as falling, the falling of Dasein who is time, that is *ipseity*.

Programs and the Improbable

The clock *sent* us *back* to Dasein. In a gesture that anticipates everything in *Being and Time*, it is a question of deciphering, starting from Dasein, not what being is but what time is—for being temporal is "the fundamental assertion of Dasein relative to its being" (Heidegger 1992, 7E). Dasein is being-in-the-world; being-with-one-another; being-together in the world in speaking as *I am*, *mineness*; mineness that always loses itself in the One; concern and care; everydayness; foreunderstanding of being-there by itself *in terms of* and *through* tradition, in other words, *concealing* of being. As for this last characteristic, it could be said that tradition is here program: it marks the explicitly pro-grammatic character of Dasein.

The difficulty of apprehending Dasein "is grounded not in the limitation of . . . our cognitive faculty" (Heidegger 1992, 10E) but rather in the fact that

> Dasein is determined by its perpetuity (*die Jeweiligkeit*); in so far as it is what it can be, it is perpetually mine. . . . Yet how is this entity to be apprehended in its being before it has reached its end? After all, I am still underway with my Dasein. It is still something that is not yet at an end. (10E)[7]

Mineness is being in perpetuity, that is, in mortality: finitude is the infinitude of the finite, or rather of the radical end as what comes to fulfillment in *not* fulfilling itself, in deferring itself. *Being and Time* will say that Dasein, as long as it exists, is not yet something. It cannot be grasped in its totality: it exceeds itself, and its end belongs to this excess—death. It finds itself in "perpetual incompletion." Ceasing to exceed itself, it is no longer there. This makes Dasein incomparable with a *what* and gives it a privileged and exemplary status among beings by its having access to being. Dasein is a being whose possibility is a "character of being" that cannot be understood under categories of reality that apply to the present-at-hand and the ready-to-hand, but is rather to be considered from out of the phenomenon of care, itself grounding "dying" and thereby the temporality whose essential phenomenon is the future. The vulgar understanding of time in terms of the now must therefore be criticized. The lecture does not yet explicitly engage in such a critique.

Since Dasein can never be deferring, that is, "toward its end," Dasein is improbable, which is to say, unprogrammable. This would seem to contradict the possibility of a constitution of the *who* (improbable) by the *what* (pro-grammatic). Perpetual mineness is the radical mark of an originary befalling, as the *improbability* of Dasein—of what it in the end is: namely, death, mortality. We will determine later the improbability of mineness as idiomaticity: *incalculability, unprogrammability, untranslatability.* But we will do so to show that the improbable is entirely programmatically destined, that the elementary *is* the supplementary, in the same strictly improbable way that says: fulfillment is only accomplished by not being accomplished. This, of course, is the very structure of delay, or of the *après-coup*, though not in terms of the successivity that would precede them and from which they would depart "afterward," but on the contrary as the origin of this successivity that covers over the structure that bears it and of which Epimetheus and everything that *ēpimētheia* stands for, in contradistinction to Prometheus, are the trace. This constitutive delay will bring to light in *Being and Time* why time cannot be thought in terms of now; and, perhaps more obviously than in *Being and Time*, the delay can be seen to emerge from the lecture as différance.

The sense of perpetuity as end without end, that is, as a limit that delimits nothing but weaves away, is mortality. It is in terms of mortality alone, and of mortality as a *knowing*, that mineness, or idiomaticity, is formulated:

> I never *am* the other. The less one is in a hurry to steal away unnoticed from this perplexity, the longer one endures it, the more clearly one sees that in whatever creates this difficulty for Dasein, Dasein shows itself in its most extreme possibility. The end of my Dasein, my death, is not some point at which a sequence of events suddenly breaks off, but a possibility which Dasein knows of in this or that way. (Heidegger 1992, 11E)

Neither the passage of my death nor that of the death of the other, since death is always mine, are experiencable (there is no "there," site of all experience). Since it is always mine and, therefore, unrepresentable, as *Being and Time* will say—thereby reformulating "I never am the Other"—

my death is improbable and yet certain: which explains at the same time the improbability of Dasein itself, its indeterminacy, that is, its absolute différance. This unrepresentability is the very ground of the principle of individuation, of differentiation. The structure Heidegger describes is indeed that of différance: *because* there is *deferment*, there is *differentiation.*

This structure only makes sense as *ēpimētheia*: just as différance is articulated upon a (pro)gram, the not-yet that is the excess is symmetrical with an already that is itself *prosthetic.* This prostheticity also means nonaccomplishment, lack of being, that is, being-in-de-fault.

Dasein is becoming: it is to be its not-yet. The structure is not that of life: the maturing fruit comes to completion, while Dasein is always in incompletion. Being by existing, Dasein is *already* its end, already its not-yet (such is the existential sense of the already-there of what has been), and "the ending designated by death does not mean Dasein's being-at-an-end but its being-for-the-end." The end pre-cedes Dasein as its possibility—its extreme possibility, that is, its own. As unsurpassable possibility, it is also the impossibility of Dasein. Improbable, it is impossible: its possibility is *only* differing and deferring.

Knowledge and Withdrawal

The knowledge of this *possibility* is the knowledge from which proceed all other forms of knowledge. How does it come about, how does it come to light, this knowledge that is the how (the *wie*) of Dasein?

The end is an (originary) certainty, a certainty, however, that is totally undetermined,[8] certainty as the very indeterminacy of the being that it certifies as being what it is. "The most extreme possibility of being has the character of a standing-before in certainty, and this certainty for its part is characterized by an utter indeterminacy" (Heidegger 1992, 11E). "How does this concern our question of what time is, and especially the following question of what Dasein is in time?" (11E).

This knowledge is the knowledge of a nonknowing (completion as knowledge of an essential incompletion); it is the improbable knowledge of the improbable, for the limit that, undetermined, neither delimits nor determines anything is radically improbable, a knowledge, always already lost and covered over, of what is never reached or of what when reached is extinguished. And this knowledge is endless; it is endlessness itself—or necessity. It is knowledge as such, *as* time, that is, as anticipation, given that "the fundamental phenomenon of time is the future" (Heidegger 1992, 14E):

> Dasein, as always perpetually mine, knows of its death and does so even when it wants to know nothing of it. What is it to have one's own death in each case? It is Dasein's *running ahead* [*Vorlaufen*, anticipation] to its past, to an extreme possibility of itself that stands before it in certainty and utter indeterminacy. (12E, my emphasis)

It is a different certainty from that of the *ego sum* which here appears as the ground of Dasein. This certainty, an originary *fact*, is just as much an originary disturbance or opacity, an originary uncertainty: it does not ground any calculation; in fact it grounds nothing, it constitutes incalculability, and yet, this incalculability merges into calculation, is tempered and forged in it. It is here rather than elsewhere that Descartes is overturned, that the ground is made groundless. Obviously, this reversal is neither a sublation nor a negation. The overturning of the *I am* results in the structure of différance that articulates anticipation. It is the being-possible that marks Dasein, and this possibility is always such that it "knows of death." But the I "knows of death in the manner of a knowing that shrinks back" (Heidegger 1992, 12E). In 1924 the *withdrawal* is already being thought—in terms not of being *qua* the withdrawal of being but of time itself considered from the perspective of mortality as the *knowledge* of death. It is the forgetful character of mortality with which the theme of *elpis*, articulated in its duplicity (hope and fear), between *ēpimētheia* and *promētheia*, has already made us familiar. It is the certain knowledge of an uncertain difference, difference that "shrinks back" and that in this very withdrawal is this différance in the Derridean sense: temporalization and spacing, datability and significability, falling and publicness[9]—but also *putting into reserve for the possibility of a singular return.*

Improbability forms the destiny of Dasein: destiny is the nonpredestination that being-mine, or having to be, expresses. Having to be (for Dasein, potentiality-for-being what it has to be) lies in the withdrawal of Dasein; it constantly conceals itself, *disappears*, as a result of which Dasein is improbable, susceptible to falling, to a not-being-there or a being-there by de-fault (for which it is precisely im-probable). *Being and Time* will say that "if Dasein exists, it has already been *thrown* into this possibility" (Heidegger 1967a, 251); in other words, Dasein is thrown forward to its end *as* it is thrown into the already-there of the factical world. If this is so, the essentially factical dying of Dasein is "more often" falling into a concern programmed by public and determinable discourse and time. To think of a possibility that is not secondary and derived, but is originary, and for which, precisely, being is a potentiality: it is on the basis of an originary *programmability* that there is an originary improbable; this improbable is not the contrary of this programmability but forms its truth.

The mark of Dasein's improbability is its loneliness (which befalls it), the lot of mineness. "This being-past, as the 'how,' brings Dasein harshly into its sole possibility of itself, allows it to stand entirely alone with respect to itself" (Heidegger 1992, 13E). This unique rest is an ipseity or an idiocy [*une idiotité*], a "freedom" or an "autonomy" only as *Unheimlichkeit*, uncanniness, not-being-at-home. The strange if not fatal *Eigentlichkeit* of idiocy always already—or always still—idiomaticity and being-in-the-world, not having, rigorously speaking, its origin in itself, only being *its* past, which is nevertheless not its own (being-thrown is also a projection):

> Dasein is authentically alongside itself, it is truly existent, whenever it maintains itself in this running ahead. *This running ahead* is nothing other than *the authentic and singular future of one's own Dasein.* In running ahead Dasein *is* its future, in such a way that in this being futural it comes back to its past and present. (Heidegger 1992, 13E)

It is in terms of anticipation, "running ahead," that *Eigentlichkeit*, idiomatic idiocy and the improbable are thought. The originary improbability can only link onto the already-there of a past after the event, onto what has already happened, onto the inherited passive stock of the effects of failure. Dasein is futural: it is the originary phenomenon of the future. Furthermore,

> anticipation of one's uttermost and ownmost possibility is coming back understandingly to one's ownmost "been." Only so far as it is futural can Dasein *be* authentically as having been. The character of "having been" arises, in a certain way, from the future. (Heidegger 1967a, 326)

This granted, must not the originary improbability that makes up *Eigentlichkeit* ground itself, in a manner just as originary, in the actual, concrete, and historico-technical possibility of a *repetition* of the past that provides the possibility of an access to this having been forming the already-there?

Real-Time Clocks of the Blank "*Geschlecht*"

Does not repetition in which the past projects itself forward as the opening of the originarily possible being-past *take* like a culinary sauce or a graft; does it not *rush* headlong into the entirely technological grammatics of active programs in which being-in-the-world and the worlding of the world are from the first deployed? The question of repetition includes here that of "reproducibility," which should be analyzed, reading Benjamin and Blanchot, as the very condition of producibility before any other determination. The question of repetition immediately connotes the question of *tekhnē*; indeed it is this question. The mythical and sacrificial source of the notion of *ēpimētheia*, the very meaning of which is to repeat the fault, and then ruminate it after the event, brings out strongly this condition of repetition.

Concern-ful from the moment Zeus has hidden the *bios*, *disappearing* in the same facticity that also provides the ground for its potentiality-for-being, humanity invents and produces expedients that compensate for its de-fault of qualities. The stamp that marks it is the prosthesis, this *what* that constitutes the very being of the outside of the *who*—movement outside of the self [*mise hors de soi*], that is, the ecstatic and temporal transcendence of Dasein. The *unheimlich* character of all prostheses is, besides, what Dasein, with its eye "on the simple fact of existing as such," cannot endure while being from the start supported by it. "Such a look" is "nothing less in essence than the fact of staring at its own mortality" (Heidegger 1982, 21). To compensate for the fault of Epimetheus—and we can now understand this—Prometheus doubles up on the act of forgetting, bestowing upon mortals the "gift" of technicity constitutive of mortality. Anticipation, as source or support of *Eigentlichkeit*, that is, of the handicapped, failing, unequal, different, idiomatic, idiotic nature of improbability, amounts to an immersion in the knowledge of nonknowing, which is nothing other than prostheticity from which *there is* being-outside-oneself, ec-stasis, mortality, and time. Time itself both deploys prostheticity in its concrete effectivity and deploys itself within it. The concrete effectivity of the prosthetic play of traces, of the referrals and recalls that make up repetition, return to the past and to the present (to the gift of the de-fault). Prior to the metaphysical forgetting of its tragic meaning, this process of anticipation, return, and withdrawal in return—which is nothing but a detour—bears the name of *ēpimētheia*, knowledge after the event.

A consequence is to be drawn from the preceding—one we will appropriately return to in the second volume—which concerns an important criterion by which contemporary technics can be specified: the precipitate nature of anticipation *qua ēpimētheia* is an essentially deferred time. Thus, if the "futural character" of Dasein is constituted in the "authentic" repetition of "having-been," if this deferred repetition, after the event, of what has been, is also what grants Dasein's difference, its idiomatic selfhood, the consistency of its *who*, then the question must emerge: what would be the effects of a dynamic of the *what* that short-circuits the work of différance?

The Dasein that comes to be in anticipation—in différance—is not given its being through the clock; rather, it loses itself in the clock. Its temporality is its future. The generation of today's "time," our *Geschlecht*, says flatly: *no future*. What is affirmed here at the same time as it is refused? Does this slogan mean that there is no différance or no longer any différance in the extrapolation of the present as *Gegenwart*—that in "real time," which is nothing but this extrapolation, *there can be no future*?

If such a question invited a response, indeed an affirmative one, it would not mean simply saying that *tekhnē* conveys the power that propels the *who* to its falling, and that such is the weight of the *what* in its ability to drag the future down into its fall, and this, precisely because it is *tekhnē* that *gives différance*, that *gives time*. With this hypothesis we embark properly upon our critique of the Heideggerian analytic, in other words, the effects of his forgetting of the meaning of *ēpimētheia*. This critique will become more sharp with our reading of *Being and Time*, despite the fact that the work is so closely engaged with the themes we are at present introducing.

We have seen why the understanding "of time starting from time" had to start in turn from a clock. The referral to the *who* as a now had been made possible and necessary by the fact that now is "fixed" durably by the clock. Now, what does "fix" mean here? And what does fix "durably" mean? What does "to fix" mean when the "object" of this fixing forms one of the three modalities of the temporal ecstasis? What would to fix the "past" mean—to record or register [*enregistrer*] it: what does to register what has passed mean? What is to rule [*régir*]; what are a register, a registrar, a control room?

The whole of Heidegger's analysis of the *what*'s referral to the *who* consists in showing that whereas the now can be fixed, a fixing of the past, and *a fortiori* of the future, is inconceivable. In *Being and Time* Heidegger goes on to draw the consequence that Dasein is ultimately not the now, and that the analysis of time that starts from the now is exactly what encloses metaphysics within a vulgar comprehension of time. "The clock shows us the now, but no clock ever shows the future or has ever shown the past" (Heidegger 1992, 17E). As for this last affirmation, which seeks to ground the privileging of the *who* over the *what*, the question is to know what one means by a clock. Even if we provisionally accept that a clock tells us nothing about the future, is not being-futural one of a clock's modalities, not only in a technico-temporal sense (for example, following what Evans Pritchard says of the Nuer tribe, for whom "the cattle clock determines the time" [1950, 103]) but in a much more technological and historico-technical sense (which the rest of the quotation from Evans Pritchard also suggests: "The Nuer have no expression equivalent to 'time' [in our language], and they cannot, therefore, as we can, speak of the time as though it were something actual, which passes, can be wasted, can be saved, and so forth" [103])? The understanding *of* time that always makes up time, *qua* a relation to the future and to the past, and that Heidegger will show being expressed as language (Heidegger 1967a, §§32–35), is *constituted* for the Nuer tribe by the clock-cattle.

Everything today would seem to confirm with still-unsurpassable strength the direction of Heidegger's analysis. And yet, the *no future* remains to be thought (as "real time" in the sense of the nondeferred): it reveals a techno-logico-instrumental condition in which *time is the technological synthesis of, and in, mortality.* Does the time without time of *no future* translate the error of technics, or does it translate, more profoundly, *the techno-logical fate [Ge-schick, errancy] of Dasein itself*? And why does this fate also take the name of "the end of history," declaring itself to be an end, that is, the fulfillment of metaphysics? Is not "to think being without beings" to acknowledge this absence of time, of this disappearance of time in time itself? Does not this "time without time" or "this absence of time" require that the thought of being, of time and the *Zeit-raum,* starts from technics? Is it not the revelation of the withdrawal for a Blank Generation, itself nothing but the name of the being that is given and, in the same gesture, withdrawn by Prometheus, that is, a mortal? Blank Generation—or Blank "*Geschlecht*"—is the name that the Punk movement gave itself, "no future" being its antislogan. "Blank" is to be understood here as "dumb" as much as "empty": without qualities, left *without voice*, if not without *logos*, indeed without "conscience" (of the being-at-fault-or-in-debt taken to its most extreme possibility), for this *aphony* is no longer that of the Heideggerian "voice of conscience" (*Gewissen*).

From 1924 onward, Heidegger aimed in a sense at what we are here calling "real time"—which remains to be thought both in *and* outside his terms. It is the question of the *Gegenwart*, of the present, or rather, following the French translation of *The Concept of Time* by Michel Haar and Marc B. de Launay (1983, 33–54), of "present actuality," which designates, in what we sense of this translation, as much the present as a moment of temporal ecstasis as the present as news or information, actuality in the sense of news.

Fixing and Determination

To fix does not mean to determine but to establish. The tool of what is established is the vice that fixes the object of work, that makes *possible* both a determination and, through articulating the *who* with the very possibility of a *what* and inversely, the *indetermination* of the multiplicity of possible determinations. If the *what* of the clock is considered pejoratively by Heidegger in the preparatory understanding of time regarding the analytic of *Dasein* and the question of being, it is because Heidegger simply identifies fixing and determination.

"The fundamental phenomenon of time is the future. . . . It is manifest that the original way of dealing with time is not a measuring" (Heidegger 1992, 14E), for to want to measure time is to want to determine the indeterminate, that is, to take flight *before the end* and *in concern*. Dasein is thrown to its end as it is thrown into the already-there of the factical world. As a result, the fundamentally factical dying of Dasein is most often falling into concern. Concern "evades [this daily being-for-death] by conferring determinateness upon it" (Heidegger 1967a, 258), through measure. Measure, the loss of (originary) time, is secured in the clock, which determines the understanding of time.

Yet is measure the *only* meaning of a clock, and, more generally, of fixing? Is not a measure, on the contrary, the possibility of an effacement, a forgetting, a veiling, and a vulgarization of a time that would not originate elsewhere than outside, otherwise than as outside, but that would be *constituted*, precisely, by the *grammē* as such and in general, that of grammar as well as that of the kilogram or photogram, initial condition of any temporalization? The measure of the clock is anticipated in the calendar, the names of saints, or holy dates in which common temporality is inscribed. Writing in general (in the current sense of the term) was firstly a site of measuring, as Wittfogel (1977) and the archaeologists of Babylon have shown concerning the rhythms of flooding. Consequently, should one not say that *writing is a clock*, thus echoing what the Egyptian attributes to Solon in the *Timaeus*? There, we recall, the clock that allows for the calculation of possible floods in the Nile valley, through their being fixed in a durable record, *also* says something of the past and the future:

> O Solon, Solon, you Hellenes are never anything but children, and there is not an old man among you. Solon in return asked him what he meant. I mean to say, he replied, that in mind you are all young; there is no old opinion handed down among you by ancient tradition, nor any science which is hoary with age. And I will tell you why. There have been, and will be again, many destructions of mankind arising out of many causes; the greatest have been brought about by the agencies of fire and water, and other lesser ones by innumerable other causes. There is the story which even you have preserved, that once upon a time Phaethon, the son of Helios, having yoked the steeds in his father's chariot, because he was not able to drive them in the path of his father, burned up all that was upon the earth, and was himself destroyed by a thunderbolt. Now this has the form of a myth, but really signifies a declination of the bodies moving in the heavens around the earth, and a great conflagration of things upon the earth which recurs after long intervals; at such times those who live upon the mountains and in dry and lofty places are more liable to destruction than those who dwell by rivers on the seashore. And from this calamity we are preserved by the liberation of the Nile, who is our never-failing savior. When, on the other hand, the gods purge the earth with a deluge of water, the survivors in your country are herdsmen and shepherds who dwell on the mountains, but those who, like you, live in cities are carried by the rivers in to the sea. Whereas in this land, neither then nor at any other time, does the water come down from above on the fields, having always a tendency to come up from below, for which reason the traditions preserved here are the most ancient. The fact is that wherever the extremity of winter frost or of summer sun does not prevent, mankind exist, sometimes in greater, sometimes in lesser numbers. And whatever happened either in your country or in ours, or in any other region of which we are informed—if there were any actions noble or great or in any other way remarkable, they have all been

> written down by all of old and are preserved in our temples. Whereas just when you and other nations are beginning to be provided with letters and the other requisites of civilized life, after the usual interval, the stream from heaven, like a pestilence, comes pouring down and leaves only those of you who are destitute of letters and education, and so you have to begin all over again like children, and know nothing of what *happened* in ancient times, either among us or among yourselves. . . . The survivors of that destruction died, leaving no written word. (Plato 1961, *Timaeus*, 22b–23c, my emphasis)

Does not Galen also speak of such a general horological possibility of recording and measuring? One that, if general, is nevertheless here singularized as Greek? Of course it is important to know here what one means by "Greek." For as far as *we* are concerned, we have aged: we are no longer Egyptian nor Greek. Writing is no longer, for us, of "recent constitution." And we must know what that means.

The "clockness" of the *grammē*, or rather the *grammē* or programness of the clock, also forms the meaning of the Augustinian question of time. This, in a passage (which Heidegger does not quote) in which the now and the *extensio* are thought in terms not of a sandglass or a water clock but of a poem—that is, of a pro-gramme (Augustine, *Confessions*, bk. 11, par. xxvii). Husserl in *The Origin of Geometry* makes a similar gesture, one to which we will return.

What, then, is Heidegger aiming at in the clock and its measure, which would concern the *grammē* in general, such that the *letter* and the *number* would from now on always have to be thought together?

> "Running ahead to" collapses if it is understood as a question of the "when" and "how much longer" of the past, because inquiries about the past in the sense of "how much longer" and "when" are not at all alongside the past in the possibility we have characterized; they cling precisely to that which is not yet past and busy themselves with what may possibly remain for me. This questioning does not seize the indeterminacy of the certainty of the past, but precisely wishes to determine indeterminate time. (Heidegger 1992, 14E)

Here, improbability, that is, temporality, is concealed in what constitutes it—namely, the possibility of fixing durably the now (whatever the apparatus of inscription); but that also of recording the past and of constituting thereby all that *Being and Time* will call later the "world-historial," and of entering into its consideration, that is, in the event, of experiencing the *as such* of nondurability, or of *revolution*, which is being-on-the-way toward the end. The possibility of access to the as-such is at the same time the loss of the as-such, its forgetting, its disappearance. Possibility, then, as much as impossibility. The concealment lies in the wish to calculate the incalculable and to prove the improbable rather than experience it—to take flight from experience. We call *ēpimētheia* this experience, an empiricity before the empirical-transcendental divide or the *indeterminate* opening of what has happened.

To calculate means to eliminate différance—the delay. "Real time" is that: it looks for synchronization, which is what all calculating anticipation amounts to. But is it the clock as such that is the problem here? If, firstly, it is argued that writing is a kind of clockwork, of objective memory (and the issue of memory is inevitable when one addresses the question of the past, present, and future of anticipation), and if, secondly, it is shown that writing forms the (entirely techno-logical) dehiscence of différance in its *historical* "as such" (and as the inception of "the history of being") and, thereby, a condition (of the impossibility) of the very opening of the historial—if both these arguments make sense, then the Heideggerian themes of *Eigentlichkeit* and falling can only become coherent from the perspective of an understanding of technics that is not metaphysical, one that is never escaped completely either by Heidegger or by all those who, perhaps imagining that they precede him, actually follow in his wake.

Self-Individuation

In 1987, a contraption was set up in front of the Georges Pompidou Center in Paris that could be considered the monument of the century—a monument of disappearance, of nothing-at-hand, apocalyptic. Given the name "Gentitron," it is an electronic chronometer that counts down the seconds to the year 2000. One might say that the contraption calculates improbable death; it presents time by fleeing it and flees it by presenting it. It calculates for nothing or *almost* nothing; sponsored by the firm Cointreau, for ten francs it hands you a card indicating the number of seconds separating you from the end ... of the century.

> Time authentically has no time to calculate time. . . . Yet we become acquainted with Dasein, which itself is supposed to be time, as reckoning with time, indeed even measuring it with the clock. Dasein is there with the clock,

> albeit only the most proximate, everyday clock of day and night. Dasein reckons with and asks after the "how much" of time, and is therefore never alongside time in its authenticity. (Heidegger 1992, 15E)

While making explicit this fundamental loss of time, *the originary absence of time in which only time presents itself,* Heidegger describes the flight before being-past in terms of *Gegenwart,* present actuality. In this context, various political groups and people in France are demanding that the principle of the people's referendum be widened, while the French television program *L'heure de vérité* in fact prefigures and already satisfies, through opinion polls in real time, the wish of the watchmakers: direct democracy, nondeferred, "in real time."[10] It is in what one calls "direct," or "live," which is nothing but the most immediately and dramatically perceptible effect of the *speed* governing the contemporary world, reconstituting the synthetic "living present" (but we will attempt to show that every synthetic living present is constituted in the death of such a synthesis), that the true stake lies, rather than in the question of calculation as such. For it is also calculation, insofar as it is implied by any clock, by any process of making discrete,[11] by any dissemination, and finally by any writing, that gives the possibility of *fixing durably,* that opens up the "as such," difference, deferred time.

Calculation, aimed at in the expression that characterizes technics as modern, grounded in the *ego sum,* could be said, then, to be itself directed at something else than calculation, and this would be *real time.* To say this, however, also means that the concept of calculation does not exhaust the richness of the effects engendered by fixing.

> The question of the "when" of the indeterminate past, and in general of the "how much" of time, is the question of what still remains for me, still remains as present. To bring time into the "how much" means to take it as the now of present. To ask after the "how much" of time means to become absorbed in concern with some "what" that is present. Dasein flees in the face of the "how" and clings to the specific "what" that is present. . . . It thus encounters the time itself that Dasein in each case is, but is as present. (Heidegger 1992, 15E–16E)

This possibility of calculation does not arise all of a sudden; it is not specifically trapped in technical measuring instruments. It forms *the tradition itself* for which the above instruments open up a publicity, a datability, a significability, and in the everyday that lives with the clock as with the daily newspaper, with, that is, the printing of the day [*l'impression du jour*] (mobilizing today so many printing techniques, the whole tabloid press, everything from marble to pixels):

> Dasein, determined as being-with-one-another, simultaneously means being led by the dominant interpretation that Dasein gives of itself; by whatever *one* says, by fashion, by trends, by what is going on: the trend that no one is, whatever is the fashion: nobody. In everydayness Dasein is not that being that I am. Rather the everydayness of Dasein is that being that *one* is. And Dasein, accordingly, is the time in which *one* is with one another: "one's" time. (Heidegger 1992, 17E)

This "one" is also the tradition in general; it is therefore part of the whole question being opened up:

> The current interpretation of Dasein is most often dominated by everydayness, by what one traditionally thinks of existence and human life: it is dominated by the "one," by tradition. (Heidegger 1992, 17E)

It is clear that what Heidegger aims at in the "one" of present actuality and of *his* present actuality (the very one that was to produce that great exploiter of the radio, Hitler—*and we are doing nothing here but asking ourselves why the analytic of everydayness did not protect Heidegger from the effects of this present*) is found as a singular modality in what is called today the *media*, or *program industries.*[12] And it is just as clear that this must be analyzed in its own terms, as a failure of tradition, although proceeding from it enigmatically. This industrial "one" proceeds from the watch: "The clock that *one* has, every clock, shows the time of being-with-one-another-in-the-world" (Heidegger 1992, 17E).

It is *historiality* that is in question here—as well as history—harboring the question of *individuation*, which is itself constituted in *repetition*:

> The past remains closed off from any present so long as such a present, Dasein, is not itself historial. Dasein, however, is in itself historial in so far as it is its possibility. In being futural Dasein is its past; it comes back to it in the "how." The manner of its coming back is, among other things, conscience {*Gewissen*}. Only the "how" can be repeated. The past—experienced as authentic historiality—is anything but what is past. It is something to which I can return again and again. (Heidegger 1992, 19E)

The issue is that of the already-there, which announces itself as being-at-fault-and-in-need through the aphonic voice of conscience (*Gewissen*).[13] This essential possibility of a *return* is itself threatened by the dominant understanding of the present:

> The present generation thinks it is . . . overburdened with history. . . . *Something is called history which is not history at all.* According to the present, because everything is dissolved into history, one must attain the supra-historial again. (Heidegger 1992, 20E, my emphasis)

It remains to be known what makes this nonrepetition, this nonreturn, possible *today*, and firstly what makes the deferring and differing repetition of the how *actually* possible. "Our" present generation no longer believes that it belongs to anything; in its eyes, no longer is anything wanting: the default has become general [*ça fait défaut*]. The Blank "*Geschlecht*" is the generation of de-fault. The "present generation" that Heidegger has in view anticipates this *Geschlecht*. And the stake is history—the différance of deferred time, the time of repetition returning not to the same but to the other, to difference, proceeding from the how, from mortality as originary improbability as much as from mortality as pro-grammability—and this programmability is precisely what the how of the improbable Blank "*Geschlecht*" cannot not feel as such. The time of the present generation is the time of the present [*l'actualité présente*] in the sense that one speaks of televised news [*actualités télévisées*]. But its scope is much wider than this, embracing what is called "real time," the system of industrial production that covers televised news as much as the numerical databanks working in "real time" and the type of information particular to the world financial-military-industrial complex.

"The past as authentic history is repeatable," but not repeatable in just any old manner: "repeatable *in the how.*" In the repetition of the past "as true history" within the what, what reemerges is being-mine as "the possibility of access to history {that} is grounded in the possibility according to which any specific present *understands* how to be futural" (Heidegger 1992, 20E, my emphasis). However, is this possibility, in its dehiscence, not in turn grounded in the pro-grammability of this being-mine, of the being idiomatic of idiocy or selfness? Is there not, furthermore, a historial, techno-logical characterization (which would be what the "world-historial" profoundly means) of this *idios*?

Idiocy and idiomaticity are what Heidegger talks about under the name of individuation, under the name of time in that time is always *individuated* (which ensues from the affirmation that time is Dasein, Dasein being alone, split [*déshérant*], and *différant* in its perpetuity or its being-toward-the-end, that is, its improbability). There follows a long passage, one of fundamental import, which carries four theses.

1. The being of temporality means nonidentical actuality—deferred and thereby differentiated:

> Time is Dasein. Dasein is my perpetuity, and this can be perpetuity in what is futural by running ahead to the certain yet indeterminate past. Dasein always is in a manner of its possible temporal being. Dasein is time, time is temporal. Dasein is not time, but temporality. The fundamental assertion that time is temporal is therefore the most authentic determination—and it is not a tautology, because the being of temporality signifies non-identical actuality. (Heidegger 1992, 21E)

2. In the sense that time is Dasein, which is itself nothing but its already-there, it can be said that time is the *principium individuationis.*

> Dasein is its past, it is its possibility in running ahead to this past. In this running ahead I am authentically time, I have time. In so far as time is in each case mine, there are many times. *Time itself* is meaningless; time is temporal. If time is understood in this way as Dasein, then it indeed becomes clear what the traditional assertion about time means when it says that time is the proper *principium individuationis.* (21E)

3. Dasein is time insofar as it is being-futural: anticipation, improbability, différance—both deferring in time (anticipating) and being different, affirming a difference *qua* a "unique time," a singularity:

> To what extent is time, as authentic, the principle of individuation, i.e., that starting from which Dasein is in its perpetuity? In being futural, in running ahead, the Dasein that on average is becomes itself; in running ahead it becomes visible as this one singular uniqueness of its singular fate in the possibility of its singular past. (21E)

4. This individuation belongs, however, and in the same movement, to a community: that of mortals. Différance is affirmed by being felt as identity—in the improbable that is not the improbable Dasein but that differs from every other Dasein, being its end:

> This individuation . . . strikes down all becoming-exceptional. It individuates in such a way that it makes everyone equal. In being together with death everyone is brought into the "how" that each can be in equal measure; into a possibility with respect to which no one is distinguished, into the "how" in which all "what" dissolves into dust.[14]

This "individual" is less a subject than an instantiated idiomatic difference—seized, of course, in a *logos*, that is, firstly, in a *relation* (which means also an idiom), which is necessarily common, not different relative to those it gathers into their différance, and which should be understood in terms of *the community of a de-fault.* This need is being-toward-the-end *qua* facticity. One could have equally said that it is *ēpimētheia* in prostheticity (in *promētheia*) as it appeals to the figure of *Hermes,* referring back to *Hestia,* where *aido* and *dikē* spring from technics and double it up. This is idiomatic difference (hermetic and babelesque), eventually instantiated in what we would call a "subject," which we would, however, prefer here to call a "citizen." Citizenship consists in belonging to an *isonomy* in and through which an *autonomy* is affirmed. This is dated, datable, as the opening of history itself; not of historiality, which belongs to Dasein at all times, but of the epoch of historiality called "history"—which is the history of being and the suspension of one form of historiality by another. By what other? How can this epoch of historiality, the history of being, open up?

We would knowingly affirm here, in plain and somewhat brutal terms, that it is a form of writing, linear and phonological, that *gives* this opening. Such writing constitutes the first case of what we will define later as what stems from the *principle of a deferring and differing identity.* This first case is achieved by what we will call, to designate the completed form of alphabetic writing (phonological writing), *literal synthesis.* A temporality that is deferred belongs in principle to literal synthesis. In the second volume of this work we will develop the notions of *analogical* and *numerical synthesis,* which dominate contemporary technology, oriented, inversely, by an asymptotic tendency toward real, live temporality, temporality without detour, that is, toward *a particular atemporality*—one that does not exclude the work of différance but conceals it in an essential manner. In tracing these distinctions our project of apprehending temporal synthesis—that is, synthesis as such—in terms of *tekhnē qua* synthesis becomes more sharply delineated.

The Deferred Time of the History of Being

Dasein is the being who differs and defers [*l'étant qui diffère*]. A being who differs and defers should be understood in a twofold sense: the one who always puts off until later, who is essentially pro-jected in deferral, and the one who, for the same reason, finds itself originarily different, indeterminate, improbable. The being who defers by putting off till later anticipates: to anticipate always means to defer. Dasein has to be: it is not simply—it *is only* what *it will be*; it *is* time. Anticipation means being-for-the-end. Dasein knows its end. Yet it will *never* have knowledge of it. Its end is that toward which it is, in relation to which it is; yet its end is what will never be *for* Dasein. Dasein *is for* the end, but its end *is not* for it. Although it knows its end absolutely, it will always be that in relation to which it will never know anything: the knowledge of the end always withdraws, is concealed in being deferred. The end of Dasein is the indeterminate. It knows this. What Dasein knows, and knows radically, is the indeterminate, what cannot be calculated, and what, for Dasein, cannot essentially be proved. Of course it has the experience of the end of others, of those that it is not itself. But its end is, precisely, what can only be its own insofar as it remains essentially in concealment from it. This never-being-finished constitutes the mark of Dasein's finitude, the infinitude of the finite, that is, of the radical end as what can only be completed in being deferred [*en se différant*]. This deferral and this difference that I am as being-mine, this différance is anticipation. As the infinite finitude of Dasein, anticipation is the mark of indeterminacy *qua* originary knowledge of being-there. Being for its end, Dasein projects this end. It can only project it *authentically* as *its* end: im-probably, in solitude, from out of its lack of predestination, its having-to-be. It can only be in deferring and differing [*en différant*], both in the sense of putting off until later, of a putting into reserve and of an essential reserve, of a deferral, and in the sense of a *differentiation*: time as Dasein is the true principle of differentiation.

Because of this double and insoluble articulation of the two meanings of *différer*, time is essentially a deferred time. Being-toward-the-end is to have to be. It is to be *not yet*. But having-to-be *also* means to be-in-facticity, or, as we prefer to say following the myth of Prometheus, to be-in-prostheticity. Dasein is essentially in-the-world; this means that the world is already there for Dasein. Now, this being-already-there of the world is constituted notably as a being with others, the tradition and traditional foreunderstanding of one's being, or the One. Therefore, in this being-already-there the knowledge of having-to-be is transmitted and concealed at one and the same time. What is concealed is being-mine, the having-to-be-toward-the-end. Most often, Dasein is "programmatically," it is constituted, that is, according to modes of being particular to facticity in its banality. So, anticipation always takes place, but in the mode of calculation, in concern, a mode that wants to determine the indeterminate, thereby concealing individuation and the improbability of the end. "Anticipation of *collapses*" (Heidegger 1992, 14E) when it is understood as *calculation*. Questioning in a calculating manner "does not grasp the indeterminacy of the certitude of the past, but precisely wishes to *determine indeterminate time*" (14E), to calculate the incalculable, to program the unprogrammable, to prove the improbable. Possibility is most often understood in this way. This average possibility belongs to the extreme possibility that is the end. For Dasein, having-to-be is always *being-in-facticity*.

Hence, if, following Heidegger, anticipation is always for Dasein *return* to its past and to its present, this return to its past and its present can only be the return to a past that is not *its* past—which means for us, in terms of *ēpimētheia*, that it can only be a pros-thetic return. The past of Dasein and for Dasein is its facticity because it cannot be *stricto sensu*, as such, *its* past. This past is transmitted to it: it is its own only insofar as Dasein *is* its past, that is, it anticipates from it. The past of Dasein is necessarily outside of it. And yet Dasein is *only* this past that it is *not*. It can only be it by deferring and differing it, by being-in-ownness from out of what it is not, or rather, from out of what it is "programmatically," *not yet*. It can only be what it has to be by anticipating it, by being improbably what it still only is programmatically: it must *double up* on its pro-gram—*just as (the fault of) Prometheus doubles up on (the fault of) Epimetheus.*

"To have to be" means, then, two things: firstly, Dasein is already what it is; secondly, what it already is it only is in facticity, only is as what is not its own: it is in the mode of what is not proper to it. Yet it is nothing else but that.

In short, "Dasein," the *who*, is in de-fault of being. Heidegger says: it is at fault; Dasein is being-at-fault [*Schuldigsein*]. It is in these terms that the analytic of being-toward-the-end, starting from "moral consciousness," is conducted in the second part of *Being and Time*. The outcome of everything above is that the structure of anticipation and of deferral that Dasein is for itself is also the structure that carries and is carried by its past, including the past that exceeds it. This is why the fault is never only my fault, and why it is nevertheless always my fault. This is what leads Heidegger to the question of the history of being, the history of a forgetting, one begun in *Being and Time* and returning in "Time and Being" as the question of time within the horizon of modern technics. The "history of being" is the past "of" Dasein that is not *its* past and that, as past, anticipates and defers. Here also in two ways: authentically (as the transmission of the question of being) and in being concealed (as the metaphysical transmission, as the Epimethean forgetting of being). This past forms the *historiality* of Dasein. When this historiality has been disclosed as such to Dasein, Dasein has entered properly into the history of being.

And yet, what is this disclosure due to? What is an epoch of being; what is the epochal? Epochality is always an epochal Epimethean doubling-up (of the fault of Prometheus, which is itself doubling up the originary fault of Epimetheus).

Consequently it is no longer simply "the being that we ourselves are" that is deferring and differing; it is the history of being itself. This history is transmitted to Dasein, as tradition, firstly as concealment, that is, as *forgetting* and as *uprooting*:

> [Not only is] Dasein . . . inclined to fall back upon its world (the world in which it is) and to interpret itself in terms of that world by its reflected light, but also . . . Dasein simultaneously falls prey to the tradition of which it has more or less explicitly taken hold. This tradition keeps it from providing its own guidance, whether in inquiring or in choosing. This holds true—and by no means least—for that understanding which is rooted in Dasein's ownmost Being, and for the possibility of developing it—namely, for ontological understanding.
>
> When tradition thus becomes master, it does so in such a way that what it "transmits" is made so inaccessible, proximally and for the most part, that it rather becomes concealed. Tradition takes what has come down to us and delivers it over to self-evidence; it blocks our access to those primordial "sources." . . . Indeed it makes us forget that they have had such an origin. . . . Dasein has had its historiality . . . thoroughly uprooted by tradition. (Heidegger 1967a, 21)

But how is the tradition, which at the same time conceals and holds in reserve what it conceals, *transmitted* to Dasein? As far as the history of being is concerned, it can only be transmitted as the *historio-graphy* that Dasein has to interpret: it is in the presence of a "historical consciousness," and in it alone, that there is a history *of being*. An epoch without historiography is historial, but it is not yet historial as the history of being. That said, a question, which does not seem to be of concern to Heidegger, necessarily arises: given that it is through the "durable fixing of the now" that a clock can bring us to recognize time in Dasein, who is outside the now, *then what can the durable fixing of the past teach us in turn*? And in what does such a fixing of the past in its concrete actuality—pro-grammatic from the perspective of the elaboration of time as anticipation—consist? How does Dasein, on the basis of its essential temporality, gain access to its historiality? How is this historiality essential to its temporality, if not through a durable, necessarily pros-thetic fixing of the past, or rather of the "before" as what has happened [*comme ce qui s'est passé*]? "Ce qui s'est passé": what does the impersonality of this reflexivity, caught by the French idiom, imply?[15]

Dasein is outside itself, in ec-stasis, temporal: its past lies outside it, yet it is nothing but this past, in the form of *not yet*. By being actually its past, it can do nothing but put itself outside itself, "ek-sist." But *how* does Dasein eksist in this way? Prosthetically, through pro-posing and pro-jecting itself outside itself, in front of itself. And this means that *it can only test its improbability pro-grammatically.*

1. Dasein, essentially factical, is pros-thetic. It is nothing either outside *what* is outside of it or *what it* is outside itself, since it is only through the prosthetic that it experiences, without ever proving so, its mortality, only through the prosthetic that it anticipates.

2. Dasein's access to its past, and its anticipation as such, is pros-thetic. In accordance with this condition, it accedes or does not accede to this past as it has been, or not been, durably fixed, and to which, at the same time, Dasein is to be found, or not found, durably fixed.

The différance that Dasein is can only be disclosed to it through a prostheticity that, if it most often conceals différance as calculation, measure, or determination, also puts it into actual play: this prostheticity effects and concretizes the endurance of the deferred and differing time that it is. The history of being is a recorded, delegated, impersonal history: it is the history of that impersonal knowing of which Blanchot talks, which can only be written, however, in the form of personal pronouns—a knowledge of mortality that can only be lived personally. As far as the history of being is concerned, it is this recording that realizes the paradox of what we are calling deferring and differing identity [*l'identité différante*], in which identity and difference are posited at one and the same time.

Linear and phonological writing is a programmatic *ēpokhē*. It suspends the forms of a tradition that is itself programmatic, but that does not appear *as such*. In this suspension, it programs another, a new endurance of the past, of anticipation and of the present, primordially as presence, *ousia*—in the now, the now become historical. This endurance can only be that of Dasein, of the now as it dissolves into its future returning to its already-there: it is *as such*, that is, *as citizenship*, the doubling-up of the technological or prosthetic *ēpokhē*. This endurance proceeds as an experience of the différance of the text that is read, which is also that of the reader-text (and its pre-text), the one putting in play and being put in play by the other—textualities that are realized together, just as in Aristotle the act of the sensible and the act of sense absolutely coincide. This forms a paradox because it is by identifying the text read letter for letter, unequivocally, without hesitation, with exactitude because *ortho-graphically*, that the reader is produced as différance, that is, as a reading that is always different, unceasingly to be resumed and deferred as the unceasing itself. Through its being identified, what the text discloses is the *elementary contextuality* of its reading, its integrity from being in a here and a now that are nothing but the ex-position of the anticipatory finitude of the reader in its *there*. Writing ex-poses différance—at the same time concealing it. Anticipation is prostheticity (ex-position, temporalization as spacing), that is, *promētheia* and *ēpimētheia*. It is fulfilled according to the actual conditions of the pros-thesis, of this techno-logical pro-position that comes from the past to anticipation and goes from the person who anticipates to what he or she anticipates (the past, that is prostheticity itself). Anticipation cannot be anything else than prosthetic; improbability cannot be anything other than programmatic—but only as *doubling-up*. Our question comes together, then, in that of the meaning of such a doubling-up: the advent of linear writing does *not explain* the inaugurality of history.

Pros-thesis means "placed-there-in-front." Pros-theticity is the being-already-there of the world, and also, consequently, the being-already-there of the past. *Pros-thesis* can be literally translated as pro-position. A prosthesis is what is proposed, placed in front, in advance; technics is what is placed before us [*la technique est ce qui nous est pro-posé*] (in an originary knowledge, a *mathēsis* that "pro-poses" us things). Knowledge of mortality is knowledge of pro-position, but through these kinds of knowledge that are *tekhnai*; in a profound and diverse manner, it is the knowledge of a "primordial" de-fault: the de-fault of quality, of having-to-be, destiny as predestination. The pro-position or technicity summons time. In the Protagorean myth, Hermes and *hermēneia* proceed from Prometheus. It is also political knowledge, the hermeneutic and hermetic knowledge of *aido* and *dikē*, "shame" or "honor" and "justice" or "law" [*droit*], a knowledge that is common to all, unlike the specialized forms of knowledge of the *tekhnai*: knowledge of a de-fault that in this context is *not* moral conscience *but the politicalness of the citizen.*

Promētheia and *ēpimētheia* thread the couple that constitutes the proposed and techno-logical form of knowing made up by temporalization in the anticipation of the indeterminate. *Ēpimētheia* is what designates thought *qua* meditation after the event ... *of the pro-position.* Prometheus and Epimetheus constitute anticipatory reflection, which is particular to mortals since it proceeds from *tekhnē qua* a deferred, differing, differentiated pro-position, that is a pro-position that is *doubled-up.* Epimetheus doubles up Prometheus just as Dasein doubles up its past. And yet, the *conditions* (of impossibility) of this doubling-up are techno-logical. *Tekhnē*, *logos* and *hermēneia* form together the horizon of all anticipation, time as mortality, *care.*

"Time is Dasein" (Heidegger 1992, 21E) means: time is the relation to time. But this relation is always already determined by its techno-logical, historial conditions, *effects* of an originary techno-logical condition. Time is each time the singularity of a relation to the end that is woven technologically. Every epoch is characterized by the technical conditions of actual access to the already-there that constitute it as an epoch, as both suspension and continuation, and that harbor its particular possibilities of "differ*a*ntiation" and individuation. Political citizenship, which is contemporaneous with the opening of the history of being, belonging itself to the history of différance, is a case in point.

This is why we could write: "Nothing can be said of temporalization that does not relate to the epiphylogenetic structure put in place each time, and each time in an original way, by the already-there, in other words by the memory supports that organize the successive epochs of humanity: that is, technics."[16] But the prior elucidation of the possibility of anticipation (of the possibility of possibility), as the existential analytic reinterpreted in terms of our understanding of *ēpimētheia*, has shown us that time is deferred. There is time only as this deferral that generates difference(s). This différance is a referral, a reflection of the *who* in the *what* and reciprocally. The analysis of the techno-logical possibilities of the already-there particular to each epoch will, consequently, be that of the conditions of reflexivity—of mirroring—of a *who* in a *what.*

Neglecting the tragic meaning of the figure of forgetting, Heidegger maintains that the principle of individuation is constituted outside the publicity of the One. But the truth is quite the opposite. The gift of différance is technological because the individual constitutes itself from out of the possibilities of the One, from the relation with one another each time allowed for by the particular technological set-up. One is individuated *sooner* than when the individual à la Heidegger falls into the publicity and chitchat of the One; "authentic temporality" always comes too late (it is always already "inauthentic," factical): this is *ēpimētheia.* No mortality is originarily absolutely alone: it is only alone *with* others. When Heidegger says that the clock is the time of the with-one-another, he means that technological time is public time. Now, it is in this common, public time, according to its possibilities, which are each time unique, that a time is constituted that is not "private" but *deferring and differing* [*différant*]. The calculation of time is thus not a falling away from primordial time, because calculation, *qua* the letter-number, also *actually* gives access in the history of being to any différance.

The Price of Being

In the following chapter this entire question will turn around the "meaning of being" that *Being and Time* grants to the world-historial, that is to say, the trace of past *whos*:

> *With the existence of historial being-in-the-world, what is ready-to-hand and what is present-at-hand have already, in every case, been incorporated into the history of the world.* Equipment and work—for instance, books—have their "fates"; buildings and institutions have their history. . . . These beings within the world *are* historial as such, and their history does not signify something "external" which merely accompanies the "inner" history of the "soul." We call such beings "the world-historial." (Heidegger 1967a, 388)

The world-historial (*weltgeschichtlich*) is not simply the result of what falls behind the temporalizing *who* in the form of traces. Rather, it constitutes the *who* in its proper temporality, one that is always properly epochal, in other words, im-proper or insufficiently proper (to come). Orthographic writing, as the *grammē* that makes calculation possible, is the recording of what has happened, and thereby makes possible for the *who* a particular type of access to itself through the mirror of a *what*. Through this mirror the *who* gains access to a form of "tality," of as-ness (Heidegger 1967a, §§32–33), which is not simply the thesis of the apophantic statement of theoretical knowledge but the work of difference as différance.

Textualized ortho-graphically when the book of history (the book of Herodotus) opens, what happened, far from ending up more determined for the one whose past it is, is on the contrary more *indeterminate*, although, like the end, more *certain*. The contextualization (dissemination) of the exact text, far from turning the having been into one voice, opens up possibilities of indefinite variation. In the following volume, we shall show that any exact, *ortho-thetic* memorization thereby engenders a disorientation in which the straight is always becoming crooked, and that this is the price (to pay, but also to cash in) for epochal doubling-up.

§ 3 The Disengagement of the *What*

Dasein accedes to its deferring and differing individuation by being-at-fault, or being-guilty, *Gewissen*.[1] We shall interpret this *existentiale* once we have commented upon the analytic of everydayness that forms the first section of *Being and Time*. The "voice" that is heard in being-at-fault is what leads Dasein to the anticipatory doubling-up of its having-been. This chapter makes an analysis of this doubling-up in terms of (i) the analysis of everydayness with regard to its "disengagement" of the *what*; (ii) the structure of being-at-fault as "engagement" in the *what*; and (iii) the question of the historical constitution of historiality as a new configuration of the *what*.

The Analysis of Everydayness *qua* Disengagement of the *What*

The Différance of the 'Who' and the 'What'

That it is impossible to question the meaning of being without having a prior understanding of it, mediated and delivered by the everydayness of Dasein (Heidegger 1967a, §2), is nothing but a resurgence of the question of Meno. Being only gives itself in the delay of an *après-coup*: we meet again the question of Epimetheus. The thematic common to the figures of Meno, Epimetheus, and Dasein is that of a form of knowing that is originarily forgetting. One "Epimethean" consequence of this fore-knowing, always assumed in an "average understanding," is that "evident" understanding is mediate, traditional as well as historial—a "mediation" that is forgotten as such.

To overcome this forgetting is to take up the ontological difference. This difference passes in turn through a difference between the *who* (Dasein) and the *what qua* a "being-ready-to-hand," itself distinct from a "being-present-at-hand." Presentness-at-hand considers the *what* in such a way that it misses the *what* as such. The "as"-ness of the *what* is its worldhood.

Being is the being of a being (phenomenological intentionality maintains that consciousness is consciousness *of* something). In order to accede to the question of the meaning of being, one must start from a being without thereby reducing being to the realm of beings. In this context there is an *exemplary* being: the *who* (Dasein). For Heidegger, this *who* is to be radically distinguished from the *what.* It is on the tenor of this distinction that we wish the discussion to bear.

The having-to-be of the *who* determines its mineness, its individuation, which we prefer to call idiomaticity or idiocy rather than ipseity, a term that betokens separation from the *what*: the idiot that is Epimetheus is caught up in the *what,* is constituted in the *what* radically. Whereas, for Heidegger, the advent of Dasein is only possible through its tearing itself away *from* the *what.*

The greatest point of proximity between existential analytic and Epimethean thanatology—one that also harbors the greatest divergence—is the theme of the "already-there": "Dasein has either chosen [its] possibilities itself, or got itself into them, or grown up in them already" (Heidegger 1967a, 12). Even those that Dasein chooses always originate from the world that is already there: every "understanding of the being of those beings . . . become[s] accessible within the world" (12).

To accede to the *who* (Dasein) is to approach this *who* in its "average everydayness." Now, must not this access include not only average [*moyen*] types of access but also Dasein's *means of access,* that is, its average already-there constituted by the means of this already-there? If so, this necessity is not correctly inscribed in the constitutive existential structures. If the already-there is what constitutes temporality in that it opens me out to my historiality, must not this already-there also be *constitutive* in its positive facticity, both positively constitutive and historially constitutive, in the sense that its material organization in form constitutes historiality itself, prior to and beyond history? Although Heidegger provides the major terms for an affirmative response to this question, he is forced to exclude the hypothesis.

The temporality of Dasein is its historiality: its factical emerging. Let me quote again the following passage:

> In its factical being, any Dasein is as it already was, and it is "what" it already was. It *is* its past, whether explicitly or not. . . . Dasein has grown up both *into* and *in* a traditional way of interpreting itself: in terms of this it understands itself proximally and, within a certain range, constantly. By this understanding, the possibilities of its being are disclosed and regulated. Its own past—and this always mean the past of its "generation"—is not something which *follows along after* Dasein, but something which already goes ahead of it. (Heidegger 1967a, 20)

This is one of the most important passages of *Being and Time.* Dasein is a past that is not its own, or which is only its own if it is past (if Dasein *is* its past—*après-coup*). The point will have major consequences for the conditions in which the already-there is constituted as such, for its "having-been" as such, predicated on the *instrumental possibilities* of access to the past. These conditions—of the order of the intratemporal and the "world-historial"—remain, for Heidegger, banal with regard to an authentic temporality, insofar as this temporality qualifies a being that is *neither* "present-at-hand" *nor* "ready-to-hand," that is, a *who* who is without doubt in singular relation to the *what* but is constituted by its very difference to it. How, however, can a positive "making the past our own" (Heidegger 1967a, 21) not be affected by the positive possibilities of an *access* to the past? This question concerns that of the factical transmission of facticity. Hermeneutical possibilities are concealed within it. In the case of orthographical writing we shall see that the difference between the *who* and the *what* is inextricably the différance of the *who and* the *what.*

The Confusion of the 'Who' and the 'What' in Everydayness and Concern in Being-in-the-World 'qua Elpis'

As the possibility of discharging one's having-to-be, tradition is what pulls Dasein down, makes it "fall"—and yet, as the very configuration of the already-there, tradition is also, alone, what releases this having-to-be. Transmission is forgetting. This is the Epimethean structure: the experience of accumulated faults that are forgotten as such. Paradoxically, tradition is also uprooting. A fundamental ontology therefore requires, for

Heidegger, a destruction of the tradition which is the history of ontology. For

> despite all its historical interests and all its zeal for an interpretation which is philologically "objective," Dasein no longer understands the most elementary conditions which would alone enable it to go back to the past in a positive manner and make it productively its own. (Heidegger 1967a, 21)

This return to the past must be a return to what has occurred (particularly within the history of the understandings of being), to what has "happened," also, to being, to its historial temporality. But what has occurred means originary "passibility" [*passibilité*] fallibility, failure, and deficiency—the de-fault to which we are giving the name of *ēpimētheia*. There is no tradition without *ēpimētheia*—without "epiphylogenesis," without the accumulated experience (trial) of the (improbable) de-fault. "Any being is either a *who* (existence) or a *what* (presence-at-hand in the broadest sense). {What is} the connection between these two modes of the characters of being[?]" (Heidegger 1967a, 45). This is indeed the question; and it is with regard to the development of its formulation that we diverge from *Being and Time*: the divergence is central.

A thanatological analytic opens up the question of access and, through it, that of animality and life (Heidegger 1967a, §9). For us, the thanatological question of access is the Epimethean one of *tekhnē*. What we are given—before any bio-anthropological positivity—is the question of our origin, and of the time thereby taken away. But this question comes to us from an already-there that is not only the generality of the question of being but that also of its various formulations [*mises en forme*], one of which is biological theory. We cannot simply suspend these forms since it is only on their account that we can experience the (de-fault of) origin in the first place. The point implies a question of apriority (in Rousseau's sense). This apriority is here stymied by technicity. The moment of being stymied is a meeting point between the empirical and the transcendental, which gives rise to the two by separating them out; it is this that calls for analysis. Which means that we are concerned with death. Death is to be understood according to a prior understanding [*pré-compréhension*] of life; death is life when life is also nonlife, is no longer simply life but is pursued by "means" other than life. The question is that of access, of prostheticity. What, therefore, precedes all (possibility) of biology is indeed fundamental ontology and the preparatory existential analytic;

but only if one also takes into account the "technology" in which such an analytic consists, a technology thought in terms of epiphylogenesis. Considered *from this perspective*, epiphylogenesis is a transcendental concept. But this concept undermines itself at one and the same time, suspending the entire credibility of the empirico-transcendental divide.

The destiny of the *who* (Dasein) is "tied" to intraworldly being, that is, to the *what*: it is what is "included" by its facticity (Heidegger 1967a, §12). There then follows the question of the spatiality of Dasein, which is grounded on its being-in-the world, without relation to the mind-body, inside-outside division and which radically troubles—and it is patent in everydayness—any clear distinction between the *who* and the *what*. To accede to originary temporality is to think prior to everydayness, everydayness accordingly appearing as nothing but the "result" of such a confusion—or rather, as one effect of an originary confusion. Now, and against this result, if the *what*, structured in the world and constituting the already-there of Dasein, is indeed what gives access in the first place to Dasein, should one not ask the question as to a *dynamic* of the *what* that would determine the most originary sphere? There is, indeed, a type of being of which the existential analytic cannot take full account: the organized inorganic, designated precisely as readiness-to-hand, and which is "animated" by a dynamic unto itself. Heidegger's reflection upon equipment will bring nothing new in this regard, avoiding completely proper consideration of the dynamic of *organization*—and, therefore, of the already-there as such.

If being-in-the-world is always in some sense concern, and if "the being of Dasein itself is to be made visible as care" (Heidegger 1967a, 57), then care is the structure of *elpis*. Carelessness is a privative modality of care. Now, *ēpimētheia* means carelessness as well as careful rumination of the faults engendered by such carelessness—while concern takes hold of *promētheia* as foreseeing anticipation.

The Hand as (Com)prehension of the System of the 'Whats' by the 'Who'

Heidegger shows that knowing interpretation *qua* ontic knowledge has always already forgotten the originary complicity, that it has lost it (Heidegger 1967a, §13). This is not the sense of *ēpimētheia*; in the language of *Being and Time* it is "ontological knowledge." Yet it is on the basis of such ontological knowledge that any particular knowledge is possible. If one is right to claim that the already-there, giving access in its prostheticity to the world, is, in a sense, forgotten by Heidegger himself, then it is incumbent upon us to understand the necessity of this forgetting, just as Heidegger himself proposes to assume a similar task with regard to the forgetting of the world by theoretical knowledge (§14). The very name of Epimetheus speaks to the necessity of this forgetting. Everyday being-in-the-world is made up of use (§15). Use encounters tools that are always "something in order to": they *refer*—and firstly, "to other equipment," such as an inkstand, a pen, and so forth. The *what* is always a totality, a system of *whats.* In (their) use, tools disappear. Their mode—the mode of *what*—is being-ready-to-hand, a mode ignored by theoretical knowledge. Tools are foresight—*promethes* is the foreseeing one.

It is therefore the hand in general that articulates upon the *who* the *what* in general (from the ready-to-hand to the present-at-hand, whose essence is concealed by knowledge). The *who* is opposed to the *what* in that it has hands, being itself neither present-at-hand nor ready-to-hand. Having hands, it has *whats* present at and ready to hand. This *what* that the hand handles makes up a system. It is a "technical system" that completely saturates the world. The "system" will come to be called *Gestell qua* modern technics, worsening in its *calculating* and *determining* systematicity, and considered as the fulfillment of metaphysics. Yet this system will never have had in Heidegger's thinking any *dynamic specificity.* It will have done nothing but follow the logic of the temporal fall into the historial forgetting of being *qua* the actuality of the forgetful and dissimulating attitude of concern. It will never have had the least *properly* unconcealing quality. In Heidegger the *what* has no other dynamic than that of an inversion of the "authentic" dynamic of the *who.* But does not the dynamic of the *who,* on the contrary, vouch for a maieutic of the *what*?

A being-ready-to-hand is a being that can go missing, be in default (Heidegger 1967a, §16). This deficiency constitutes the very condition of appearance (vanishing) of worldhood. It is a modification, a disturbance, what comes to suspend the execution of a program. The system of references that is thereby disturbed becomes explicit, revealing a totality in which the world comes to the fore, as well as the factical character of the world that makes it both appear and disappear. This break in *promētheia* (circum-spection, foresight) is the daily effect of the fault, of the de-fault, brought forward in the *après-coup, qua après-coup,* of *ēpimētheia.* It is made possible only because fore-sight is originarily lacking in foresight, has not foreseen everything—always remaining caught in the indeterminate—and is in fact grounded on the fault of Epimetheus, the initial act of forgetting that incessantly returns, casting the already-there into facticity. Already-there always means "not yet" there (in-determinate). Not only does Heidegger think the instrument; he thinks *on the basis of it.* Yet he does not think it fully through: he fails to see in the instrument the originary and originarily deficient horizon of any discovery, including the unforeseen; he fails to see in the instrument what truly sets in play the temporality of being, what regarding access to the past and, therefore, to the future, is constituted through the instrument techno-logically, what through it constitutes the historial as such. He always thinks tools as (merely) useful and instruments (merely) *as* tools, and he is as a result incapable of thinking, for example, an artistic instrument as something that *orders* a world. Now here, less than ever can the needed analyses of "utilizing" correspond to utilitarian concern; here, more than ever, with instrumental implementation [*la mise en oeuvre instrumentale*] as such, the worlding of the world takes place. Further, a break or suspension can only take place *through* instrumental implementation. This instrumental epochality is of a type untheorized by Heidegger; it embraces instrumental-ity as such, indeed it is this instrumental-ity.

The Husserlian Conception of Memory and the System of 'Whats' as References

The Heideggerian concept of a sign, an exemplary tool for references, covers signals as much as relics and documents (Heidegger 1967a, §17). Now, (1) the confusion between a sign and a signal ignores the dynamic of sign-aling, of sign-ifying, just as it ignores idiomatic opacity as the play of an already-there of significations (which will be brought up later with regard to language) and just as the dynamic of the *what* in general is ignored; and (2) the singularity of a document as "image-consciousness," in the Husserlian sense, has no inherent consistency. Heidegger remains faithful here to his teacher.

Husserl's *On the Phenomenology of the Internal Consciousness of Time* sets out to criticize the concept of "originary association" by which Franz Brentano attempts to take account of temporality. This association, effected by the imagination, produces a "representation" of the temporal moment, of the past character of the present that comes and attaches itself to it (Husserl 1991, §6). For Husserl it is a matter of criticizing in the concept of "originary association" the role that Brentano grants to the imagination in order to explain the phenomenon of retention. The argument consists basically in saying that by attributing an imaginary character to the moment of the past, Brentano makes any distinction between present, past, and future impossible, except in the claim that the past and the future are "unreal": to which Husserl objects that the temporal phenomenon—thought on the basis of the temporal object, melody—must be conceived as a process of modification in which, at every present moment, with each "originary" impression, are attached a retention and a protention that are *constitutive* of this present. Retention belongs to this "now," which Gérard Granel calls the "large now" and Husserl represents as a "comet's tail." This retention, which is part of the now of the temporal phenomenon, is called *primary memory.*

In §12 of the first part of the *Internal Consciousness of Time,* Husserl explains the fact that retention, which is not perception but *refers back* to it, and which is not a production of the imagination either since it is part and parcel of the real phenomenon of time, is neither a "secondary memory" (a rememorization of a past temporal phenomenon that could come back into presence) nor the consciousness of an image—a general case of what we will call *tertiary memory*:

> The retentional tone is not a present tone but precisely a tone "primarily remembered" in the now: it is not really on hand in the retentional consciousness. But neither can the tonal moment that belongs to this consciousness be a different tone that is really on hand; it cannot even be a very weak tone equivalent in quality (such as an echo). A present tone can indeed "remind" one of a past tone, exemplify it, pictorialize it; but that already presupposes another representation of the past. The intuition of the past cannot itself be a pictorialization. It is an originary consciousness. . . . The echoing itself *and after-images of any sort left behind by the stronger data of sensation, far from having to be ascribed necessarily to the essence of retention, have nothing at all to do with it.* (Husserl 1991, 33, my emphasis)

Husserl adds in §13 that memory in general, whether it be primary or secondary,

> —and this is equally true of retention—is not image-consciousness; it is something totally different. . . . Just as I see being-now in perception and enduring being in the extended perception as it becomes constituted, so I see

> the past in memory, insofar as the memory is primary memory. The past is given in primary memory, and givenness of the past is memory. (36)

Primary memory is what is constituted in the originary impression. It is impossible to conceive

> a retentional consciousness that would not be the continuation of an impressional consciousness . . . for every retention intrinsically refers back to an impression. "Past" and "now" exclude one another. Identically the same thing can indeed be now and past, but only because it has endured between the past and the present. (36)

Retention is not a re-presentation. Otherwise, one could no longer speak of a "large now" or oppose the psychologism of Brentano. Retention and secondary memory must not be confused, the last distinguishing itself in turn from any image-consciousness in that it is originarily constituted in an originary impression. This is never the case of a tertiary memory; secondary memory is a "recollection."

> Let us consider a case of secondary memory: we recall, say, a melody that we recently heard at a concert. It is obvious in this case that the whole memory-phenomenon has exactly the same constitution, *mutatis mutandis*, as the perception of the melody. Like the perception, it has a privileged point: to the now-point of the perception corresponds a now-point of the memory. We run through the melody in imagination; we hear, "as it were," first the initial tone then the second tone, and so on. At any particular time there is always a tone (or tone-phase) in the now-point. The preceding tones, however, are not erased from consciousness. Primary memory of the tones that, as it were, I have just heard and expectation (protention) of the tones that are yet to come fuse with the apprehension of the tone that is now appearing and that, as it were, I am now hearing. The now-point once again has for consciousness a temporal fringe which is produced in a continuity of memorial apprehensions. . . . Everything is *like* perception and primary memory and yet is not itself perception and primary memory. Of course, we do not actually hear. . . . The temporal present in recollection is a remembered, re-presented past but not an actually present past, not a perceived past, not a past primarily given and intuited. (Husserl 1991, 37–38)

It is perception, therefore, which distinguishes primary and secondary memories:

> Perception . . . is the act that places something before our eyes as the thing

> itself, the act that *originarily constitutes* the object. Its opposite is *re-presentation* [*Vegegenwärtigung, Re-presentätion*], understood as the act that does not place an object itself before our eyes but precisely represents it; that places it before our eyes in image, as it were, although not exactly in the manner of a genuine image-consciousness. . . . If we call perception the *act in which all "origin"* lies, the act that *constitutes originarily*, then *primary memory* is *perception*. . . . On the other hand, recollection, like imagination, merely offers us re-presentation. (43)

Given these distinctions, §28 opposes "image-consciousness" to primary memory as much as to secondary memory. Regarding the re-presentation in which secondary memory consists, what

> is not in question is a re-presentation by means of a resembling object, as in the case of conscious depiction (paintings, busts, and the like). In contrast to such image-consciousness, reproductions have the character of the re-presentation of something itself. (Husserl 1991, 61)

It is easy to see in what Heidegger's critique of Husserl *ought* to consist: the historial conception of temporality such as it constitutes the *who* would demand that the already-there that is *not lived* but inherited, constituted outside any perception, is nevertheless constitutive of presence as such—and this is why temporality cannot be conceived in terms of the "now." The response would be an argument in favor of a radical revision of the oppositions between the primary, the secondary, and the tertiary. Without such a critique the concept of facticity is empty of all content. And yet, we shall see how Heidegger holds to these divisions.

Let us now return to §17 of *Being and Time*:

1. By taking the example of the arrow of the motor car, Heidegger empties the sign of all dynamic, of all thickness; and by understanding the ready-to-hand in terms of his prior definition of the sign, he will do as much with his understanding of instrumentality, a pure chain of "significances" finalized by concern.

2. With the placing of documents under the category of sign, considered in terms of a signal, and with the consequent determination of the understanding of instruments as the understanding of memory—notably tertiary memory and image-consciousness, though Heidegger's move has consequences for the understanding of memory in general—it is the understanding of everything of the order of epiphylogenesis (of the already-there) that is affected.

> A sign is not a thing which stands to another thing in the relationship of indicating; it is rather *an item of equipment which explicitly raises a totality of equipment into our circumspection so that together with it the worldly character of the ready-to-hand announces itself.* . . . The south wind may be meteorologically accessible as something which just occurs; but it is *never* present-at-hand *proximally* in such a way as this, only occasionally taking over the function of a warning signal. On the contrary, only by the circumspection with which one takes account of things in farming, is the south wind discovered in its being. (Heidegger 1967a, 80–81)

With such analyses, which always foreground and highlight the privilege of concernful finality, Heidegger shows ultimately that worldhood is constituted by anticipation (mortality). But he also wants to show that this initial relation to mortality, which the sign introduces through its publicity [*Öffentlichkeit*],[2] is always already a kind of nonrelation, resoluteness only constituting itself to one side of this form of anticipation. As soon as Heidegger makes this move, the sign is on the side of *falling*—justified by the fact that reference as such could not be a *what* since it constitutes every *what*:

> The reference or the assignment itself cannot be conceived as a sign if it is to serve ontologically as the foundation upon which signs are based. Reference is not an ontical characteristic of something ready-to-hand, when it is rather that by which readiness-to-hand itself is constituted. (Heidegger 1967a, 83)

"In anything ready-to-hand the world is always 'there,'" (83) and the already-there of the world has for support instrumentality, beings-ready-to-hand. This precedence is called "reference" in that it opens up a "totality of involvements" or a "finality."[3] This finality refers to the ultimate instance of the end whose meaning will only be revealed in the second part of *Being and Time qua* being-toward-the-end, where reference functions in relation no longer to a being-ready-to-hand but to a being-in-the-world, Da-sein, or *who*. This "finality" consequently appears to precede the possibility of an already-there of the *what*-ready-to-hand. However, this is far from the case—a crucial point since it indicates that finality (being-toward-the-end) and the facticity of an *already-there* are inextricable: "As the being of something ready-to-hand, a finality is itself discovered only on the basis of the prior discovery of a totality of finalities" (85). As for the end, it is transcendence and the announcement of (the meaning of) being, insofar as being exceeds any *what*, and the *who* itself is its extreme possibility: the end here is called the "toward-which." The understanding of the end of Dasein is itself only delivered and deliverable by a *what* already there, one already working within, and working out finality as such:

> Dasein always assigns itself from a "for-the-sake-of which" to the "with-which" of a finality; that is to say, to the extent that it is, it always lets beings be encountered as ready-to-hand. (86)

This finality, experienced in both a prior and actual manner by Dasein in all the relations it encounters within-the-world, is an understanding pro-posed by the play of relations that make up the world, signification. The totality of these relations forms the significance that makes the meanings of words possible: the Husserlian eidetic, and consequently intentionality, must be conceived on the basis of being-toward-the-end. This is a thesis of the first importance since it would allow for an (epi)genetic of the idiomatic—subject to qualification—that is impossible from within Husserlian phenomenology.

The De-severant Forgetting of Heidegger

With the further argument that spatiality is constituted as ready-to-hand, that is, closeness—the hand consequently being constitutive of space—the spatiality of *who* is characterized as de-severance.[4] In the *who*

> there lies an essential tendency towards closeness. All the ways in which we speed things up, as we are more or less compelled to do today, push us on towards the conquest of remoteness. With the "radio," for example, Dasein has so expanded its everyday environment that it has accomplished a de-severance of the "world"—a de-severance which, in its meaning for Dasein, *cannot yet be visualized.* (Heidegger 1967a, 105, my emphasis)

Every reach of the hand implies a closeness that only comes to the fore from an originary de-severance. Every reach of the hand has *in the end* a nothing-at-hand that is given. There is only nongiving that is given. As a gift there is only the inaccessible as such of a something present-at-hand. It is in this something that the hand *reaches.* De-severance is accompanied by prostheses, of which the radio is but one case (singular, for sure, whence the difficulty of seizing its "existential meaning"), together with glasses or even simply the street. These prostheses are forgotten, in an essential manner:

> Seeing and hearing are distance-senses [*Fernsinne*] not because they are far-reaching, but because it is in them that Dasein as deseverant mainly dwells. When, for instance, a man wears a pair of spectacles which are so close to him distantially that they are "sitting on his nose," they are environmentally more remote from him than the picture hanging on the opposite wall. Such equipment has so little closeness that often it is proximally quite impossible to find. Equipment for seeing—and likewise for hearing, such as the telephone receiver—has what we have designated as the inconspicuousness of the proximally ready-to-hand. So too, for instance, does the street, as equipment for walking. (Heidegger 1967a, 107)

Here we have, in primordial terms, the naturalized character of prostheses, through whose naturalization we see, feel, think, and so on. This is particularly true of writing, of a document, of the already-there in general, more specifically of the already-there that gives access to having-been-already-there as such, to the as-such of the past, to its passage and its being-past. If this were not the case, the having-been would present itself to the *who*, through these traces, not *as* having-been but as the *facticity* of this having-been—as the possibility of not having-been. The specificity of image-consciousnesses and other tertiary memories is here lost: owing to a necessity that Heidegger describes without *seeing* what he is describing, in the de-severant look that he himself casts on Dasein. It is indeed quite remarkable that Heidegger remains in this inattentive attitude to the *what*, an attitude all the more essential in that it sets itself up to explain the already of the already-there as such. The forgetting that later marks the analyses of history, of the ancients, and so on is an integral part of this "inconspicuousness," this essential inattention characteristic of *ēpimētheia*, which Heidegger does nothing but describe, submitting himself thereby to it.[5] This forgetting is brought about by Heidegger when, in hasty concern, he maintains that de-severance is sorted out by concern.

De-severing, Dasein orients itself on the basis of signs that open up access to the "regions." In the matter of orientation and access, however, the actual opening up of the "region" is determined yet again by the attention provided by the supports of having-already-been *qua* access-givers—as much "images" that resituate and reconstitute as "tools of navigation" and piloting programs that make up so many prior understandings that Dasein has of its being: reading programs, telecontrols of (the understanding of) being. In this perspective, for example, there is a programmatic specificity to orthographic writing, "restituting" on the basis of a certain *exactitude* the specificity that allows Galen to (re)read Plato, the having-been of philosophy and more generally of an already-there that con-stitutes, as re-stitution, the *who* in its being—a specificity dependent on a particular telecontrol: the history of being. This analysis has as its major consequence that no access is ever possible to a pure constitutivity: *constitution is always reconstitution*, less genetic than *epigenetic*—or, as Nietzsche would say, *genealogical.*

The Programmatic Neutrality of the 'Who'

If the question concerning Dasein is *who*, it is because its being is always "mine." "The *who* is what maintains itself as something identical throughout changes in its experiences and ways of behaviour, and which relates itself to this changing multiplicity in so doing" (Heidegger 1967a, 114). But the *who* of everyday Dasein—and Dasein must be understood in terms of its everydayness, that is, its facticity, since it is in the world, being "first and foremost as well as most frequently" seized by the world—is not, however, the *who* as mine. This implies on the part of phenomenology an abandoning of all egology: the access to the *who* cannot be effected by bracketing the world and other *whos* (egos) who meet each other in it. An existential phenomenology does not aim at the acts of an egological intentionality. One must substitute existence for lived experience. This *who* is it not, then, that of impersonal knowledge à la Blanchot—a neutral *who*? The answer is both yes and no. For "the One" does not die in Heidegger. "The One" only dies in Blanchot.[6]

Others are not determined firstly as non-I; on the contrary they are met as "those over against whom the 'I' stands out" (Heidegger 1967a, 118). The place of Dasein is determined (in the world) by what it does; others are met at work. It is true, however, that Dasein always lives in difference to others, a difference that it can widen or reduce: Heidegger calls this "distantiality" [*Abständigkeit*] (126). This means that Dasein is immediately under the sway of others and is not itself. "What the *who* is" is the One; "the *who* is the neutral." It carries within it an essential tendency toward the mediocre leveling of all possibilities of being (differences): it is "publicity" (or "public opinion") that governs from the outset every "way of interpreting the world and Dasein" (127), divesting it of responsibility "in its everydayness." Dispersed in the One that "articulates the referential context of significance" (127), Dasein, distracted, must find itself again. The rediscovery is "a clearing-away of concealments and obscurities" and "a breaking up of the disguises with which Dasein bars its own way" (127). The return is made in the lack of mood in which "Dasein becomes satiated with itself. Being has become manifest as a burden" (134), the burden of the *what* in which the *who* is taken up, the weight of the *what* as (*possibility* of) the *who*. In this mood Dasein is "disclosed"—to its having-to-be ... a *who*. "The phenomenal fact of the case, in which the being of the 'there' is disclosed moodwise in its 'that-it-is' . . . we call it '*thrownness*' [*Geworfenheit*]" (135). "The expression 'thrownness' is meant to suggest the *facticity of its being delivered over*" (135, my emphasis): the factuality of its lack of quality, prosthetic technicity. This factuality is also one of forgetting, of *ēpimētheia*, since "the way in which the mood discloses is not one in which we look at thrownness, but one in which we turn towards or turn away" (135). What the mood discloses is the totality of being-in-the-world, in other words, the *possibility* of Dasein that is not that of the what, "on a lower level than actuality and necessity" (143), while "possibility as an *existentiale* is the most primordial and ultimate positive way in which Dasein is characterized ontologically" (143–44). The existential structure of understanding is the project that presupposes being-thrown: which is why this understanding is most often articulated in "a totality of finalities already understood," and why it is at the very same time grounded on an act of anticipation that is borne by this fore-sight.

This structure of "fore-having" marks all interpretation, textual interpretation for example. Consequently, "any interpretation that is to contribute to understanding, must have already understood what is to be interpreted" (Heidegger 1967a, 152)—a circularity that already formed the aporia of Meno. To remove this aporia from the Platonic temptation that disavows mortality, opening up in the same gesture the metaphysical epoch of thought, is directly to confront the question of the already-there. Historiality is recurrence: it is comprehensible on the sole condition that an analysis of the pro-grammatic, of the facticity of the already-there *qua* bearer of *ēpimētheia*, is made. Historiality is epiphylogenetic in the sense that the forestructure of understanding must vary with respect to possibilities inherent in such and such a support of the already-there. These *possibilities* of the *what* are not those that simply stem from the actuality that Heidegger distinguished from the possibility of a *who*—all the more because this programmatic character is constitutive of language itself that "hides in itself a developed way of conceiving" (157). In 53 Heidegger writes: "The closest closeness which one may have in being towards death as a possibility is as far as possible from anything actual." This entire discourse describes the structure of différance. Now, does not the deseverance of the actual, in which this possibility consists, affect just as remarkably the textual *what, indeed any "world-historial" trace*? The possibilities of the *what* are constitutive of the very possibility of the *who*—in other words, the possibility of the *what* (and the same is no less true for the *who*) is neither that of the Kantian substance nor of the "categories" of reality (see §43).

The Tool as "Image-Consciousness"

The programmatic character of language mobilizes a listening that is itself programmatic in a pre-predicative way:

> What we "first" hear is never the noises or complexes of sounds, but the creaking coach, the motor-cycle. . . . The fact that motor-cycles and coaches are what we proximally hear is the phenomenal evidence that in every case Dasein, as being-in-the-world, already dwells *alongside* what is ready-to-hand within-the-world; it certainly does not dwell proximally alongside the "sensations"; nor would it first have to give shape to the swirl of sensations to provide the springboard from which the subject leaps off and finally arrives at a "world." (Heidegger 1967a, 163–164)

The *hylē* of intentionality is always already intentional. By maintaining that listening only takes place on the basis of the originary proximity of the ready-to-hand, thereby criticizing the form/matter opposition, Heidegger allows us to introduce the question of this "to-hand." It is a memory that is neither primary nor secondary; it is completely ignored in Heidegger's analyses, as it was in those of Husserl, and yet it is immediately there in a tool; indeed it is the very meaning of a tool.

A tool is, before anything else, memory: if this were not the case, it could never function as a reference of significance. It is on the basis of the system of references and as a reference itself that I hear the "tool" that is "the creaking coach." The tool refers in principle to an already-there, to a fore-having of something that the *who* has not itself necessarily lived, but which comes under it [*qui lui sous-vient*][7] in its concern. This is the meaning of epiphylogenesis. A tool functions first as image-consciousness. This constitutivity of "tertiary memory" grounds the irreducible neutrality of the *who*—its programmaticality, including above all the grammar governing any language.

The Care(less) Idiocy of the Idiom Outside Itself and the Term of Death

The programmatic character of language is the publicity of the "One" (what we shall call for our part *signification*, which inhabits the *who* at all levels, including that of its radical solitude, that is, its "inside" as well as its "outside": the *who* is idiomatic; it is idiom, inhabited, even within its withdrawal, by a publicity that is "its," being truly irreducible). We will deal with this constitutivity of the *intimate publicity* of the *who* under the name of "idio-textuality," referring also to the idiocy of Epimetheus. This publicity is essentially repeatable. Thus, in Heidegger there are two figures of repetition, given that repetition will come to constitute also the possibility of resoluteness *qua* the recurrence of having-been [*Gewesensein*] in the instant. Uprooting, machinelike repetition is gossip, of which the written word is an extension. It is on the basis of this (fallen) possibility of extension that we will always understand what is of the order of tertiary memory, which Heidegger names the world-historial and, more generally, everything that constitutes the being-there of the already-there.

It is here that Heidegger stresses the essential falling of existence, its being-in-de-fault so near to the Promethean-Epimethean structure, and introduces the theme of care. The being of Dasein is care. Hence,

> because the ontological problematic of being has heretofore been understood primarily in the sense of presence-at-hand . . . while the nature of Dasein's being has remained ontologically undetermined, we need to discuss the ontological interconnections of care, worldhood, readiness-to-hand, and presence-at-hand (reality). (Heidegger 1967a, 183)

To accede ontologically to care is a matter of hand. What of the hand? And what of the *what* concerning the *who*? That which understanding articulates through the hand, the *who* and the *what*, is the truth that tradition has always understood as truth of the *what*, itself understood in the restrictive terms of the "present-at-hand." Now, truth is that of the *articulation* of the *who* and the *what*, which is the term of death.[8] In fear, Dasein is before a *what*. In anxiety, it is before its own "who," which presents itself to it as it were interrogatively, which does not present itself: its *who* is its "*who*?" The "*who*?" turns to the *what* in order to flee its "?" This "?" is its indeterminacy, with respect to which the finalities within-the-world collapse, the world assuming a "character of total insignificance." But this "?" is also "being-in-the-world as such." In short, to be anxious is disclosure to the world.

Anxiety isolates and thereby discloses the possible. Loneliness is not solipsism but being-in-the-world, which is, nevertheless, a not-being-at-home. The familiarity of the collapsing world becomes being-outside-oneself, the Epimethean situation.

> That kind of being-in-the-world which is reassured and familiar is a mode of Dasein's uncanniness [*Unheimlichkeit*], not the reverse. From an existential-ontological point of view, the "not-at-home" must be conceived as the more primordial phenomenon. (Heidegger 1967a, 189)

There is an uprooting more originary than that which, as in the uprooting particular to the idiotic publicity of the One, still consists of a certain familiarity.

Careful, Dasein is in advance of itself and beyond itself—outside itself, the ontological meaning of which is advance, a temporality whose essential phenomenon is the future. "'Being-ahead-of-itself' means . . . : 'ahead-of-itself-in-already-being-in-a-world'" (Heidegger 1967a, 192): in being-born. The already means that everything has always already begun, whereas the indeterminacy of the anxious person is just as much that nothing has ever begun in the very fact that nothing will end—Dasein will never have finished (being), remaining always for itself its "?" It finds itself without end, in the face of the nothing of "without-end," the unceasingness of nothing and the nothing of the unceasing, in front of the impossibility of the end that is itself certain and indubitable. "To put it otherwise, existing is always factical. Existentiality is essentially determined by facticity" (192). Yet the possibility of Dasein's "return" in isolation, insofar as it eludes any world-historiality, is not what we are aiming at with *ēpimētheia*—and in this context the Heideggerian discourse on "uprooting" remains fundamentally ambiguous.

Having fashioned *homo*, *Care* takes hold of him throughout his life, whereas at his end his soul returns to Jupiter and his body to the ground. The Greek name for *Care*, which here assumes the role of Epimetheus, is *elpis*, as much forgetting and knowledge as hope and fear, error and truth—*alētheia* retrieved from oblivion. The oblivion is originary, just as the fault of Epimetheus means the originary de-fault of origin, and this is why the "originary disclosure is essentially factical"; "Dasein is already both in the truth and in untruth" (Heidegger 1967a, 222). The structure of care affirms the unity of *promētheia* and *ēpimētheia*. The Promethean experience, the first moment of *ēpimētheia*, is wandering, primordial failing on account of which alone something takes place or is. On the basis of a radical empiricity [*empēreia*] that is always a fault (covering by uncovering, the gesture that makes up any disclosing of a site), the reflection *après coup* of being in de-fault as such is possible. It is the reason why even in the repetition of gossip,

> Dasein speaks over again what someone else has said, it comes into a being-towards the very beings which have been discussed. But it has been exempted from having to uncover them again, primordially, and it holds that it has thus been exempted. (223)

The possibility of such a repetition is itself grounded in the *epiphylogenetic* structure. Such a repetition of experience, which is also the covering-over of this experience, remains at the horizon of any outside-oneself *qua* instrumental. Historiality, the horizon of every truth, also proceeds originarily from this repetition that governs both the possibility of an access (to the already-there as already-there) and a concealing that is this very disclosure: the *grammē* is simultaneously calculation, determination and letter, indeterminacy. Here the understanding of *alētheia* as *adaequatio* cannot be isolated from the constitution of an orthothetic already-there. We designate by this term all forms of memory, "exact" forms of recording—for example, orthographical—from those of phonological and linear writing, through photography and phonography, to that of computer processing. If Galen can say "thanks to the written works, and to the use of his hands, you may converse with Plato, Aristotle, Hippocrates, and the other Ancients," including Galen himself, but also with Heidegger, indeed with the having-been of any "itself," and in a mode that leaves no doubt as to the literalness of these remarks, from Plato to "oneself," it is because orthothetic writing, when it records, *sets down exactly*. Only an orthothetic reification of any uncovering makes possible at one and the same time an understanding of the truth in terms of a being "present-at-hand" or "sub-sistent" and as exactitude (*orthotēs*): there is only sub-sistence *on*, starting from and through a support, as a particular relation to a particular support. A critique of exactitude—especially that of the clock—and a critique of substantialism, which always defines here metaphysics, are related.

Temporality is, then, repetition. As an idiot, an idiom repeats (itself). Just as there are two figures of repetition, so there are two figures of uprooting. This duplicity stems from a "being-guilty," "being-in-debt," or "being-at-fault" [*Schuldigsein*], which we prefer to name *being-in-de-fault.*

The Structure of Being-at-Fault *qua* Engagement in the *What*

Being in De-fault 'qua' Programming of the Possible Suspension of any Program

Mortal, the *who* exceeds itself *qua* indeterminate possibility, and the meaning of falling (gossip in concern, curiosity, and so forth) is the fleeing in the face of the indeterminate, the attempt to determine the end, the leveling of "differences."

The improbability of the *who*, its nonpredestination, its destiny, is grounded in the indeterminacy of death—a structure that is constituted in *promētheia/ epimētheia*, where *Elpis* has the ambiguous attributes of *Care.* Grounded on the programmability of the already-there, it *doubles up*, without ever overcoming, irreducible facticity *qua* a particular suspension of active programs, a kind of *epochality* that is existential (and historial, and, in terms of a particular form of datability, it can be considered as the history of being). This happens as the conscience (*Gewissen*) of a fault or debt. "Death does not just 'belong' to one's own Dasein in an undifferentiated way; death lays claim to it as an individual Dasein" (Heidegger 1967a, 263). One's ownmost possibility lies in the epochal suspension of the programs of everyday publicity. For Heidegger, this possibility is the extraordinary and constitutive possibility of the *who*, "freedom for death," in that it suspends the ordinary neutrality of the *who.* The suspension constitutes ipseity *qua* the modification of a *who* since "for the most part *I myself* am not the 'who' of Dasein; the One is its 'who'" (267). The One constitutes the being-already-decided as to the factical "being-able" of the *who*—in the form of rules, criteria, and so on, which distract it from making any explicit choice, and which function as a program—one that Dasein can suspend. This suspension or rupture with the "mishearing of the self which is the hearing of the One" finds its possibility in a "call" that calls from out of being-in-fault, in-debt, or in-de-fault. *That which* "hears" the call is "resoluteness."

Faults are forgotten as they accumulate, covering each other over. A moment arrives in which the fault is experienced: not this or that fault, but the fault of being-at-fault as such—originary de-fault as de-fault of origin, which Heidegger calls *Gewissen*. The *who* called, discussed, put in question is Dasein itself. This *who* "maintains itself in conspicuous indefiniteness" (Heidegger 1967a, 274). "*Consciousness manifests itself as the call of care*," and "the 'voice' of conscience speaks of a 'debt' or a 'fault'" (277). If *ēpimētheia* is to be thought in terms of the articulation of the *who* and the *what qua* the term of death, the *who* that is calling is what precedes the divide between *who* and *what*—the strange "that" of being-outside-oneself, of the originary de-fault of origin.

> In its "who," the caller is definable in a "worldly" way by *nothing* at all. The caller is Dasein in its uncanniness [*Unheimlichkeit*]: primordial, thrown being-in-the-world as the "not-at-home"—the bare "that-it-is" in the "nothing" of the world. The caller is unfamiliar to the everyday one-self; it is something like an *alien* voice. What could be more alien to the "one," lost in the manifold "world" of its concern, than the Self which has been individualized down to itself in uncanniness and been thrown into the "nothing"? (Heidegger 1967a, 276–77)

This nothing of the *who* says that the *who* is nothing, remains nothing, and will always be nothing; that it has never begun, will never have finished, "thrown" outside of any self that is won in actuality, the "self" being nothing but its différance. The mark of a de-fault of identity that structures the identical *who* as having always already actualized itself in multiple, disseminated occurrences, it thereby learns in its unitary consistency to be forever *only to come.*

Rather than debt or fault, we hear in *Schuld* de-fault. That said, a debt is itself due to the divine gift of the de-fault, and the fault is theft consequent upon a forgetting. Undoubtedly, de-fault must not be understood as lack of a being present-at-hand, and

> the idea of debt must not only be raised above the domain of that concern in which we reckon things up, but it must also be detached from relationship to any law or "ought" such that by failing to comply with it one loads oneself with debt (guilt). (Heidegger 1967a, 283)

It is nevertheless true that a debt or a fault has "the character of not."

> Hence we define the formally existential idea of the "in-debt" as "being-the-basis for a being which has been defined by a "not"—that is to say, as "being-the-basis of a nullity." . . . Being-in-debt does not first result from an indebtedness, but, on the contrary, indebtedness becomes possible only "on the basis" of a primordial being-in-debt. . . . Thus "being a basis" means *never* to have power over one's ownmost being from the ground up. (283)

This is nothing but the de-fault of quality and the community of de-fault (the banality of uncanniness). "Not" is a Promethean/Epimethean trait. *Ēpimētheia* implies différance because it means the essential unfinishing, the essential accidentality (failing) of Dasein, of the *who.*

The itself that makes up the "autonomy" of Dasein "is neither substance nor subject" (Heidegger 1967a, 61). Being-in-the-world is not a substance-subject. The "work" of the true—time—is a deviation rooted in singularity, individuation, an "autonomy" incompatible with dialectical synthesis. That said, the question should be put as to whether another interpretation of the meaning of substance in Hegel is relevant here, especially if resoluteness is constitutively linked, in its possibilities, with the "actuality" as well as the inactuality of "subsistent" beings, which the already-there delivers in its alreadyness—an already (for a *who* plunged into the *not yet*) that defines the substantiality of sub-stance. In this reading, autonomy would be constituted through its heteronomy, and not only by accepting it but by listening to this heteronomy's very *dynamic*—without presupposing the dialectical necessity of such a "maieutic."

The de-fault of origin (which is debt) and the end (which is always defaulting) form two aspects of one and the same relation: technics is the vector of any anticipation, only insofar as there is only de-fault of origin (*there is* only "debt" or "fault") *qua* facticity, the experiencing of the situation of an occurrent already-there. "Only on the basis of Dasein's whole being does anticipation make being-in-debt manifest. Care harbors in itself equiprimordially both death and debt" (Heidegger 1967a, 306). If the fault-debt is indeed de-fault, the prostheticity of the already-there is the truth of care.

The Ways of the Hand and the In-finitude of the 'What'

Dasein is futural: it is so starting out from the originary phenomenon of the future as return to having-been. Return to having-been is being-having-been *qua* assumption (of the facticity) of the already-there:

> Taking over thrownness signifies *being* Dasein authentically *as it already was.* Taking over thrownness, however, is possible only in such a way that the futural Dasein can *be* its ownmost "as-it-already-was"—that is to say, its "been" (*sein "Gewesen"*). Only in so far as Dasein *is* as an "I-*am*-as-having-been," can Dasein come towards itself futurally in such a way that it comes *back*. . . . Anticipation of one's uttermost and ownmost possibility is coming back understandingly to one's ownmost "been." (Heidegger 1967a, 325–26)

Dasein has the character of recurrence: access to its future is only possible through access to its having-been; access to its having-been is access to its future. The origin is at the end, and the end at the origin—with this one différance that there is time (that of the return, time as deferral), that is, facticity (itself deferred: effaced, forgotten). The point is here all the more that of access to having-been since Dasein does not have *its* having-been on its own accord. It is a past that it has not lived; it is more than *its* past. Here again we are looking at an excess that Heidegger is unable to think through entirely, all the while intimating the need to do so in his very demonstration that the consideration of time in terms of the vulgarly understood ecstases, including Husserl's, must be relinquished. Being-already as being-having-been should not be thought in terms of the past, no more than "anticipation" should be understood in terms of the future, or tarrying "alongside" in terms of the present: Dasein is not *in* time since it is neither present-at-hand nor ready-to-hand. The *what* would be "in" the time that makes up the *who* in its ec-stasis. And yet, if indeed it is true that the *what*'s possibility cannot always be reduced to actuality thought under the categories of reality, is the *what* simply *in* the time that the eks-istent *who* is? Is not the *what* in some manner the time *of* this *who*—in the manner of its hands? The future of Dasein is not that of something present-at-hand because it is *being-able.* However, its having-been is not its "past" either, since its having-been is insofar as it exists, whereas the past of the present-at-hand no longer is. Dasein never finds itself except as having-been-thrown. But what is true of the past of Dasein is also true of this past that is not its lived past and that nevertheless remains, and more than any other, *its* past as *already-there*, its *there* properly speaking. Now, the singularity of this having-been is not envisaged by Heidegger in its own terms.

These shifts concerning the comprehension of the three terms of extendedness nevertheless expressly imply the inscription of temporality in facticity:

> *In the state-of-mind in which it finds itself,* Dasein is assailed by itself as the being which it still is and already was—that is to say, which it constantly is as having been. The primary existential meaning of facticity lies in the character of "having been." In our formulation of the structure of care, the temporal meaning of existentiality and facticity is indicated by the expressions "before" and "already." (Heidegger 1967a, 328)

"*Ekstatikon* pure and simple," "temporality is the primordial outside-of-itself and in and for itself," in accordance with the end.

> The question is not about everything that still can happen "in a time that goes on," or about what kind of letting-come-towards-oneself we can encounter "out of this time," but about how "coming-towards-oneself" is, as such, to be primordially determined. (Heidegger 1967a, 329)

This remark is problematic: resoluteness can only make sense through its projection into in-finitude, which is what is encountered in the very endurance of finitude, into the beyond of the self (after the self, such that the deluge must not happen, heroism giving the exemplary, and highly ambiguous, sense of resoluteness). This kind of *negligence* on Heidegger's part (regarding the beyond of the self that the outside-itself implies) is symmetrical with that mentioned earlier concerning the already-there in its accessibility. The accessibility of the already-there was only made possible through the experience of in-finitude (of past experience, of the accumulation of inherited faults) in the ordeal of enduring the end itself. The question is all the more essential since it also commands the whole dynamic of the *what*: it is because resoluteness projects itself beyond the *who,* as well as the other *who* present, for the *who* to come, that the *who* takes care of the *what,* together with its becoming, pro-jecting another horizon of *what(s),* affirming an infinite finality of the *who-what* totality, past, present, and future. Attentiveness, *cura*, the concernful care of the *what,* is perhaps not simply turning away from a having-to-be.

Such "carelessness" would no longer have in mind what Husserl thinks under the name of science as infinite reactivation, nor the process of dissemination that Plato denies, constituting, in Blanchot's terms, impersonal knowledge, knowledge older than the nonknowledge of death. Rather, is not the consideration of *tekhnē*, as the originary horizon of any access of the being that we ourselves are to itself, the very possibility of disanthropologizing the temporal, existential analytic? When "Time and

Being" gives itself the task of thinking being without beings (without Dasein), is it not a question, ultimately, of radically shifting the above understanding of time in terms of *this* finitude?

If a "finitude" of Dasein may give the understanding of the phenomenon of time, it is on the basis of an in-finitude of the *what,* which bequeaths it a *heritage* having-been before it, that it can only *be* (in view of a) beyond itself. This originary temporality is therefore not originary enough, even if we are not contesting the fact that

> only because primordial time is *finite* can the "derived" time temporalize itself as *infinite*. . . . Time is primordial as the temporalizing of temporality, and as such it makes possible the constitution of the structure of care. Temporality is essentially ecstatical. Temporality temporalizes itself primordially out of the future. Primordial time is finite. (Heidegger 1967a, 330–31)

This finitude is, however, constituted in the *what* that is, *qua* epiphylogenetic projection, indefinite and thereby *promised* to an hypo-thetical infinitude that exceeds the finitude of Dasein. Otherwise nothing of what, after the "failure" of *Being and Time* and the relinquishment of the project to write the final part, will come to constitute the *Kehre* would be possible.

Repetition as Recall—and the Invention of the Other

Coming to oneself from the future is a returning to the already (where Dasein can be its "there"): this repetition is having-been. If it is also a matter here of the "already" of the world as much as the "already" of the "lived" of Dasein, the conditions of this return, repetitive "reproduction," cannot remain trivial: the inclusion of the nonlived in the "instant" of resoluteness implies that these "memories" that are neither primary nor secondary, and that Husserl excluded, reestablish the threshold of time. Heidegger, who will never make this step, introduces precisely *here* the theme of memory: concernful memory is constituted on the basis of a forgetting of being-having-been, while the "recall" (of the de-fault) is the return of being-having-been, a return that grounds anxiety.

Temporality, in each of its modalities, made up respectively of understanding, the mood of the situation (state-of-mind), and falling, is each time totally determined in terms of one of the ecstases, given that it is not a succession (of nows). It can *not be* and *cannot* be succession because being-having-been incorporates the nonlived having-been of Dasein, the already-there as such in the radicality of its already. Always already "before me," preceding any identity of the *who*, the difference of *whats* that are already there has marked it, has *already* altered it—the *who*'s nomination under the name of a saint, ancestor, or father or a name given by its father does nothing but synthesize this difference—something that Heidegger had indicated as early as §6 of *Being and Time*. The traces of materiality, of "there has been," belong originarily to the phenomenon of temporality; yet to accept this demands a general critique of the Husserlian conception of memory that not only is not taken up here by Heidegger, or even sketched-out, but is on the contrary excluded.

Concern is always inscribed in a complex of tools, and a tool is always inscribed in a finality that itself stems from a mode of temporalization of temporality. This mode is a forgetting. But is not this forgetting of the Self salutary, referring to a more originary temporality? According to Blanchot, commenting on Hegel: "A person who wishes to write is stopped by a contradiction: in order to write, he must have the talent to write. But gifts, in themselves, are nothing. As long as he has not yet sat down at his table and written a work, the writer is not a writer and does not know if he has the capacity to become one. He has no talent until he has written, but he needs talent in order to write" (Blanchot 1981, 23). Blanchot adds in a note: "In this argument Hegel is considering human work in general" (23, n. 1). The writer exemplifies with rigor the question of invention *qua* the paradox of the *après-coup*—a matter of the beginning, of production, of the new, quite simply, of time. It is here that the writer puts his or her talents to work:

> That is, he needs the work he produces in order to be conscious of his talents and of himself. The writer only finds himself, only realizes himself, through his work; before his work exists, not only does he not know who he is, but he is nothing. He only exists as a function of the work; but then how can the work exist? . . .
>
> {The man who writes, remarks Hegel,} "has to start immediately, and, whatever the circumstances, without further scruples about beginning, means, or end, proceed to action" [*Phenomenology of Spirit*, chap. 5, sec. 1a]. (Blanchot 1981, 24)

This means that there is neither middle, nor end, nor simple beginning. What is true of the person who writes is true of humanity in general *qua* an organism that invents and produces. *This* question of writing is nothing but a radicalization of that of the memory of the human. It is the reason why,

> if we see work as the force of history, the force that transforms man while it transforms the world, *then a writer's activity must be recognized as the highest form of work.* . . . For example, my project might be to get warm. As long as this project is only a desire, I can turn it over every possible way and still it will not make me warm. But now I build a stove: the stove transforms the empty ideal which was my desire into something real; it affirms the presence in the world of something which was not there before, and in so doing, denies something which was there before; before, I had in front of me stones and cast iron; now I no longer have either stones or cast iron, but instead the product of the transformation of these elements—that is their denial and destruction—by work. Because of this object, the world is now different. . . . But what is a writer doing when he writes? Everything a man does when he works, but to an outstanding degree. The writer, too, produces something—a work in the highest sense of the word. . . . When he writes, his starting point is a certain state of language, a certain form of culture, certain books, and also certain objective elements—ink, paper, printing presses. . . . Before I wrote {this book}, I had an idea of it, at least I had the project of writing it, but I believe there is the same difference between that idea and the volume in which it is realized as between the desire for heat and the stove which makes me warm. (Blanchot 1981, 33–34)

To work [*oeuvrer*] is to forget the self, to let one's other be—but an other who is not a self, nor one's own, but quite other. (Knowing whether Hegel reduces (sublates) this figure or not matters little here.) This other is at the heart of the idiom. Moreover, and most importantly, this other sweeps the whole question of work [*du travail et de l'ouvrage*] and invention, of the new, far away from the sense given it by Heidegger in his analysis of curiosity.

The issue of work is indeed what Heidegger misses, especially when he talks about it in thematic terms in 15 of *Being and Time*—an issue that, when formulated by Blanchot, becomes an originary one.

These objections relate to Levinasian arguments concerning the death of the other (Levinas 1990, 15 and 17) and with the phenomenology of photography developed by Barthes in *Camera Lucida: Reflections on Photography* [*La chambre claire*, 1979]: through the photo-graphic support, Barthes wrests thanatology and the there-has-been from ipseity that remains radically identity-based and egological. The Barthesian there-has-been only finds its full force in the factum of photo-graphic possibility (in terms of a tertiary memory of a type whose specificity is to be analyzed phenomenologically—that is, here, *also and irreducibly technologically*—for a proper account of the phenomenon), of seeing what could not be experienced, of seeing the past life of the other, its death as other, and, by projection, my alterity in my own photo-graphic mortality: "all photography is this catastrophe" (Barthes 1979, 148). This catastrophe is the experience of a repetition in which, within the *punctum*, the ordeal of the idiocy of the photo-graphic already-there and that of the return of death are radically indissociable—call *qua* recall, *Gewissen* in terrible silence, suffering without voice, the work of mourning, incalculable guilt.

That said, Blanchot's reading also means a "conversion"[9]—one that never forgets, however, the outside-of-itself: it is not a return to self but a moving-outside into effects (of writing), a moving toward the world. With Blanchot, writing (and all that it designates: the outside *qua* instrumentality, *tekhnē*) is the originary horizon, that is, constitutive of temporality as such. Publicity is essential to this "conversion"—for such is the direction and sense of all writing.

Instruments and the Hands of Science

Science is born with the suspension of handling: it constitutes a "withdrawal of the hand." But it is more than that, being also a *praxis* that employs instruments. It remains in this positive sense a *handling*. It reassumes the hand once it has withdrawn it. To thematize beings it must take them into hand, that is, make them at-hand. This remainder of the hand is of the greatest interest to us:

> Even in the "most abstract" way of working out problems and establishing what has been obtained, one manipulates equipment for writing, for example. However "uninteresting" and "obvious" such components of scientific research may be, they are by no means a matter of indifference ontologically. The explicit suggestion that scientific behaviour as a way of being-in-the-world, is not just a "purely intellectual activity," may seem petty and superfluous. If only it were not plain from this triviality that it is by no means patent where the ontological boundary between "theoretical" and "atheoretical" behaviour really runs! (Heidegger 1967a, 358)

The consideration of the technicity of knowledge is only apparent here: knowledge *qua* knowledge is not *constituted*—in its proper temporality—by its instrumentality. The relation between a result, fixing [laying something down on a support], and a pencil not only should be *found* in the temporal phenomenon but should *constitute* and *organize* the latter. When we address the originary phenomenon of time that is constitutive of the temporality of science, we shall see that this instrumentality is given a derivative status. The project of science grounds itself in originary existential temporality, and the thematization of the *what* that is ready-to-hand *as* present-at-hand—a thematization that takes place with exact instruments, handled concernfully by science in its wish to achieve *faultless* results—has *already* left the originary ground.

The Question of the Historical Constitution of Historiality as the New Configuration of the *What*

The Secondarity of the World-Historial 'What'

Dasein cannot escape everydayness as habit. Or as program (Heidegger 1967a, §71). Everydayness is the inauthentic modality of the historiality of Dasein that is neither in time nor in history, but is temporal and historial. Its being "in" time is, however, possible, indeed unceasing: one need only think of the clock and the calendar. That said, its temporality makes intratemporality possible in the first place, and not the reverse—while being co-originarily intratemporal:

> Since time as intratemporality also "stems" from the temporality of Dasein, historiality and intratemporality turn out to be co-originary. Thus, within its limits, the ordinary interpretation of the temporal character of history is justified. (377)

The analytic of the historial must be grounded in that of the originary temporality of Dasein; the intratemporal "derives" as it were from originary temporality; and at the same time, there is co-originarity. But this co-originarity remains a kind of inert contiguity, without engagement (in the *what*): it is informed by an alternative between the *eigentlich* and the *uneigentlich* that rules out consideration of the dynamic of intratemporality as being, if not located at the source of historial emergence, at least co-implied by it (owing to the complication and complicity of this co-originarity). The already-there of the historial, in its intratemporal modalities of recording, has no claim to any proper temporal opacity: it is a pure accident, being-thrown into the inauthenticity of facticity. *Eigentlichkeit* remains understood as the possibility of a *who* released from the *what*, its having-been thereby being, be it only for an *instant*, the "instant" of resoluteness, redeemed of its facticity.

From here, the Heideggerian critique of historical science has the disastrous consequence that the questioning of the positivity of facts and traces ends up excluding these from any ontological dimension, in the name of their belonging to intratemporality. What makes "antiquities" possible, both present and past, is that their world

> is no longer. But what was formerly *intratemporal* with respect to that world is still present-at-hand. . . .
>
> Thus the historical character of the antiquities that are still preserved is grounded in the "past" of that Dasein to whose world they belonged. But according to this, only "past" Dasein would be historical, not Dasein "in the present." However, can Dasein be *past* at all, if we define "past" as "now *no longer either present-at-hand or ready-to-hand.*" Manifestly, Dasein can *never* be past, not because Dasein is non-transient, but because it essentially can never be *present-at-hand*. Rather if it is, it *exists*. A Dasein which no longer exists, however, is not past, in the ontologically strict sense; it is rather having-been-there. (Heidegger 1967a, 380)

The having-been of a Dasein that *is no longer* is, however, not past, but is being toward a Dasein who *is*; in other words, it remains having-been for another Dasein, as this past that is now this other's without this other "having had" it, that is, lived it.

It is here that the *who* and the *what* must be both distinguished and brought together, for the having-been-there is the general possibility of the there-has-been—literal-orthographic, photographic, or more generally objective: antique, a there-has-been that is older than the separation between my lived past and my inherited past. Heritage is what is at stake. This there-has-been, and the whole generality of having-been, has its possibility of constitution in this singular *what*—neither present-at-hand nor *simply* ready-to-hand—that is assumed by the being in the role of tertiary memory: a role that can happen to any *what* whatsoever, to *anything whatsoever*. This anything whatsoever is archaeological material *par excellence*. It is nevertheless true that among this bric-a-brac beings ready-to-hand are privileged (by the archaeologist, the historian, but also the philosopher, and more generally the Dasein who pursues one who is no longer). We are back at the whole question of access to the already-there insofar as this access is nothing but (the actuality of) its access. This singular being is the "world-historial." And yet Heidegger immediately limits its privileged status, does not encompass within it this question of access, but relegates it under the category of secondarity:

> We contend that what is *primarily* historial is Dasein. That which is *secondarily* historial, however, is what we encounter within-the-world—not only equipment ready-to-hand, in the widest sense, but also the environing *Nature* as "the very soil of history." Beings other than Dasein which are historial by reason of belonging to the world, are what we call "world-historial." *It can be shown that the ordinary conception of "world-history" arises precisely from our orientation to what is thus secondarily historial* {my emphasis}. World-historial beings do not first get their historial character, let us say, by reason of a historical [*historisch*] objectification; they get it rather *as those beings* which they are in themselves when they are encountered within-the-world. (Heidegger 1967a, 381)

Being-thrown is a heritage from which the *who* is handed over only when it comes back to it, handing it over itself authentically (Heidegger 1967a, §74). This thematic of heritage is that of the already-there, thought according to the epochality in which "resoluteness" consists—our whole question being to know how this epochality, in its properly historial character, never given in advance by a transcendentality that would erase its indeterminacy, is constituted by the already-there as a world-historial *what.*

"Fate" means "Dasein's originary historizing, which lies in authentic resoluteness and in which Dasein hands itself over to itself, free for death, in a possibility that it has inherited and yet has chosen" (Heidegger 1967a, 384). This structure is *ēpimētheia* insofar as "the blows of fate" dealt to the *who* are the engendered faults of the de-fault and of all the attempts to make up for it. This fate is itself a shared fate, "historizing of the community, of the people," and "Dasein's fateful destiny in and with its 'generation' goes to make up the full authentic historizing of Dasein" (384–85). From our perspective, this is the question of the community of those who have no community, of the de-fault of community and of the community of the de-fault, one that, addressed in these terms, necessarily poses the question—itself singular and to be thought idiomatically—of the relationship between convention and idiom.

If "the resoluteness which comes back to itself" is "the authentic repetition of a possibility of existence that has been—the possibility that Dasein may choose its hero" (Heidegger 1967a, 385), if that is indeed the consequence of having a past that is not mine (that I have not lived, but without which my past is nothing), then such a repetition can only make sense for itself within an epiphylogenetic horizon, each time singular in that it is shot through by the dynamic of a *what*—or a tertiary memory from which the *who* can never disengage itself.

The Leveling of the World-historial as Forgetting of Tertiary Memory

This constitutive engagement is what §75, already quoted, *ought* to have indicated:

> *With the existence of historial being-in-the-world, what is ready-to-hand and what is present-at-hand have already, in every case, been incorporated into the history of the world.* Equipment and work—for instance, books—have their "fates"; buildings and institutions have their history. And even nature is historial . . . as a countryside, as an area that has been colonized or exploited, as a battlefield, or as the site of a cult. These beings within-the-world *are* historial as such, and their history does not signify something "external" which merely accompanies the "inner" history of the "soul." We call such beings "the world-historial." (Heidegger 1967a, 388)

Constitutive of the historial, but only in a secondary sense, the world-historial does not engage any resolutory dynamic and remains without ontological reach. Heidegger seems, however, to indicate that a specific analytic of the world-historial would be necessary, recognizing in any case its originality in respect of beings-ready-to-hand:

> The historial world is factical only as the world of beings within-the-world. That which "happens" with equipment and work as such has its own character of movement, and this character has been completely obscure up till now. . . . Quite apart from the fact that if we were to follow up the problem of the ontological structure of world-historial historizing, *we would necessarily be transgressing the limits of our theme, we can refrain all the more because the very aim of this exposition is to lead us face to face with the ontological enigma of the movement of historizing in general.* (Heidegger 1967a, 389, my emphasis)

We can only regret this refusal on Heidegger's part, for it constitutes a decisive choice concerning the core of fundamental ontology. First, because it allows in principle for the possibility of a disengagement of "historizing in general." Second, and more seriously, because the world-historial constitutes before anything else the vector of the fall of historiality.

> Because factical Dasein, in falling, is absorbed in that with which it concerns itself, it understands its history world-historially in the first instance. And because, further, the ordinary understanding of being understands "being" as presence-at-hand without further differentiation, *the being of the world-historial is experienced and interpreted in the sense of something present-at-hand which comes along, has presence, and then disappears.* (Heidegger 1967a, 389, my emphasis)

But does not Heidegger himself end up leveling *in principle* the specificity of the world-historial by ignoring the dynamic of the *what* that is already there? Does he not himself end up understanding the world-historial in terms of the present-at-hand?

The vulgar understanding always apprehends time starting from the now as a moment inscribed in a flux (Heidegger 1967a, 75 and 81). It is nevertheless true that the historial, if it is not to be thought of in these terms, conserves the character of a flux *qua* heritage. It is a matter of the flux of historical vortexes, ruptures, epochs, broken or suspended movements that can always be reassumed—the only "hope" that the question of being can be reopened is precisely that the historial is a "current" in this sense. "In the fateful repetition of possibilities that have been, Dasein brings itself back 'immediately'—that is to say, in a way that is temporally ecstatical—to what has *already been before it*" (391, my emphasis). The historial "flux," unceasingly broken, suspended, exposed to its interruptions, yet essentially reconstitutable (indeed presupposing and actualizing itself through a constant reconstitution of the having-been, inherited as this reconstitution (repetition)), could never be made up of a succession of nows; it is the linking of phenomena of recurrences. This understanding undoubtedly refers to the Husserlian thematic of a "large now" of geometry, of the sciences, of philosophy, which is not a simple flux like internal time-consciousness but an unceasing reinauguration, one that will be thought by Heidegger in terms of the "history of being," outside all teleology, in the shelter of, and sheltered from, metaphysics (that is, protected both by and from metaphysics). The issue here is indeed that of knowing what *forms* "the steadiness of existence," on what basis it is formed, and, importantly, that this basis is *not* the now:

> The steadiness of existence . . . is not first formed either through or by the adjoining of "moments" one to another; but these arise from the temporality of that repetition which is futurally in the process-of-having-been—a temporality which has *already been stretched along.* (391)

There is recurrence and différance. Différance must be inscribed in the horizon of the positive possibilities of repetition (of the *what* and the *who* in the *what*), in a *logic of the supplement* and, when this horizon becomes historical, in orthothesis.

The Exactitude of the Supplement and Restitution

It is the world-historial having-been, concretized by "remains, monuments, and records that are still present-at-hand" (Heidegger 1967a, 394), that makes historical thematization possible. But it is "the historiality of the historian's existence [that] is the existential foundation for history as a science, even for its most trivial and 'mechanical' [*handwerklich*] procedures" (394). Yet is not the historical qualification of this historiality of the historian actually constituted by the positivity of having-been in the singularity of its form—as it happens, an orthothetic form? The negligence of Heidegger here has to do with the specific character of these world-historial beings within-the-world that are made up by any surface of recording, especially one that allows for an orthothetic re-stitution (and re-constitution) of the having-been. This restitution is here named a repetition that alone, as the sole possibility of access, makes a thematization governed by concern for historical truth possible, this truth once more rooted here in the *who* disengaged from any *what*: "The possibility and the structure of historical truth are to be expounded in terms of the *authentic disclosedness* ('truth') of *historial existence*" (397). This disengagement is justified by the critique of horological instrumentality; this time, however, this instrumentality is thought exclusively in terms of its end: *exactitude.* The disengagement is based on the demonstration that exactitude is the *telos* of instrumentality (particularly that of measuring time) insofar as it is in the service of taking flight in concern, a flight that wishes to "determine the undetermined." Of course, Dasein reckons with time before any particular measuring instrument "by which time can be determined" (404), but not before any instrument: equipmentality is constitutive of being-in-the-world. There must be one instrument, any kind of instrument, provided that it is a *what* (understood as ready-to-hand), for there to be an *account* of time. This derived relation to time presupposes the hand that articulates the *who* with the *what* (and nothing more) before any chrono-instrumentality:

> Everyday Dasein, the Dasein which takes time, comes across time proximally in what it encounters within-the-world as ready-to-hand and present-at-hand. (405)

Such an insight is secured on the basis of the structure of datability, the whereas. Every instantiation of ecstasis is consequently articulated upon *something*, no matter what, calendarity being the general form of inscriptability of the *who* (*qua* temporal) in the *what* (*qua* within-the-world). Inscribed, the time of the *who* can become the time of the One, public time Heidegger 1967a, §79). This publicity constitutes social programmatics. But we need to show, further, that this publicity (re)constitutes the temporality of the *who* "itself," *as idiomatic*. Thus, the *who* is, in its very *intimacy*, structured through calendrical and temporally programmatic publicity. The improbable, which is the possible, is itself programmatic. And this publicity is what opens truly historical space: there is a specificity of historical publicity that Heidegger does not account for either in the "falling" dimensions that it liberates or in its radically original historial character, even if, in the following paragraph, he marks a difference between "primitive" Dasein and what is called "advanced" Dasein.

Just as earlier the interest of a specific study on the mobility of world-historial beings was recognized, albeit then immediately qualified as secondary, the thematic of calendarity admits, perhaps more clearly, the need for a "history of the clock," a history more worthy of figuring at the heart of an *extensive* ontological project: "Every clock as such 'has a history'" (Heidegger 1967a, 417); "the connections between historical numeration, world-time as calculated astronomically, and the temporality and historiality of Dasein *need a more extensive investigation*" (418 n. 5, my emphasis). But, once again, this type of history is nothing but a pious wish if, following a well-rehearsed gesture, it reduces exactitude to the pure concern that always wants a clock to be more exact and more easy to handle (§80). From these analyses there results a derogatory judgment of exactitude in general, highly prejudicial to an analytic of the orthothetic of the having-been. Now this world-historial form cannot be reduced to the exactitude of a measure, but (re)constitutes orthographically a *having-been* in its *as such.* It is not the exactitude of *measure* but that of *recording*, of *access.* And, as Barthes's analysis shows, it opens up a singular thanatology. We cannot, then, accept the statement that "the foundations of historical and calendrical 'chronology' can be laid bare only within the orbit of the tasks of analyzing historical cognition existentially" (418), in the sphere of a *who* disengaged from the *what*. The question of this calendarity cannot be relegated to world-historial secondarity, nor therefore follow a fundamental ontological interpretation of temporality, "formally" determined by it, and not determining it "materially."

The measure of the "transcendence of time" accentuates its publication (the loss of its originary intimacy, of its withdrawal). Time, which is neither subjective nor objective,

> is neither "inside" nor "outside" and it is "earlier" than any subjectivity or objectivity, because it presents the condition for the very possibility of this "earlier." (Heidegger 1967a, 419)

Given that the divide inside/outside, which separates firstly *the who and the what*, has to be destroyed, one might have expected that time was thought in the "before" of such a divide. But this is never the case with Heidegger because the *who* conserves its privilege over the *what*, the *what* never assuming therefore a truly constitutive role. It is true that the Husserlian divide between the immanent and the transcendent is put in question. World-time "caught in the use of the clock" has been understood since Aristotle in terms of the now and flux; the critique of this image of the flux is based on the fact that "in the ordinary interpretations of time as a sequence of 'nows,' both datability and significance are *missing* [*font défaut*]" (Heidegger 1967a, 422). But no more than in Husserl (indeed less than in "The Origin of Geometry") is any dynamic particular to the *what* taken into account. [Heidegger continues:]

> Hegel's "construction" was prompted by his arduous struggle to conceive the "concretion" of the spirit {after its fall into time, while} *the existential analytic starts with the "concretion" of factically thrown existence itself.* . . . {Far from} spirit {falling} *into* time . . . factical existence "falls" as falling *from* primor-

> dial, authentic temporality. This "falling," however, has itself its existential possibility in a mode of its temporalizing—a mode which belongs to temporality. (Heidegger 1967a, 435–36, my emphasis)

If this is so, then the objection could still be made to Heidegger that one must fully integrate the (re)constitutivity of the already-there in its "thrown" concretions—what could be thought, perhaps, through a revisiting of the question of "substance-subject," of the "speculative."

Exactitude and Possibility

Being and Time ends by both announcing the need to engage, after its preparatory analytic, in the question of being and interrogating the weight of the *what* that always propels thought toward its reification. At the same time it insists singularly on the need to disengage the specificity of the *what* as ready-to-hand, traditionally unthought under the category of substance, that is, the present-at-hand, or the possible *qua* a category of reality. Being and time are thought from out of the need to disengage the *what*: the gesture is irreplaceable and unprecedented.

Heidegger's work will continue on another path, one that will never renounce, however, the fundamental procedure of the existential analytic. The question will become that of the history of being. Now, the critique of the vulgar understanding of time is articulated upon a highly determined understanding of exactitude, one that appears characteristically as the symptom of the flight that wishes to determine the undetermined. Is not such an understanding a reification of the analytic? Furthermore, has not exactitude, brought about definitively in Greece, played a quite different role in the "history of being"? Indeed would the "history of being" be *possible* outside such exactitude?

The Heideggerian critique of exactitude is in perfect complicity (insofar as it implies a critique of phonological and exact writing, itself the index of a general fate of writing destined to exact calculation, to the typewriter and computer processing)[10] with a "logocentric" understanding of writing. The privilege of the voice and self-presence that is *still* there in the theme of the aphonic voice of conscience [*Gewissen*] is indeed the sign of Heidegger's retreat before his own undertaking to deconstruct the "metaphysics of presence," named in *Being and Time* "the vulgar understanding of time as a flowing stream of 'nows'" (1967a, 422).[11] That said, what would the logic of the orthographic supplement consist in? What—

and who in this *what*—would allow for an epochal beginning called "the history of being"?

These questions open the second volume of this work. They will be pursued through an analysis of orthotheses particular to present analogical, numerical, and biological technologies (which are nothing other than mnenotechnologies "en-gramming" [*engrammant*] the already-there). The second volume will attempt to interpret the specificity of contemporary technics from this perspective, measuring up to the following question: to what extent can the *who* that we are today double up on its *what*?

The irreducible relation of the *who* to the *what* is nothing but the expression of retentional finitude (that of its *memory*). Today memory is the object of an industrial exploitation that is also a war of speed: from the computer to program industries in general, via the cognitive sciences, the technics of virtual reality and telepresence together with the biotechnologies, from the media event to the event of technicized life, via the interactive event that makes up computer real time, new conditions of event-ization have been put in place that characterize what we have called *light-time*. Light-time forms the age of the différance in real time, an exit from the deferred time specific to the history of being that seems to constitute a concealing of différance and a threat to all kinds of difference—which is why one can speak of the end of history or of a change of epoch. Today this light-time raises demands for *exceptional* measures: hence "the cultural exception." There is therefore a pressing need for a politics of memory. This politics would be nothing but a thinking of technics (of the unthought, of the immemorial) that would take into consideration the *reflexivity* informing every orthothetic form insofar as it does nothing but call for reflection on the originary de-fault of origin, however incommensurable such a reflexivity is (since it is nonsubjective). Whence the excess of measure in this exceptional phrase inscribed on the wall of time: *no future*.

Reference Matter

Notes

General Introduction

1. Aristotle 1984, *Physics*, Book 2, §1: 329.

2. Following current usage as well as Stiegler's own practice, we have kept the Heideggerian term in its original German throughout, placing the French translation (*arraisonement*, "enframing") afterwards in parentheses wherever Stiegler wishes to play on or draw attention to the root of the French equivalent.—Trans.

3. The Heideggerian term *Geschichtlichkeit* is translated throughout by the term "historiality" and not, as in the Macquarrie and Robinson translation of *Sein und Zeit* (1967a), by "historicality." The Heideggarian term *historisch* is accordingly translated by the straightforward term "historical"—to distinguish it from "historial" (*geschichtlich*)—and not by the somewhat heavy term "historiological."—Trans.

4. Heidegger 1972, 1959, 1977, 1969b.

5. Heidegger 1967a, 42. Following standard practice, all page references to *Being and Time* are to the German pagination found in the margin of each page of the English translation.

6. Aristotle 1984, *Nicomachean Ethics*, bk. 6, §§3 and §4.

7. Attention must be drawn here to the pejorative connotation of "exactitude." I will often dwell on this theme in the course of this study, insofar as calculation will be conceived as exactitude, and inversely—a reciprocity that gives rise to the temptation to "determine" the undetermined.

8. Aristotle 1984, *Nicomachean Ethics*, bk. 6, 4.

9. Habermas 1987, 98. Marx was of course the first to make the point, in the *Grundrisse* (1973).

10. See Détienne 1988 and Marrou 1981.

11. We coin the neologism "event-ization" to translate the Stieglerian term *événementialisation* (the taking place and time of events).—Trans.

12. We wish to stress here Stiegler's insistence throughout the work on the originary *défaut* of the human species which makes of it a technical being, in distinction to other living species, and, as a result, a contingent and undetermined being. To distinguish, therefore, *défaut* from the connotations that inform either the English term "lack" (the term has been much used in recent French thought concerning the ends of the concept of a "subject") or the work (more Derridean in tone and inspiration) on "radical lack," we believe it worthwhile to translate the term by the neologism "de-fault," thereby picking up the play between "default" and "fault," but also the connotations of "failure," "lack," "mistake," "deficiency," and "defect" which inform Stiegler's use of the French term. The concept *défaut* in fact marks a strategy in Stiegler's work which addresses, through the concomitant reflection on the originary relation between the technical and the human, the question of finitude within and across diverse fields of human thought and practice (from religion to technical and political invention in general, from the humanities to the "social" and "techno"-sciences in particular) . At the risk, then, of ugliness to eye and ear, we believe that the coining of the neologism "de-fault" is the most appropriate way to render the diversity of meanings that Stiegler wishes to give to the concept given the discursive fields in which it is operating. For the possibility of a careful reading of *Technics and Time*, it is consequently important to bring out in English the insistence of the term. Where the term *défaut* has not been translated by "de-fault," or where the term is operating in a particularly idiomatic phrase, the French original is placed in brackets afterwards. Where, however, the term is taken from another author—as will be seen in Stiegler's chapter on Rousseau—we have kept to the standard translation of the term "default."—Trans.

Part I, Introduction

1. Just as for the form/matter divide—as Simondon will develop it in a later work, *L'individu et sa genèse physico-biologique* (Simondon 1964), of which I propose in the second volume of this work a general interpretation.

2. The *Robert* dictionary of French.

Part I, Chapter 1

1. Concerning the recurrent terms "technics," "technique(s)", the "technical," and "technology," a word of clarification is needed. The French terms *une technique* and *des techniques*, referring to one or more individual, specialized "techniques," are translated as "technique" and "techniques." The French *la technique*, referring to the technical domain or to technical practice as a whole, as system or result, is translated as "technics" or "the technical." The French *la technolo-*

gie and *technologique*, referring to the specific amalgamation of technics and the sciences in the modern period, are translated as "technology" and "technological." When hyphenated (*la techno-logie, techno-logique,* etc.), the terms refer to the thinking and logic of technics and are translated as "technology."

2. The report *A Halt to Growth* [*Halte à la croissance*] was edited by D. H. Meadows and published by MIT in 1972.

3. This was François de Wendel's line of reasoning at the beginning of the nineteenth century, as Gille notes, 1978, 54.

4. "Those who so easily propose the substitution of mineral for vegetable coal seem to have no doubts that this will lead to changes in nearly everything in the furnaces, the refineries, the mechanics, the workshops, that you must be placed quite close to the coal mines producing the right kind of coal, and have the ore near the fuel, and be able to train the workers in this new type of work." Quoted in Gille 1978, 59.

5. Cf. Bourguinat 1988; Orléan and Aglietta 1988.

6. Jean-François Lyotard uses the term "development" in this sense in Lyotard 1992.

7. The concept of technical tendency owes much to the concept found in Henri Bergson's *Creative Evolution*, and this is the case not only as regards Bergsonian biology: Leroi-Gourhan analyzes matter as "the tendency to constitute isolable systems susceptible of being treated geometrically. . . . But that is only a tendency. Matter does not extend to its ultimate consequences, and the isolation is never complete" (1943, 10). The Bergsonian analysis of the relation organic/inorganic confirms later in *Man and Matter* that the concept of technical tendency as the coupling of man to matter is already found in the Bergsonian concept: "Life is, before all else, a tendency to act upon raw matter. The meaning of this action is no doubt undetermined: hence the unpredictable variety of forms that life, in evolving, sows along its path. But this action always presents, to a greater or lesser degree, a contingent character, implying at least a rudiment of choice. Now this choice presupposes the anticipated representation of several possible actions. Thus, possibilities of action must be delineated for the human being before the action itself" (ibid., 97).

The whole of Leroi-Gourhan's genetics, embedding the first elements of properly technical evolution in the most remote zoological past, comes under the point of view according to which "*life appears as a stream moving from germ to germ by means of a developed organism.* Everything happens as if the organism itself were but an excrescence, a bud brought to life by the old germ working to survive in the new one. What is essential is the continuity of progress going on indefinitely, an invisible progress that each visible organism rides during the short interval of time that he has to live" (ibid.). Leroi-Gourhan's originality resides in his analysis of the pursuit of this vital tendency outside of the organisms themselves, in inorganic matter organizing itself—this is the fact of anthropological "intentionality."

Just like the technical tendency, the biological tendency is unpredictable: "the more one's attention is concentrated on this continuity of life, the more one sees organic evolution approaching that of a consciousness, whereby the past pushes against the present, causing a new form, incommensurable to former forms, to emerge. The fact that the appearance of a vegetable or animal species is due to precise causes is well established. But what must be understood here is that, if these causes were understood in detail after the fact, we would be able to explain through them the form that has emerged; but predicting forms is out of the question" (ibid., 27). This unpredictability is linked to the tendency's irreversibility: "We undoubtedly think with only a small part of our past, but it is with the whole past, including the inscape of our native soul, that we desire, will, and act. Our past thus becomes integrally manifest in its thrust in the form of the tendency, since only a small part of this past becomes representation. The survival of the past results in the impossibility for a consciousness to cross through the same state twice. The circumstances may indeed be the same, but it is no longer the same person they influence, since they intervene at a different moment of his history" (ibid., 5).

Furthermore, the tendency poses the problem of individuation that we shall find in Simondon, and the problem of a conflictual play reminiscent of the dynamic of the technical system in Gille:

> The biologist with the geometrical approach wins out too easily over our inability to give a precise and general definition of individuality. A perfect definition only applies to an accomplished reality: but vital properties are never completely realized, but always in process, less states than tendencies. A tendency can only accomplish its aims when no other tendency obstructs it: how could such a situation present itself in the domain of life, where there are always, as we shall show, a reciprocal implication of antagonistic tendencies? In particular as regards the case of individuality, it can be said that, if the tendency to individualization is present everywhere in the organized world, it is everywhere confronted with the tendency to reproduce. For an individuality to have been perfect, no separated part of the organism should have been able to live separately. But in this case reproduction would become impossible. In fact what is reproduction, if not the reconstitution of a new organism with a separate fragment of the old one? Individuality thus harbors its enemy within. Experiencing the very need to perpetuate itself in time dooms it to perpetual incompletion in space. It is up to the biologist, in all cases, to distinguish between the two tendencies. (Leroi-Gourhan 1943, 12)

The Simondonian question of individuation, raised to the level of the contemporary technical system, could moreover be approached in light of another remark by Leroi-Gourhan: "Everywhere, the tendency to become individualized is combated and at the same time realized by the antagonistic and complementary tendency to associate, as if the multiple unity of life, drawn toward multiplicity, was all the more strenuously attempting to retract into itself" (1943, 259).

Lastly, the thematic of tendency is here clearly totally interdependent with the thematic of phylogenesis, which, as we shall see, is crucial to Leroi-Gourhan's understanding of technical evolution:

> Now, this is precisely the relation we find in the animal and vegetable realms, between what engenders and what is engendered: on the tapestry that the ancestor passes down to his descendants, and that they share, each of them embroiders something original. It is true that the differences between the descendant and the forebear are small; it can be asked whether the same living matter presents enough plasticity to cover successively forms as different as those of the fish, the reptile, and the bird. But this question receives a peremptory answer from observation. We are shown that, up to a certain period of its development, the bird embryo can hardly be distinguished from the reptile's, and that the individual develops in the course of its embryonic life in general a series of transformations that can be compared to those whereby, according to evolutionism, one species evolves into another. (1943, 23)

8. See "The Permanence of Evolution," in Leroi-Gourhan 1943, 39.

9. Paleontology . . . has discovered that through numerous channels the construction plan of animal species is modified to achieve a more efficient contact with the exterior milieu. These modifications always lend themselves to a mathematical analysis of forms, each species being at a moment of its history the embodiment of a multitude of physical laws whose harmonious linkage suggests a state of equilibrium. The modification of the slightest detail leads consequently to that of all the others.

> The fusiform profiles of aquatic animals, the encompassing twist of the shell of gastropods, the limb segmentation of walking animals are the plans of general construction to which respond in coherent formulas the diverse species in their different conditions of life. In these general plans, which for example provide fish, reptiles, and aquatic mammals with a similar architecture, a long, cone-shaped body, the play of the tendency has the mammal, originally little different from terrestrial mammals, acquiring progressively in its aquatic life an evermore hydrodynamic cone shape. (Leroi-Gourhan 1945, 337)

10. "Culture ignores in technical reality a human reality" (Simondon 1958, 9).

11. "The machine takes the human's place because the human accomplished a function of the machine, that of tool bearer" (ibid., 15).

12. "Industrialization is made possible by the formation of stable types" (ibid., 24).

13. Just as the copy errors of the genotype engender mutants among the living.

Part I, Chapter 2

1. Cf. Blanchot 1982b.

2. "L'avenir de la Terre" (The future of the Earth), in Reeves 1981, 135–40.

3. "Biosphere 2," a technologico-scientific experiment in survival, was inaugurated in France in the late 1980's to test the physical, mental, and ecological potential of artificial colonies having to function in conditions totally alien to those of the earth.—Trans.

4. That is, eidetic characteristics: can one vary the *eidos* of the world without kinship, without a body proper, without distinct proximity in a distance, and so on, and come up with an *invariant substrate*?

5. So as to continue on the subject of stars and the becoming-astral of man, Michel Deguy comments on an article in *Le Monde* on "spatial art." See Deguy 1985, 189–90.

6. See Lyotard 1992.

7. We have hitherto chosen to translate Stiegler's "l'homme" by either "the human" or "humanity." However, in the following sections devoted to an analysis of Rousseau's thought, we shall retain the classic translation: "man." —Trans.

8. Throughout the book we will maintain the French term *différance.* Given its broad acceptance in Anglo-American culture, a translation seems unnecessary. —Trans.

9. We obviously do not want to say that the empiricist philosophy of Hume remains fundamentally transcendental, but that it is philosophical in the sense that it seeks principles; through its concept of experience, that it aims at a constitution, the reason for which Husserl will be able to claim filiation with Hume. The Humean subject "who invents and who believes is constituted in the given in such a way as to be able to turn the given itself into a synthesis, into a system. . . . In the problem posed in this manner, we find the absolute essence of empiricism. It can be said of philosophy in general that it has always sought a plan of analysis from which to undertake and conduct an examination of the structures of consciousness, that is, from which to submit it to criticism, and justify the entirety of experience. What first opposes critical philosophies is thus a difference in plan. We are doing a transcendental critique when, placing ourselves on a methodically reduced plan that thereby affords us an essential certitude, a certitude of essence, we ask: how can the given be, how can something give itself to a subject, how can the subject give something to itself? Here, the critical demand is that of a constructive logic whose type is found in mathematics. Critique is empirical when, placing oneself in a purely immanent vantage from which, however, a description is possible, whose rule is found in determinable hypotheses and its model in physics, we ask concerning the subject: how does it constitute itself in the given? The construction of the latter yields to the constitution of the former. The given is not given to a subject; the subject is constituted in the given. Hume's merit is to have brought out this problem in a pure state, keeping it distant from the transcendental, as well as from the

psychological" (Deleuze 1953, 92). Humean thought would thus be the first non sophistic anthropology.

10. "Religion commands us to believe that, *God Himself having taken men out of a state of nature immediately after the creation*, they are unequal only because it is His will they should be so: but it does not forbid us to form conjectures based solely on the nature of man, and the beings around him, concerning *what might have become* of the human race, if it had been left to itself" (Rousseau 1973, 51, my emphasis).

11. On the constitutively aporetic character of this question concerning humankind, see Blanchot 1951 and the commentary by Roger Laporte in Laporte 1987, 36–37.

12. Rousseau wrote, in the *Essay on the Origin of Language*, "It is in order to achieve repose that everyone works" (Rousseau 1966, 39).

13. "By becoming domesticated, [man] . . . grows weak, timid, and servile; his effeminate way of life totally enervates his strength and courage" (Rousseau 1973, 57).

14. It would be necessary here to analyze and compare this theme of distancing in authors as different from each other as, on the one hand, Benjamin (exposition value in reproducibility), Lyotard (telegraphy), and Virilio, for example, and on the other, Heidegger (*Ent-fernung*), Derrida (différance and dissemination), and Deleuze (deterritorialization).

15. This is precisely the structure of *elpis*, which characterizes, in *Works and Days*, the duplicitous condition of mortals struck simultaneously by *promētheia* and *ēpimētheia.*

16. "Where there is no love, of what advantage is beauty? Of what use is wit to those who do not converse, or cunning to those who have no business with others?" (Rousseau 1973, 81).

Part I, Chapter 3

1. See Prochiantz 1988.

2. Aristotle also characterizes noetic life as movement and conquest of mobility.

3. See Maturana and Varela 1987.

4. "Pondering the nature of human intelligence is the most personal of problems. Do we not exist only by virtue of our own awareness of existing?" (Leroi-Gourhan 1993, 104).

5. Ibid., 255; cf. 404.

6. Ibid., 107; cf. 110–11.

7. This is why, for Husserl, "the act of expression is . . . an experience [*vécu*] whose specificity is to speak the essence or the general form, entering into the knowledge of what is aimed at" (Schérer 1967, 127).

8. The French expression is *être à l'article de la mort,* meaning to be close *to the point of death.*—Trans.

Part II, Chapter 1

1. "Since from now on through Prometheus's scheming, mortals have cattle meat to eat, by the will of Zeus, they will no longer have at hand, within immediate reach, the wheat they need to subsist" (Vernant 1979, 59).

2. See Loraux 1981.

3. "The fire of Prometheus is not that of the gods (Zeus's thunderbolt, the lightning of Athena). . . . It is a perishable fire: engendered, starved, precarious, like all mortal creatures; . . . the *tekhnai* that men have at their disposal are not less equivocal than the Titan who provided them with these. . . . Not only because 'the ardor of a ceaseless fire' harbors a power that escapes human control but, more precisely, because this force contains something mysterious, a supernatural quality . . . that adds a new dimension to the features of animal wildness and the assets of human culture" (Vernant 1979, 64).

4. "Since, through the fault of Prometheus, the cereals no longer grow on their own accord, their seed has to be buried in the womb of the earth, to be seen to disappear in silos, and cereal food in the womb of women . . . [and] the procreation of children occurs henceforth in sexual union" (ibid., 105).

5. "In the human world, in which fortune and misfortune are found intimately mixed without either being foreseen with total assurance, in which the spirit of men, when they peer into the future, falls between the exact foresight of Prometheus and the total blindness of his brother, it is in the ambiguous form of *elpis,* of an expectation at times vain, at times well-founded, sometimes good, sometimes bad, that the horizon of the future for mortals is drawn up" (ibid., 132).

6. "For those who are immortal, like the gods, there is no need of *elpis.* No Elpis either for those who, like the beasts, do not know that they are mortal. If man, mortal like the beasts, foresaw the future in advance like the gods, if he was wholly on the side of Prometheus, he would have no force to live, for failure to be able to look at his own death in the face. He is aware, however, that he is mortal without knowing when nor how he will die, and Elpis, foresight, but blind foresight, necessary illusion, good and ill at one and the same time, Elpis alone allows man to live the ambiguous, split existence that the Promethean fraud brings about when it institutes the first sacrificial meal. From that moment on everything has its inverse side" (ibid.).

7. See the previous chapter, §§10–13.

8. Georges Bataille, quoted in Blanchot 1988, 9.

9. "The immortality of the Promethean liver corresponds to the mode of ex-

istence of those natural phenomena that, without ever disappearing, can only subsist in fact through periodic renewal" (Vernant 1979, 90).

Part II, Chapter 2

1. See Heidegger 1992.

2. If the question is indeed that of deciding in philosophy—a deciding that makes philosophy immediately political—here it will be one of deciding about a mythical reference, between Athens and Mycenae, no matter what Heidegger's reading of *Antigone* in *An Introduction to Metaphysics* (1959) is. For, if it is true that the question of orginary uprooting is thematized in this work, the Heideggerian discourse on uprooting remains as a whole oriented by a myth of autochthony of Athenian descent (such as Nicole Loraux has reconstructed it in *Les enfants d'Athéna* [1981]). By according it this privilege in his politics, Heidegger will have *forgotten* the Promethean myth of originary uprooting, which is, that said, so close to his interpretation of time. Heidegger's reading of *Antigone* in *An Introduction to Metaphysics* admittedly interprets both the origin as a tearing away or an uprooting and Dasein, that is, time, as originary violence. Without doubt the analysis of *deinon* and *deinotaton* in the context of Sophocles's poem as well as what emerges from this analysis, the historial as unearthing / making-strange [*dépaysement*], shows that for Heidegger, in 1935, chthonic myth does not prevail in any simple sense. A highly detailed reading is needed here. And yet, Heidegger will always privilege such a myth, from *Being and Time* (1967a) through *An Introduction to Metaphysics* (for example, "From a metaphysical point of view, Russia and America are the same; the same inconsolable technological frenzy, the same *rootless* organization of standard man," 1959, 37, my emphasis), through to the end (for example, statements in the *Spiegel* interview). The reason for this is that he will have never thought time from out of [*à partir de*] *promētheia*, an absence translated into the conflict that opposes *dikē* and *tekhnē* (1959, 160–65). The latter admittedly appear together *in* and *as deinon*, but *tekhnē* is never considered as the source of un-earthing / making-strange [*dépaysement*] *qua* good un-earthing, not that of being torn away but that of the return to the most strange, to the most far, which is always the most familiar, concealed by its everydayness. The thematic is played out again, for example, in the words "habitual" (*gewohnt*) and "dwelling" (*wohnen*), in "Building, Dwelling, Thinking" (1954). It is not our desire here to evacuate the possibility of an irreducible, territorializing, "chthonian" drive, which would always already inhabit, as the very condition of its being borne out, the differing and deferring movement of uprooting. Rather, it is the originary tension between these two movements that needs to be thought, today more than ever. It is a question of thinking, then, the articulation between time and technics, of

conceiving technics as the very source of *dé-paysement* in the insoluble complexity of its effects.

3. Notably Heidegger 1967a, §§6, 35, 36, 38, 44.

4. See Zarader 1976, 114 and, especially, 124.

5. We understand the word ["inventor"] in the sense that it designates for Husserl the "proto-geometrician" in *The Origin of Geometry* (Derrida 1989).

6. This installation is the object of §§71–80 of *Being and Time* and of §19 of Husserl's *The Basic Problems of Phenomenology* (Husserl 1982).

7. With the translation of *Jeweiligkeit* by "perpetuity," and not, as is standard practice in English translations of Heidegger, by "specificity," we follow Michel Haar's French translation of *Der Begriff der Zeit*, "Le concept du temps" (Haar and de Launay 1983). This is the translation with which Stiegler is working, and it has the merit of stressing the temporal aspect of the German word.—Trans.

8. Similarly, anxiety is the experiencing of indeterminacy: "The before-which of anxiety is completely undetermined" (Heidegger 1967a, §40). Indeterminacy is what speaks in the voice of conscience (§57), that is, in being-in-de-fault. What makes one anxious is the de-fault.

9. We take up here the terms of §§16, 27, 35, 38, 51, 55, and 79–81 of *Being and Time*.

10. Almost all politicians have adjusted themselves to this time.

11. A process which not even the sandclock can escape—it has to be turned over—even if the process of making discrete in its diverse technical modalities is exactly what determines that the appearance of a phenomenon is each time singular.

12. A singularity that §23 of *Being and Time* rightly insists on.

13. On this point, see *Being and Time*, §§54–58, and the following chapter.

14. Heidegger 1992, 21E. The term "individuation" is used in §§25, 61, and 66 of *Being and Time*.

15. Is not the pro-venance of being, as it is given in the third-person singular of the indicative, to be sought, precisely, in this reflexivity which precedes that of Dasein?

16. Above in the Introduction to Part II, p. 183.

Part II, Chapter 3

1. In the following, Heidegger's existentiale of *Schuldigsein*, with regard to which conscience [*Gewissen*] finds voice, will be predominantly translated as "being-at-fault" and not, as in the English translation, as "being-guilty." Stiegler's work on the relations between this existentiale and the originary default, that is, his epiphylogenetic reading of the Heideggerian thematic of already-there, will thereby be maintained.—Trans.

2. While the English translation of *Öffentlichkeit* in *Being and Time* is "pub-

licness," we have remained faithful to the French *publicité* since the latter term, with its connotations of advertising and public relations, immediately evokes the logic of repetition prior to any distinction between Dasein and the One.—Trans.

3. The translation of *Bewandtnis* ("involvement," Heidegger 1967a, 84) by *finalité* is to be found in Boehm and Waehlens's French translation of *Sein und Zeit.* Stiegler exploits this translation at length in the following with regard to the second half of *Being and Time,* so it is appropriate to translate *Bewandtnis* here by "finality."—Trans.

4. We follow the English translation in rendering *Ent-fernung* (French: *é-loignement*), together with its derivatives, by "de-severance," "de-severant," etc., when the French equivalent suggests in the context of Stiegler's argument the active and privative mode of *anticipating* a distance. Otherwise, again following the English translation, we will translate *é-loignement* by "remoteness" ("remote," etc.).—Trans.

5. This inattention is still visible today in the "cognitive sciences": see *La technique et le temps. Tome* 2 (Stiegler 1996).

6. "It is the fact of dying that includes a radical reversal through which death, which was the extreme form of my power, not only becomes that which undoes me, throwing me out of my power to begin and even to finish, but becomes that which is without any relation to me, without power over me—that which is stripped of all possibility—the unreality of the indefinite. I cannot represent this reversal to myself; I cannot even conceive of it as definitive. It is not the irreversible step beyond which there would be no return, for it is that which is not accomplished, the interminable and the incessant. . . . Time without present, with which I have no relation, that toward which I am thrown, for I cannot die in (it), I have fallen from the power of dying, in (it) one dies, one does not stop dying. . . . Not the term but the interminable, not proper but featureless death, and not true death but, as Kafka says, 'the sneer of its capital error'" (Blanchot 1982b, 106 and 154).

7. Stiegler plays here on the analogy between support (*support, soutien*), remembering (*se sou-venir de*), and memory (*le sou-venir*). The tool as memory is a mnesic archive.—Trans.

8. *L'article de la mort,* from the French idiom *être à l'article de la mort* (literally: "to be on the verge of dying"). The translation loses Stiegler's point that the instant of death is itself articulated through the articulation between the human and the prosthetic.—Trans.

9. Compare the texts on "use" in Blanchot 1982b.

10. Cf. Derrida 1987.

11. See Derrida 1974, 20–28.

Bibliography

Dates given in square brackets refer to the original editions of cited works.

Aristotle. 1984. *The Complete Works of Aristotle.* 2 vols. Ed. Jonathan Barnes. Princeton, N.J.: Princeton University Press.

Augustine. 1961. *Confessions.* Trans. R. S. Pine-Coffin. Harmondsworth, Eng.: Penguin.

Barthes, Roland. 1979. *La chambre claire.* Paris: Gallimard, Le Seuil.

———. 1981. *Camera Lucida: Reflections on Photography.* Trans. Richard Howard. New York: Hill and Wang.

Bataille, Georges. *Lascaux ou la naissance de l'art.* In Georges Bataille, *Oeuvres complètes,* vol. 9. Paris: Gallimard.

Blanchot, Maurice. 1951. *Au moment voulu.* Paris: Gallimard.

———. 1969. *L'entretien infini.* Paris: Gallimard.

———. 1981. *"The Gaze of Orpheus" and Other Literary Essays.* Ed. P. Adams Stirney. Trans. Lydia Davis. New York: Station Hill.

———. 1982a. *La bête de Lascaux.* Montpellier: Fata Morgana.

———. 1982b. *The Space of Literature.* Trans. Ann Smock. Lincoln: University of Nebraska Press.

———. 1988 [1984]. *The Unavowable Community.* Trans. Pierre Jons. New York: Station Hill.

Boirel, Réné. 1961. *Théorie générale de l'invention.* Paris: Presses Universitaires de France.

Bourguinat, Henri. 1988. "La finance globale." In *Encyclopaedia Universalis.*

Châtelet, François. 1965. *Platon.* Paris: Gallimard.

Deguy, Michel. 1985. *Le temps de la réflexion*

Deleuze, Gilles. 1953. *Empiricisme et subjectivité.* Paris: Presses Universitaires de France.

———. 1983 [1962]. *Nietzsche and Philosophy.* Trans. Hugh Tomlinson. London: Athlone.

Derrida, Jacques. 1974 [1967]. *Of Grammatology.* Trans. Gayatri Spivak. Baltimore: John Hopkins University Press.

———. 1982 [1972]. *Margins of Philosophy.* Trans. Alan Bass. Chicago: University of Chicago Press.

———. 1987. "*Geshlecht II*: Heidegger's Hand." In *Deconstruction and Philosophy: The Texts of Jacques Derrida,* ed. John Sallis, trans. John P. Leavey, pp. 161–96. Chicago: University of Chicago Press.

———. 1989 [1962]. *Husserl's Origin of Geometry: An Introduction.* Trans. John P. Leavey, Jr. Lincoln: University of Nebraska Press.

Détienne, Marcel. 1988. *Les savoirs de l'écriture en Grèce ancienne.* Villeneuve d'Ascq: Presse Universitaire de Lilles.

———. 1979. "Pratiques culinaires et esprit de sacrifice." In *La cuisine du sacrifice,* ed. J.-P. Vernant, pp. 21–32. Paris: Gallimard.

Dreyfus, Hubert. 1992. "History of the Being of Equipment." In *Heidegger: A Critical Reader,* ed. Herbert Dreyfus and Harrison Hall, pp. 173–85. Oxford: Blackwell.

Febvre, Lucien. 1935. *Annales d'histoire économiques et sociales, sous la direction de Lucien Febvre et Marc Bloch.* Special issue of *Histoire des Techniques.* Paris: Armand Colin.

Ferry, L., and A. Renaud. 1988. *Heidegger et les modernes.* Paris: Grasset.

Foucault, Michel. 1973 [1966]. *The Order of Things.* Trans. Alan Sheridan. New York: Vintage Books.

Gille, Bertrand, ed. 1978. *Histoire des techniques.* Paris: Gallimard, Encyclopédie de la Pléiade.

Granel, Gérard. 1976. Preface to his translation of *La crise des sciences humaines et la phénoménologie transcendentale,* by E. Husserl. Paris: Gallimard.

Haar, Michel, and Marc B. de Launay, trans. 1983. "Le concept du temps," by M. Heidegger. In *Cahier de l'Herne: Heidegger,* ed. Michel Haar, pp. 33–54. Paris: Editions de l'Herne.

Habermas, Jürgen. 1987 [1968]. "Technology and Science as 'Ideology.'" In J. Habermas, *Towards a Rational Society,* pp. 81–127. Cambridge, Eng.: Polity.

Heidegger, M. 1954. "Building, Dwelling, Thinking." In M. Heidegger, *Basic Writings,* ed. and trans. David Farrell Krell, pp. 323–39. New York: Harper and Row, 1977.

———. 1927. *Sein und Zeit.* Tübingen: M. Niemayer.

———. 1959 [1935]. *An Introduction to Metaphysics.* Trans. Ralph Manheim. New Haven, Conn.: Yale University Press.

———. 1962 [1929]. *Kant and the Problem of Metaphysics.* Trans. James S. Churchill. Bloomington: Indiana University Press.

———. 1964. *L'être et le temps.* Trans. Rudolf Boehm and Alphonse de Waehlens. Paris: Gallimard.

———. 1967a [1927]. *Being and Time.* Trans. John Macquarrie and Edward Robinson. Oxford: Blackwell.

———. 1985. *Etre et temps.* Trans. Emmanual Martineau. Paris: Joel Lechaux and Eric Ledru.

———. 1967b. *What Is a Thing?* Trans. W. B. Barton and Vera Deutsch. Chicago: Regnery.

———. 1969a. "The End of Philosophy and the Task of Thinking." In M. Heidegger, *Basic Writings*, ed. and trans. David Farrell Krell, pp. 369–92. New York: Harper and Row.

———. 1969b [1957]. *Identity and Difference.* Trans. Joan Stambaugh. New York: Harper and Row.

———. 1972 [1962]. "Time and Being." In M. Heidegger, *On Time and Being*, trans. Joan Stambaugh, pp. 1–24. New York: Harper and Row.

———. 1977. *"The Question Concerning Technology" and Other Essays.* Trans. William Lovitt. New York: Harper and Row.

———. 1982 [1933]. "L'auto-affirmation de l'université allemande" [French trans. of the lecture "Die Selbstbehauptung der deutschen Universität," known as the Rectorate Discourse]. Trans. Gérard Granel. Mauzevin: T.E.R.

———. 1985 [1933]. "The Self-Assertion of the German University" [English trans. of the lecture "Die Selbstbehauptung der deutschen Universität," known as the Rectorate Discourse]. Trans. Karsten Harries. *Review of Metaphysics*, 28, no. 3: 470–80.

———. 1989. *Überlieferte Sprache und technische Sprache.* Sankt Gallen: Erker Verlag.

———. 1992 [1924]. *The Concept of Time.* Trans. William McNeill. Oxford: Blackwell.

Husserl, Edmund. 1970 [1954]. *The Crisis of the European Sciences and Transcendental Phenomenology.* Trans. David Carr. Evanston, Ill.: Northwestern University Press.

———. 1982. *The Basic Problems of Phenomenology.* Revised edition. Trans. Albert Hofstadter. Bloomington: Indiana University Press.

———. 1991 [1966]. *On the Phenomenology of the Internal Consciousness of Time: 1893–1917.* Trans. John Barnett Brough. Boston: Kluwer Academic Publisher.

Jacob, François. 1973 [1970]. *The Logic of Life: A History of Heredity.* Trans. Betty E. Spillmann. New York: Pantheon Books, Random House.

Ladrière, Jean. 1977. *Les enjeux de la rationalité.* Paris: Aubier Montaigne.

Laporte, Roger. 1987. *L'ancien, l'effroyablement ancien.* Montpellier: Fata Morgana.

Leroi-Gourhan, André. 1943. *L'homme et la matière.* Paris: Albin Michel.

———. 1945. *Milieu et techniques.* Paris: Albin Michel.

———. 1993 [1964, 1965]. *Gesture and Speech.* Trans. Anna Bostock Berger. Cambridge, Mass.: MIT Press.

Levinas, Emmanuel. 1990. *La mort et le temps.* Paris: Livre de Poche.

Lévi-Strauss, Claude. 1978. *Anthropologie structurale II.* Paris: Plon.

Loraux, Nicole. 1981. *Les enfants d'Athéna.* Paris: La Découverte.

Lyotard, Jean-François. 1992 [1988]. *The Inhuman: Reflections on Time.* Trans. Geoffrey Bennington and Rachel Bowlby. Stanford, Calif.: Stanford University Press.

Marcuse, Herbert. 1964. *One Dimensional Man: Studies in the Ideology of Advanced Industrial Society.* Boston: Beacon Press.

Marrou, Henri. 1981. *Histoire de l'éducation dans l'Antiquité.* Paris: Ed. du Seuil.

Marx, Karl. 1973. *Grundrisse.* Trans. Martin Nicolaus. Harmondsworth, Eng.: Penguin.

———. 1976. *Capital.* Vol. 1. Trans. Ben Fowkes. Harmondsworth, Eng.: Penguin.

Maturana, Umberto, and Francisco Varela. 1987. *The Tree of Knowledge.* Boston: New Science Library.

Nietzsche, Friedrich. 1961. *Thus Spoke Zarathustra.* Trans. R. J. Hollingdale. Harmondsworth, Eng.: Penguin.

———. 1986. *Human, All Too Human.* Trans. R. J. Hollingdale. Cambridge University Press.

Orléan, André, and Michel Aglietta. 1988. *La violence de la monnaie.* Paris: Presses Universitaires de France.

Plato. 1961. *The Collected Dialogues.* Ed. Edith Hamilton and Huntington Cairns. Bollingen Series LXX. Princeton, N.J.: Princeton University Press.

Pritchard, Evans. 1950. *The Nuer: A Description of the Modes of Livelihood and Political Institutions of a Nilotic People.* Oxford: Clarendon.

Prochiantz, Alain. 1988. *Les stratégies de l'embryon.* Paris: Presses Universitaires de France.

Reeves, Hubert. 1981. *Patience dans l'azur.* Paris: Le Seuil.

Ricoeur, Paul. 1983. *Temps et récit.* Vol. 1. Paris: Le Seuil.

Rolland, Jacques. 1986. "Technique et invention démocratique." In *Heidegger: Questions ouvertes,* ed. Yves Duroux, pp. 161–72. Paris: Osiris.

Rousseau, Jean-Jacques. 1966. *Essay on the Origin of Language.* In J.-J. Rousseau, *Two Essays on the Origin of Language.* Trans. John H. Moran. Chicago: University of Chicago Press.

———. 1973. *Discourse on the Origin of Inequality.* In J.-J. Rousseau, *"The Social Contract" and "Discourses,"* trans. G. D. H. Cole, Rev. J. H. Brumfitt, and J. C. Hall. London: Everyman's Library.

Schérer, René. 1967. *La Phénoménologie des recherches logiques.* Paris: PUF.

Simondon, Gilbert. 1958. *Du mode d'existence des objets techniques.* Paris: Aubier.

———. 1964. *L'individu et sa genèse physico-biologique.* Paris: Presses Universitaires de France.

Sophocles. 1954. *Antigone.* In *Sophocles 1,* ed. David Grene and Richard Lattimore, trans. Elizabeth Wykoff. Chicago: Chicago University Press.

Stiegler, Bernard. 1996. *La technique et le temps. Tome 2: La désorientation.* Paris: Galilée. (English translation forthcoming from Stanford University Press.)

Taminiaux, Jacques. 1983. "L'essence vraie de la technique." In *Cahiers de l'Herne: Heidegger,* ed. Michel Haar, pp. 263–84. Paris: Editions de l'Herne.

Vernant, Jean-Pierre. 1979. "A la table des hommes." In *La cuisine du sacrifice,* ed. J.-P. Vernant. Paris: Gallimard.

———. 1982. *Mythe et pensée chez les Grecs.* Paris: Maspero.

Weber, Max. 1958. *The Protestant Ethic and the Spirit of Capitalism.* Trans. Talcott Parsons. New York: Charles Scribner's Sons.

Wiener, Norbert. 1950. *The Human Use of Human Beings.* New York: Houghton Mifflin.

Wittfogel, Karl. 1977. *Le despotisme oriental.* Paris: Minuit.

Zarader, Marlène. 1976. *Heidegger et les paroles de l'origine.* Paris: Vrin.

MERIDIAN

Crossing Aesthetics

Bernard Stiegler, *Technics and Time, 1: The Fault of Epimetheus*

Werner Hamacher, *pleroma—Reading in Hegel*

Serge Leclaire, *Psychoanalyzing*

Serge Leclaire, *A Child Is Being Killed*

Sigmund Freud, *Writings on Art and Literature*

Cornelius Castoriadis, *World in Fragments*

Thomas Keenan, *Fables of Responsibility: Aberrations and Predicaments in Ethics and Politics*

Emmanuel Levinas, *Proper Names*

Alexander García Düttmann, *At Odds with AIDS: Thinking and Talking About a Virus*

Maurice Blanchot, *Friendship*

Jean-Luc Nancy, *The Muses*

Massimo Cacciari, *Posthumous People: Vienna at the Turning Point*

David E. Wellbery, *The Specular Moment: Goethe's Early Lyric and the Beginnings of Romanticism*

Edmond Jabès, *The Little Book of Unsuspected Subversion*

Hans-Jost Frey, *Studies in Poetic Discourse: Mallarmé, Baudelaire, Rimbaud, Hölderlin*

Pierre Bourdieu, *The Rules of Art: Genesis and Structure of the Literary Field*

Nicolas Abraham, *Rhythms: On the Work, Translation, and Psychoanalysis*

Jacques Derrida, *On the Name*

David Wills, *Prosthesis*

Maurice Blanchot, *The Work of Fire*

Jacques Derrida, *Points ... : Interviews, 1974–1994*

J. Hillis Miller, *Topographies*

Philippe Lacoue-Labarthe, *Musica Ficta (Figures of Wagner)*

Jacques Derrida, *Aporias*

Emmanuel Levinas, *Outside the Subject*

Jean-François Lyotard, *Lessons on the Analytic of the Sublime*

Peter Fenves, *"Chatter": Language and History in Kierkegaard*

Jean-Luc Nancy, *The Experience of Freedom*

Jean-Joseph Goux, *Oedipus, Philosopher*

Haun Saussy, *The Problem of a Chinese Aesthetic*

Jean-Luc Nancy, *The Birth to Presence*

Library of Congress Cataloging-in-Publication Data

Stiegler, Bernard.
[Technique et le temps. English]
Technics and time / Bernard Stiegler ; translated by Richard Beardsworth and George Collins.
p. cm. — (Meridian)
Translation of: La technique et le temps; vol. 1 translation of: La faute d'Epiméthée.
Includes bibliographical references.
Contents: 1. The fault of Epimetheus
ISBN 0-8047-3040-7 (cl.)
ISBN 0-8047-3041-5 (pbk.)
1. Technology—Philosophy. I. Title. II. Series: Meridian (Stanford, Calif.)
T14.S7513 1998
303.48'3—dc21 97-30449
CIP
Rev.

Original printing 1998

Made in the USA
Monee, IL
16 August 2021

75821709R00187